Southern Literary Studies
Louis D. Rubin, Jr., Editor

Faulkner's "Negro"

Faulkner's "Negro"

Art and the Southern Context

———

THADIOUS M. DAVIS

Louisiana State University Press
Baton Rouge and London

Copyright © 1983 by Louisiana State University Press
All rights reserved
Manufactured in the United States of America
Designer: Joanna Hill
Typeface: Palatino
Typesetter: G&S Typesetters, Inc.
Printer and binder: Thomson-Shore, Inc.

Library of Congress Cataloging in Publication Data

Davis, Thadious M., 1944–
Faulkner's "Negro"

(Southern literary studies)
Bibliography: p.
Includes index.
1. Faulkner, William, 1897–1962—Criticism and inter-
pretation.   2. Faulkner, William, 1897–1962—Characters.
3. Afro-Americans in literature.   4. Race relations in
literature.   5. Southern States in literature.   I. Title.   II. Series.
PS3511.A86Z7817   1983   813'.52   82-7327
ISBN 0-8071-1047-7   AACR2
ISBN 0-8071-1064-7 (pbk.)

Published with the assistance of a grant from the
National Endowment for the Humanities.

For permission to quote extensively from *The Sound and the Fury, Light in August,* and
Absalom, Absalom!, acknowledgment is made to Random House, Inc.

To my Family in New Orleans

Contents

Acknowledgments

Throughout my work on this book, I have been fortunate to have a sustaining community of scholars and friends. I am particularly indebted to Emily Dalgarno of Boston University, who first encouraged me to undertake a Faulkner dissertation and who believed that I could complete it. This book owes much to Emily and to other nurturing friends, especially Leslie Sanders, who listened from the beginning, and Ralph Singfield, who understood all along. Samuel Allen, Millicent Bell, Helen Vendler, Emerson Marks, Blyden Jackson, Louis D. Rubin, Jr., and Nell Painter read portions of the manuscript and offered advice at various stages. My former colleagues and Faulkner students at the University of Massachusetts, Boston, never failed to be interested and supportive.

A grant from the American Council of Learned Societies enabled me to do research at the Alderman Library, University of Virginia, and in the Berg Collection, New York Public Library, both of whose knowledgeable staffs offered invaluable assistance. A year-long National Endowment for the Humanities seminar at Brown University gave me the opportunity to read in fields related to my subject.

I am grateful for permission to reprint segments of two chapters that appeared in the following journals: "The Other Family and Luster in *The Sound and the Fury*," *College Language Association Journal*, XX (December, 1976), 245–61; "The Yoking of 'Abstract Contradictions': Clytie's Meaning in *Absalom, Absalom!*" *Studies in American Fiction*,

VII (Autumn, 1979), 209–19; " 'Be Sutpen's Hundred': Imaginative Projection of Landscape in *Absalom, Absalom!" Southern Literary Journal*, XIII (Spring, 1981), 3–14; and "Jason Compson's Place: A Reassessment," *Southern Studies*, XX (Summer, 1981), 137–50.

I owe special gratitude to Judith Brazinsky, who typed the manuscript with more dedication and patience than I had during the final stages. The English Department of the University of North Carolina, Chapel Hill, provided both partial funding for the typing and a graduate assistant, Paula Dale, who cheerfully and efficiently helped to check references.

Faulkner's "Negro"

Preface

In this work I use both *black* and *Negro* in reference to people of African descent: *black* in a general descriptive sense; *Negro* specifically in regard to Faulkner's characters and to southern attitudes or precepts which antedate *black* as a nomenclature of self-definition and self-identification. The usage, then, of the outmoded term *Negro* is not the result of an ideological inconsistency or an insensitivity to the positive values of "blackness"; rather, it is an attempt to reflect Faulkner in his proper sociohistorical context and to suggest that the cultural myths and limitations of the period under consideration, primarily from the mid-1920s through the 1930s, which was closer, chronologically and philosophically, to the Civil War and the 1860s than to the 1980s and our present. *Negro* evokes a wide variety of traditional meanings and experiential associations that *black*, despite its inherent color symbolism, has not yet accumulated. Moreover, Faulkner's fiction makes use of an entire backlog of associative meanings acquired by *Negro*.

The distinction between *Negro* and *black* assumed in this discussion is epitomized in an exchange between Roy Wilkins of the NAACP and a predominantly black audience on April 4, 1974. Wilkins, delivering a speech in the South on the sixth anniversary of the Reverend Martin Luther King's assassination, recounted the trials and woes of black people in a hostile region. He recalled how blacks even suffered the indignity of drinking water from public fountains labeled "Black Only." At that point he was interrupted by the audience who voiced the correction, "Colored Only!" As the incident dramatizes, yesterday's racial designations may elicit painful memories in today's world, yet they represent a reality which, though wanting, existed in incontrovertible fact. Bringing contemporary knowledge and awareness to bear on historical situations (including those of the near past) can provoke fresh insights regarding both that past and our present; however, modifying the conditions or updating not just the terminology but the informing conceptions of the past can distort its meaning and substance for the present day.

Faulkner (born September 25, 1897) never knew or wrote about "black" people as we today know and understand the term. He wrote about "the Negro," the white man's own creation. The reiteration of this fact is one of the simplest ways of defining the social and cultural concerns reflected in Faulkner's world. Even while acknowledging the largeness of Faulkner's vision, we must admit that the world today is not the reality at the heart of either *The Sound and the Fury, Light in August,* or *Absalom, Absalom!,* and that Faulkner's conceptions of "Negro" characters is now part of a bygone era. Such admissions do not detract from Faulkner's true subject: what it means to be human, the infinite variety of the human condition, its tragedy as well as its comedy.

Faulkner's imaginative concern with "the South"—people, legacies, and culture—is especially evident in his preoccupation with "the Negro." From the time of his early novels of the twenties (*Soldiers' Pay, Sartoris,* and *The Sound and the Fury*), through his artistic achievements of the thirties (*Light in August* and *Absalom, Absalom!*), continuing through his emphatic statements of the forties (*Go Down, Moses* and *Intruder in the Dust*) and his morality dramas of the fifties (*Requiem for a Nun, A Fable*), to the comic finale of *The Reivers* in 1962, "Negro" is a central imaginative force in Faulkner's fiction. The Negro functions both as concept and as character and becomes an integral component of the structural and thematic patterns in much of Faulkner's art.

Any mention of Faulkner evokes the South; and the South evokes the Negro, because the two are irrevocably joined in achievement and in despair. That union, originating in slavery and continuing through the Civil War and Reconstruction, has not been an easy one. Yet, the Negro has come to represent in the postbellum, modern world a gauge of the quality of southern life, the validity of southern ideals, the morality of southern attitudes, and also the dynamics of southern culture—all of these in their negative and positive aspects. Any representation of the Negro in fiction incorporates a multitude of ideas, frequently contradictory ideas. While the multifaceted thematic and symbolic implications of blacks in southern culture and literature have been recognized, the larger function served by the Negro has not, perhaps because that function is much more difficult to define.

One way of defining the function of the Negro in southern literature and culture is set out in this book. It provides a way of seeing the Negro in the context of southern life and art. The traditional southern world is divided into two parts, one white and the other black. Granted, there are other divisions within each part (class, caste, family, sex among others), but black and white are the two major divisions. The Negro, then, is the other half of the racially divided world; he represents a natural antithesis or a counterpoint to the white world. What this division means is that, for the southerner of either race, there is usually present the alternative side and the opposite point of view, or simply put, another way of seeing, doing, living, being, or thinking.

The recognition of a divided world may be translated into an approach to Faulkner's fictional world. Contemporary critics, such as Walter Slatoff, have observed a fragmentation or division at the core of Faulkner's art. That fragmentation is intrinsic to his way of perceiving, experiencing, ordering, and presenting his materials. When, for instance, Faulkner refers to the conflicts of the human heart as the main subject of his art, as he does in his Nobel Prize speech, he reveals (whether consciously or not) the magnitude of the problem of divisiveness inherent in his art. Why is it so natural for Faulkner to think of life—individual and social—as conflict? One obvious answer is his personality, but another is quite possibly the nature of the southern world that he was born into. Recognition of the nature of Faulkner's world is, in large measure, dependent upon recognition of the place of the Negro in it.

Faulkner writes with the weight of his culture upon him, and that culture centrally involves the Negro. Because the two parts of his society encompass values and attitudes that are essentially different, they constantly provoke tensions, which are intensified by a consciousness of southern history. The racially divided South presents, then, a unique problem of perception for Faulkner as artist. His awareness of the two separate worlds and his understanding of their mutual histories lead to an intense preoccupation with wholeness— with achieving a unified vision. Basically, it is an ongoing consideration of artistic integration, in which the artist attempts to bring about a fusion of fragmented parts. His art becomes an effort to transcend the tensions and divisions emanating from his cultural heritage, as well as from his position as artist in that culture, that divided world. Coming to terms with the Negro is essential to this process and, I believe, central to Faulkner's artistic achievement.

For Faulkner, because he is a white southerner and a sensitive artist, *Negro* generally suggests the possibility of wholeness, of establishing the missing parts of his world or vision. But the suggestion does not necessarily lead to a single, unified, or even constant vision, because *Negro* stands, as well, for the unresolved tensions of southern life. Thus emerge the prevalent fragmentation and the artistic counterpoint in Faulkner's fiction. As a result of his characteristic contrapuntal designs with alternative points of view, the seeing whole or the fusion of parts lies with the reader outside of the work itself; it is, to use Faulkner's phrase, the "fourteenth image" of the blackbird.

I proceed from the assumption of the Negro's centrality to an analysis of the uses Faulkner makes of "Negro" as idea (or abstract, symbolic presence) and as character (or concrete, physical presence) in his fictional world. The special focus is an examination of the burden Faulkner places on his "Negro" in his novels, especially in the resolution of the intricate tensions and angles of vision. I do not attempt to isolate Faulkner's attitudes toward Negro characters and to glean from them his attitude toward black people outside his fiction. My concern lies with what "the Negro" as an artistic conception reveals about the form of Faulkner's novels and with how a knowledge of his "Negro" leads to an enriched understanding of the works themselves and the creative process behind them.

I concentrate mainly on the novels published during the first and most prolific decade of Faulkner's career, 1926–1936, although I also treat *Go Down, Moses* (1942). There are two reasons for devoting most of my attention to this early period. One is that from the publication of *Soldiers' Pay* in 1926 to the publication of *Absalom, Absalom!* in 1936, Faulkner seems to be involved in the creation and development of themes, techniques, and characters which he drew upon in later years. By the end of 1936, most of the major Faulkner forms, styles, and people had already found expression, albeit embryonic in some cases. For example, Nancy Mannigoe of *Requiem for a Nun* (1951) is the central figure in "That Evening Sun" (1930), and Sam Fathers, *Go Down, Moses,* appears in "A Justice" (1931). Lucas Beauchamp, *Go Down, Moses* and *Intruder in the Dust* (1948), is the one major black character introduced after 1936, but he seems to be largely a polemical creation growing out of Faulkner's attempt to explain, or perhaps expiate, the South's irresponsible and peculiarly selective morality. In addition, both Lucas and Nancy duplicate, to a large extent, the form and functions of the Gibson family in *The Sound and the Fury.* Faulkner's works after 1940 that encompass the Negro in any meaningful way seem more self-conscious, and at times even defensive, treatments by the writer as spokesman for the morally aware, responsive South. Of these works that centrally involve the Negro, only *Go Down, Moses* is a major addition to the Faulkner canon.

By the 1940s too, the transition of the South to modernity was in its middle stages so that links to the past were much less clearly defined than during the 1920s and 1930s. For instance, the South in the twenties and thirties was overwhelmingly rural, with 5.5 million people employed in agriculture in 1930, but by 1950 only 3.2 million were employed in agriculture. And it is the rural, small-town South of Faulkner's boyhood at the turn of the century and of his young manhood in the twenties that continued to provide the raw material for his fiction. In a sense, Faulkner never seemed to move beyond the thirties in his general conception of the South; for example, in 1955 at Nagano, Japan, he spoke at length on the South's economic system as the basis of racial prejudice in the region. When asked to clarify his statements, Faulkner insisted on his economic interpretation by claiming that the South has "an economy of producing cotton primarily." Yet, his claim is not at all an accurate portrayal of the South in the 1950s, or even in the 1940s, although it would be applicable to the South of the twenties and thirties. Thus, my second reason for concentrating on 1926–1936 is that this period provides Faulkner with his dominant image of the South and with a particular perspective from which he viewed both earlier and later periods in southern history.

My specific concern lies with Faulkner's "Negro" in the context of his art and the South. By treating black characters in their nexus of relationships with structure, theme, symbols, and characters in the individual novels, I show that "Negro" functions as a basic concept underlying Faulkner's fiction. Previous studies have recognized that Faulkner's blacks are portrayed primarily in terms of their connection with white characters or their association with themes; however, none has attempted to pursue this conclusion or to examine "the Negro" in these larger terms. As a result, much of the existing criticism is devoted to isolated treatments of Faulkner's blacks or to specialized aspects of individual works, while the larger relation to and construction of the whole go ignored. Charles H. Nilon's brief monograph, *Faulkner and the Negro* (New York: The Citadel Press, 1965), is the major example. Other studies have focused on sociological generalizations about the Negro. These have failed to illuminate in any coherent way the artistic burden Faulkner usually places on his "Negro" in the invention and structure of his fiction. For instance, Charles D. Peavy uses only Faulkner's nonfictional statements in order to discuss his attitudes toward race relations in *Go Slow Now: Faulkner and the Race Question* (Eugene: University of Oregon Press, 1971). There are, then, serious omissions in the criticism which deserve to be corrected. Lee Jenkins' work, *Faulkner and Black–White Relations: A Psychoanalytic Approach* (New York: Columbia University Press, 1981), constitutes what I hope will be the start of fresh reconsiderations. Published after the completion of this study, *Faulkner and Black–White Relations* is a fuller discussion than earlier studies, but the conclusions, by virtue of the approach, are different from those reached in this work.

I have confined my discussion neither to Faulkner's "Negro" in isolation nor to black characters solely in relation to other blacks. As a result of placing the Negro in the formal contexts in which he exists in Faulkner's fiction, this work contains discussions usually omitted from strictly thematic studies of Faulkner's blacks. For instance, I include lengthy discussions of Jason and Quentin Compson, Lena Grove, and Rosa Coldfield as they reflect artistic uses or aesthetic assumptions regarding the Negro. If I seem to overlook some minor appearance of black characters while devoting space to white characters, it is generally because I focus on "Negro" as both character and concept in order to demonstrate how "Negro" operates within and contributes to the entire novel—its narrative structure, thematic design, character development, or other applicable aspects of the fiction. In some minor cases I assume that the similarities of function are readily apparent and so do not repeat the discussion. Overall, my concern is not with enumerating the black figures in Faulkner's novels, but rather with what the Negro reveals about the novels and the process of creating them.

CHAPTER I

Cultural Contexts

The Artist, the South, and the Negro

Mississippi begins at the lobby of a Memphis, Tennessee hotel and extends South to the Gulf of Mexico. It is dotted with little towns and concentric about the ghosts of the horses and mules once tethered to the hitch-rail enclosing the county courthouse and it might also be said to have only those two directions, north and south. . . .

"Mississippi," *Essays, Speeches and Public Letters by William Faulkner*, p. 11.

Home again, his native land; he was born of it and his bones will sleep in it; loving it even while hating some of it. . . .

"Mississippi," p. 36.

"Art is no part of southern life," William Faulkner has asserted in an essay written during the summer of 1933.[1] In that essay, one of two extant versions of an introduction to a proposed edition of *The Sound and the Fury*, he substantiates his claim by recording his personal conceptions about art and the artist in the South. These conceptions, while essentially consistent with his later views, are limited to a specific historical context, the 1920s and 1930s. At the same time, they are especially valuable for their presentations of his most frank and cogent appraisal of art and the South, an appraisal which no-

---

1 William Faulkner, "An Introduction to *The Sound and the Fury*," *Mississippi Quarterly*, XXVI (Summer, 1973), 410. Reprinted in *A Faulkner Miscellany*, ed. James B. Meriwether (Jackson: University Press of Mississippi, 1974), 156–61.

where else, to my knowledge, has been so incisively expressed. For the most part, Faulkner's other observations on the South and aesthetics made primarily during interviews or class conferences are not wholly satisfactory if one is searching for direct expression of the theories guiding his writing. They are generally spontaneous statements, sometimes rambling homespun witticisms, often tongue-in-cheek responses.

As Joseph W. Reed has indicated, the difficulty in establishing the theoretical basis of Faulkner's art is due to his own posturing and the simplistic, frequently contradictory, nature of his interviews.[2] Even in his class discussions at Virginia, Faulkner was apt to give answers that, while ostensibly serious, were actually informed by the sense of humor of a southern storyteller; for example: "I might say that when the so called blossoming of Southern writers came along, it was a time when nobody in the South had much money, they couldn't travel, and they had to invent a world a little different from the shabby one they lived in, so they took to writing, which is cheaper than—that is, a ream of paper and a pencil is cheaper than a railroad ticket."[3] In comparison with comments such as this one, Faulkner's 1933 introduction offers a perceptive interpretation of the artist in the region, though it is most enlightening in terms of his own art.[4] For in that essay Faulkner comes closer than in any other single statement to expressing, coherently, the place of the South in his creative drives and aesthetic intentions.

When Faulkner elaborates on art in southern life, his personal vi-

2 For a detailed treatment of this subject, see Joseph W. Reed, Jr., *Faulkner's Narrative* (New Haven: Yale University Press, 1973), 1–11.
3 Frederick L. Gwynn and Joseph L. Blotner (eds.), *Faulkner in the University: Class Conferences at the University of Virginia, 1957–1958* (Charlottesville: University Press of Virginia, 1959), 43.
4 Regarding Faulkner's impressions of southern culture and literature, as well as general historical or sociological valuations, I agree with historian Thomas D. Clark that "clearly there is no single pattern of Southern culture, and no single set of facts will describe the region." *The Emerging South* (2nd ed.; New York: Oxford University Press, 1968), xiii. See also C. Hugh Holman, "The View from the Regency-Hyatt: Southern Social Issues and the Outer World," in *Southern Fiction Today: Renascence and Beyond*, ed. George Core (Athens: University of Georgia Press, 1969), 16, 18; and Holman, "Diversity Within Unity," *Three Modes of Southern Fiction: Glasgow, Faulkner and Styron* (Athens: University of Georgia Press, 1966), 1–10.

sion builds directly upon H. L. Mencken's essay "The Sahara of the Bozart," a formidable attack on the South as "almost as sterile, artistically, intellectually, culturally as the Sahara Desert,"[5] which helped to goad the region into artistic endeavors during the early twenties. Similar to Mencken's interpretation, Faulkner's analysis is not a lament but an indictment:

> But in the South art, to become visible at all, must become a ceremony, a spectacle, something between a gypsy encampment and a church bazaar given by a handful of alien mummers who must waste themselves in protest and active self-defense until there is nothing left with which to speak—a single week, say, of furious endeavor for a show to be held on Friday night and then struck and vanished, leaving only a paint-stiffened smock or a worn out typewriter ribbon in the corner and perhaps a small bill for cheesecloth or bunting in the hands of an astonished and bewildered tradesman.[6]

Art in the South, he maintains, has not been incorporated into everyday life and, therefore, must become an exaggerated display ("a ceremony, a spectacle") if it is to receive any attention at all (by attention I mean a simple notice and imply neither acceptance nor accolade). The southern artist, unlike his northern counterpart, is forced by the attitudes of his society to dissipate his creative energy in the defense of art. Society's failure to understand the aesthetic impulse alienates the artist; yet withdrawal by the artist would further remove the possibility of art from the society. Thus, though "alien

5 H. L. Mencken, "The Sahara of the Bozart," *Prejudices: Series Two* (New York: Knopf, 1920), 136, 142. This essay, originally published in a shorter version in the November 13, 1917, New York *Evening Mail*, is similar in strategy to Faulkner's. Fred C. Hobson, Jr., provides a full discussion of "The Sahara of the Bozart" and Mencken's impact on the South in *Serpent of Eden: H. L. Mencken and the South* (Chapel Hill: University of North Carolina Press, 1974), 11–32.
6 Faulkner, "An Introduction to *The Sound and the Fury*," 411. See Mencken's comparable statement, "The Sahara of the Bozart," 140. A similar view of the writer and the community appears in sociologist John Maclachlan's "No Faulkner in Metropolis," in Louis D. Rubin, Jr., and Robert D. Jacobs (eds.), *Southern Renascence: The Literature of the Modern South* (Baltimore: Johns Hopkins University Press, 1953), 109. See also Louis D. Rubin, Jr., *The Faraway Country: Writers of the Modern South* (Seattle: University of Washington Press, 1963), 5–8; and Willard Thorp, "The Writer as Pariah in the Old South," in R. C. Simonini (ed.), *Southern Writers: Appraisals in Our Time* (1961; rpt. Freeport, N.Y.: Books for Libraries, 1969), 3–18.

mummers," southern writers persist in presenting their specta-
cles; they understand and respond by calculated design to the unacknowledged needs of their community.

What Faulkner implies is that specific social constraints operate
to influence not just an artist's subject matter and theme, but the
form of the presentation as well. A concern with form, with the
whole work as an art object, is generally characteristic of the first-
generation Southern Renascence writers. For these highly conscious
literary artists (Faulkner, Katherine Anne Porter, Caroline Gordon,
Robert Penn Warren, and Andrew Lytle among others), "art was an
autotelic activity, and . . . fiction could aspire to the artistic unity,
finish, and ultimate effect normally associated with only poetry."[7]
Some measure of this concern with artistic control of the medium is,
of course, attributable to the influence of T. S. Eliot and the European literary avant garde, who considered art as autotelic; but a
large part is the result of an attempt by these writers to come to
terms with themselves as artists and as southerners, as well as to
prove Mencken (and others disparaging their region) wrong, by
effecting a revival of arts and letters in the South.

Faulkner's analysis of art in the South, however, alludes to general
social considerations as still another factor contributing to the emphasis on form. He implies, as well, a social function of art. He suggests that because art is not intrinsic to southern life, a special burden is placed on the southern artist. This burden includes the
obligation to infuse art into southern life. Concerning his creation of
Yoknapatawpha County, Faulkner states: "I was trying to reduce my
one individual experience of the world into one compact thing
which could be picked up and held in the hands at one time."[8]
Hence, evolves the creation of a South in the fiction that, like Balzac's Paris or Tolstoy's Russia, does not conform to actual human or
physical geography; a fictional South that is purely an aesthetic
achievement and not valid as either sociological or historical "fact."[9]

7 John M. Bradbury, *Renaissance in the South: A Critical History of Literature, 1920–1960*
(Chapel Hill: University of North Carolina Press, 1963), 15.
8 *Interviews in Japan* (1955), in James B. Meriwether and Michael Millgate (eds.),
Lion in the Garden: Interviews with William Faulkner, 1926–1962 (New York: Random
House, 1968), 133.
9 Ward L. Miner interprets the geography of Faulkner's Jefferson and Yoknapataw-

Faulkner's Yoknapatawpha is the most famous example, but there are others: Eudora Welty's Mississippi, Thomas Wolfe's Altamont, North Carolina, T. S. Stribling's Florence, Alabama.

A striking paradox related to the position of the artist is evident in Faulkner's contention: "Yet this art, which has no place in southern life is almost the sum total of the Southern artist. It is his breath, blood, flesh, all. Not so much that it is forced back upon him or he is forced bodily into it by the circumstance; forced to choose, lady and tiger fashion, between being an artist and being a man. He does it deliberately; he wishes it so. This has always been true of him and of him alone." The southern artist lives his art seriously, feels it intensely because he embraces it so totally (the attendant complications peculiar to the South notwithstanding). "Only Southerners," Faulkner reminds us, "have taken horsewhips and pistols to editors about the treatment or maltreatment of their manuscript." He also reveals an imaginative link between himself (and his contemporaries) and those passionate writers of an earlier day: "This—the actual pistols—was in the old days . . . we no longer succumb to the impulse. But it is still there, still within us."[10]

If art is not part of southern life, as Faulkner claims, then the distinct directions of his own art are all the more remarkable. His decision to concentrate in fiction on his own "little postage stamp of native soil," and to remain in residence there, has allied his work from the beginning with the South as a region. This alliance has been on a grand scale; perhaps only Thomas Wolfe has attempted to execute a vision of "the South" as large. More than any other writer Faulkner explored the richness and complexity of southern life in his fiction (which in itself argues his explicit rejection of alternative subject matter). Beginning with his first novel, *Soldiers' Pay* (1926), with its raw materials not yet imaginatively distilled, Faulkner has created a mythical region out of his own imagination and his creative understanding of the South, her traditions and legacies. Since then he has

---

pha quite literally in *The World of William Faulkner* (Durham, N.C.: Duke University Press, 1952), 104, 86–87. For a more recent example of literal interpretations of Jefferson and Oxford, Yoknapatawpha and Lafayette, Mississippi, see Elizabeth M. Kerr, *Yoknapatawpha: Faulkner's "Little Postage Stamp of Native Soil"* (New York: Fordham University Press, 1969).

10 Faulkner, "An Introduction to *The Sound and the Fury*," 411–12.

scrutinized his created world and set it forth in minute detail which ultimately magnifies the most significant aspects of the human situation. His characters (the Sartorises, and Compsons, Dilsey and Nancy, the Sutpens and Snopeses alike) are people caught in the act of life, and they are distinctly southern, not incidentally but by dint of his conscious, repeated design. His intense probing of the human condition urges the reader to interact imaginatively in translating the experience of the exposed people of the South into symbolic meaning.

To talk about the South is to suggest the Negro; the two collectively, in achievement and despair, are irrevocably joined. To consider the social or historical context of Faulkner's fiction is to evoke the association of "the Negro" and "the South." And at the root of the problems besetting the region defined by Faulkner, and ultimately the southern artist, is the treatment and place of the Negro.

Faulkner's notions of Negro life were shaped by a traditional society known more for its solidarity than its mavericks. The "solid South" had one clearly defined conception of what "the Negro" was: he was *not white*. Whatever else he might be issued in descending order from that conception, thereby assuring definitions and descriptions of the Negro in terms of his physical differences from the white man and his deviation from white standards. The Negro was considered inferior to whites in every area of consequence. Faulkner inherently shares this traditional view of blacks. Yet to argue that Faulkner directly transcribes the general racial precepts of "the solid South" is to deny his striking individuality and his artistry. His thinking and writing, although responding to the external world, are not rigidly *determined* by an amorphous southern tradition. His fiction is neither photographic realism nor journalistic writing, and Faulkner is neither social historian nor philosopher, particularly in regard to black people. However, he has assumed that the Negro is an essential element of the life of the South, accepting him without question as a major force in southern culture; and Faulkner has produced works intrinsically based on this preconception.

From *Sartoris* (1929, originally entitled *Flags in the Dust*) through *The Reivers* (1962), Faulkner's fiction reveals a preoccupation with the black presence in areas of southern life and thought that are crucial

to his art. Out of a subjective understanding of history and experience, he has created memorable black characters (Luster Gibson,
Lucas Beauchamp, Ned William McCaslin Jefferson Mississippi) and
also striking portrayals of the centrality of race in southern attitudes
and mores (*Light in August, Absalom, Absalom!, Go Down, Moses*).
This extensive figuring of a Negro presence is, in fact, one distinguishing characteristic of the work Faulkner produced over nearly
four decades.

In the novels of his first decade, 1926–1936, the recurrence of the
Negro makes it apparent that Faulkner has found signal inspiration in the life of blacks, and it suggests that the Negro is part of
Faulkner's creative impulse. In three of his major novels, *The Sound
and the Fury (1929), Light in August (1932)*, and *Absalom, Absalom!*
(1936), the Negro is important as a dominant thematic concern, but
even more so as an artistic conception affecting Faulkner's vision of
his work and his choices for communicating that vision. Even when
the Negro as character or theme is not the central focus, as in *Soldiers' Pay* and *Sartoris*, he remains a vital part of the texture of life
created, part of a "southern" atmosphere. Inasmuch as Faulkner's
novels of this decade evidence a painstaking concern for a surface
reality enmeshed in a complex form, they suggest the magnitude of
communicating a whole, a substantive reality in art when the external world is so fragmented, irrational, and distorted. Each of these
novels shows a struggling with the difficulty of form in art that
seems related to the struggle to understand both a society and a vision in spite of problems or imperfections. By his use of the Negro
Faulkner explores the relationship between form and the southern
experience.

Unfortunately, his "Negro" has often received critical attention
solely because of the sociological implications relating to southern
society.[11] The focus is on discovering Faulkner's "real" feelings or attitudes toward blacks, at the expense of viewing his people as characters. In addition, identifying Faulkner the Mississippian too closely with his individual characters or narrators has resulted in some

11 See, for example, Charles D. Peavy, *Go Slow Now: Faulkner and the Race Question*
(Eugene: University of Oregon Press, 1971).

hysterical and misleading writing on the race issue in his fiction. Maxwell Geismar has become the most commonly referred to example of the critical misreading involving "the Negro." He presents Faulkner as "the supreme example" of a "hatred of life so compelling . . . that there almost seems to be an inability in the writer to reach maturity itself"; moreover, he interprets Faulkner as a man driven by "twin Furies: the Female and the Negro," personal symbols of evil drawn out of a severe "cultural psychosis."[12]

Even in later criticism, views of Faulkner's "Negro" related to Geismar's have persisted. Aaron Steinberg, for instance, has probed Faulkner's attitudes toward blacks and has found a deep ingrained hostility toward them. Steinberg concludes that Faulkner's attitudes are irrational and reveal him to be a victim of himself, "trapped in the web of his own Southern fantasies."[13] What Steinberg does not go on to say is that every imaginative writer is in some way entrapped by his own fantasies, that his struggle is to order and shape them into a form which communicates with the external world. The ability to articulate fantasies that strike a responsive, or familiar, chord in individuals unable to make their own expressions is part of the artist's creative endeavor.

The emphasis on the relationship of Faulkner's black characters to thematic content has led to insufficient analysis of their place and relation to fictional structure and form. Although the separation of content and form into two distinct aspects is no longer critically viable, some studies of Faulkner's "Negro" suggest a division, or at best a separate locus in experience for matter and form, in their stressing of thematic readings. The deep personal involvement with the South and the Negro in Faulkner's artistic vision is partly responsible for the tendency. The more intimately a writer is associated with his subject the more difficult it becomes for the critic to separate

12 Maxwell Geismar, "William Faulkner: The Negro and the Female," *Writers in Crisis: The American Novel, 1925–1940* (1947; rpt. New York: Hill and Wang, 1961), 168, 181. The value of Geismar's essay, unfortunately almost forgotten, is his recognition of the importance of childhood and innocence and the special ways blacks relate to the two in Faulkner's fiction. The importance of childhood relationships and the Negro is taken up by Irving Howe, "William Faulkner and the Negroes: A Vision of Lost Fraternity," *Commentary*, XII (October, 1951), 359–68.
13 Aaron Steinberg, "Faulkner and the Negro" (Ph.D. dissertation, New York University, 1963), 362–89.

areas of emotional and intellectual responses. However, as Ralph Ellison has pointed out, "Every serious novel is beyond its immediate thematic preoccupations a discussion of the craft; a conquest of the form, and a conflict with its difficulties; a pursuit of its felicities and beauty."[14] In his attempt to confront the reality of his South, Faulkner has had both successes and failures. Nevertheless, the Negro and the South are related to the form of his novels, and to his characteristic way of perceiving experience, ordering and presenting materials. "Negro" both as character, an actual physical presence, and as a cultural concept, a disembodied myth in the South's psyche, is integral to his art. Faulkner's "Negro" is not a test of his humanity, but a measure of his creativity.

As a southerner Faulkner may have become openly embroiled in the unending controversy regarding race in the South; nevertheless, as an artist committed to communicating his vision of life, he is not so interested in blacks as individual characters as he is in formulating his aesthetic image and sense of "Negro." He has stated that his writing "could have sociological implications," but he is not absorbed in that aspect because his intention is to write about people, to create people.[15] His primary intention is not to provide sociological treatises on race and color; as he once remarked: "The writer's only responsibility is to his art. He will be completely ruthless if he is a good one. He has a dream. It anguishes him so much he must get rid of it. He has no peace until then. Everything goes by the board: home, pride, decency, security, happiness, all to get the book written. If a writer has to rob his mother, he will not hesitate; the 'Ode on a Grecian Urn' is worth any number of old ladies."[16] Because for Faulkner artistic integrity is more of a guiding principle than is social commitment, his foremost concern is neither the Negro nor any social problem.

The real issue is whether Faulkner's black characters stand or fail on their own merit as characters within the artistic context he has

---

14 Ralph Ellison, "Society, Morality and the Novel," in Grandville Hicks (ed.), *The Living Novel: A Symposium* (New York: Macmillan, 1957), 60.
15 Gwynn and Blotner (eds.), *Faulkner in the University*, 57.
16 Interview with Jean Stein (1956), in Meriwether and Millgate (eds.), *Lion in the Garden*, 239.

invented for them. If they are credible "people" within his fictional world, then in one sense at least they have succeeded. Whether they measurably enrich the reader's pleasure or understanding and how they do so are matters for critical evaluation. To say that the Negro is a central imaginative force in Faulkner's art[17] is not to say that Faulkner creates a mystique of the Negro. He does not; he does not have to. All the ingredients of a mystique are already entrenched in southern history and popular culture. While Faulkner's statements on the southern writer in "An Introduction to *The Sound and the Fury*" do not refer specifically to the Negro, they are informed by a consciousness of the tensions in southern life which result from the complicated "Negro Question."

At the base of Faulkner's analysis of southern life is an awareness of a society that is the legacy of the enslavement of human beings. Thus, in interpreting the dilemma of the southern writer in a society antagonistic to art, and to black humanity, Faulkner indicates that the process by which the southerner produces art is not just diffi-cult, it is violent: "[The southern writer] has, figuratively speaking, taken the artist in him in one hand and his milieu in the other and thrust the one into the other like a clawing and spitting cat into a croker sack. And he writes."[18] Faulkner contends that the southern artist can and does separate himself from his milieu, but that in or-der to write he must have the two come together, and that coming together is by no means an effortless union. His metaphor encom-passes violence and implies pain. The resultant work invariably ex-hibits the tensions provoking it, no matter whether the artist gives in to romantic tendencies, or takes a hard realistic approach, or strives for some taut balance between the two.

The writer's creative process duplicates the violent nature of his society. Faulkner's elaboration of his point regarding the southern writer is succinct:

17 Two early Faulkner critics, Robert Penn Warren and Irving Howe, place the Negro at the center of Faulkner's imaginative life. See Robert Penn Warren, "Faulkner: The South, the Negro and Time," *Faulkner: A Collection of Critical Essays* (Englewood Cliffs, N.J.: Prentice-Hall, 1966), 257; Irving Howe, "Faulkner and the Negroes," *William Faulkner: A Critical Study* (2nd rev. ed.; New York: Random House, 1952), 132; and Howe, "Faulkner and the Negroes: A Vision of Lost Fraternity," 367.
18 Faulkner, "An Introduction to *The Sound and the Fury*," 412.

We seem to try in the simple furious breathing (or writing) span of the individual to draw a savage indictment of the contemporary scene or to escape from it into a makebelieve region of swords and magnolias and mockingbirds which perhaps never existed anywhere. Both of the courses are rooted in sentiment; perhaps the ones who write savagely and bitterly of the incest in clayfloored cabins are the most sentimental. Anyway, each course is a matter of violent partizanship, in which the writer unconsciously writes into every line and phrase his violent despairs and rages and frustrations or his violent prophesies or still more violent hopes.[19]

The southern writer, even when he is not conscious of the fact, writes with the weight of his cultural complex upon him; for as Faulkner also points out, "it is himself that the Southerner is writing about." The impetus for his writing, despite its directions, is related to a "violent partizanship," the writer's own way of responding to his South. Significantly, it is not objective "experience," Faulkner intimates, that connects southern writers; it is the nature of their literary design. One consequence, for Faulkner (as for Eudora Welty and Carson McCullers or William Styron and Elizabeth Spencer), is a movement simultaneously toward objective works, aesthetically conceived and executed, and toward a subjective vision, involved and complex.

Faulkner's forceful repetition of *violent* underscores the tension and conflict between the artist and his milieu which collide in giving birth to his writings. The emphasis on *violent* also reinforces another of Faulkner's insights regarding the southern artist: "I do not believe there lives the Southern writer who can say without lying that writing is any fun to him. Perhaps we do not want it to be."[20] His attempt to communicate a personal vision impels his writing. This conclusion (coupled with the idea that southern writers pour such intense emotional and intellectual "sentiment" into their works) provides a writer's insight into southern fiction. He implicitly addresses the issue of the prominence of violence and grotesques in the works of novelists as diverse as Thomas Wolfe and Erskine Caldwell.

An extension of Faulkner's conclusion would suggest, too, that one index to the quality of art produced by a southerner may well be

19 *Ibid.*
20 *Ibid.*

his ability to metamorphose those tensions emanating from his cultural heritage and his position as an artist in that culture. If he is able to transcend the tensions out of which his work is created and to sublimate them into aesthetic tensions that operate somehow harmoniously whether or not resolved, then he is at once envisioning art in the southern context and replacing art in southern life. Certainly this transcendency as a process of artistic integration is one measure of the distance between Faulkner and minor figures, such as T. S. Stribling, Frances Newman, and Julia Peterkin, whose writings, though containing moments of rare, penetrating insight, all too frequently evince a distracting quality either of a fractured psyche at work or a disturbing hiatus between the idea and its expression.

The point to be emphasized, however, is that Faulkner's art creates a new experience, which in turn expands the possibilities of the South, that South necessitating "violent despairs" or "violent hopes." In essence, the South becomes revitalized through a transferral of the imaginative energy that attends first the creation of fiction, then the aesthetic experience fiction engenders. And the new experience comes into being through the artist's imaginative daring in connecting the raw materials of experience (that is, the details of southern life as the artist perceives them) to matter ordered through form (the work of art). "If the artist does not perfect a new vision in his process of doing," John Dewey states, "he acts mechanically and repeats some old model fixed like a blue print in his mind."[21] Faulkner's process is vital, as it encompasses evolving yet abiding responses to the pressures and tensions of southern life as well as to the aesthetic demands of fiction.

The tension between artist and milieu, of course, is limited neither to the South nor any one place or time; it may even be the typical state for the creation of art. Nevertheless, Faulkner is aware of the unique circumstances that make the South especially problematical for the artist. The particular bent of his comments stems from the application of his implicit aesthetic principles to the peculiar situation of the post–World War I South. Faulkner sees the writer as per-

21 John Dewey, *Art as Experience* (New York: Minton, Balch, 1934), 50.

forming a social function in expressing the materials of experience, capturing the essence of life from its flux and flow. In effect, as he has said, the aim of the artist is "to arrest motion, which is life, by artificial means and hold it fixed so that 100 years later when a stranger looks at it, it moves again since it is life."[22] For an artist of responsive sensibilities, a singular opportunity presented itself in the contemporary South, which in moving toward modernity emerged as a labyrinth of new experience, involving resistance and tensions that had not yet been adequately assimilated into the culture. These evolving materials demanded expression. The difficulty for Faulkner lay, it would appear, in holding fixed both apprehension and expression (that is, vision and form) of a whole in the midst of the tense, contradictory condition of southern life.

Historically the South has been painfully aware of the critical flux of things, especially time and fortune; however, the specific South to which Faulkner addresses himself was beset by more immediate strife—that of a culture at once dying and regenerating. Consciousness of change was one dominant characteristic of the times. This characteristic was part of the aesthetic problem pointed out by Faulkner, in that the relinquishing of forms and concepts no longer valid and the struggle to create or rediscover appropriate replacements made the writer's task especially challenging. The problems of race relations, caste privilege, and agrarian reform in a region becoming industrialized and urbanized were compounded by resistance to change. Two conflicting images of the region informed Faulkner's view: "The benighted (or embattled) South" and "the progressive New South."[23] Both economic and social change were considered disruptive by various elements of southern society. Among the most prominent reactionaries were the Ku Klux Klan and the fundamentalists, whose greatest anxiety was over the disintegration of traditional culture. Their opponents, the advocates of the "New

22 Interview with Jean Stein, in Meriwether and Millgate (eds.), *Lion in the Garden*, 253.
23 George Brown Tindall, *The Emergence of the New South, 1913–1945*, Vol. X of Wendell Holmes Stephenson and E. Merton Coulter (eds.) *A History of the South* (Baton Rouge: Louisiana State University Press, 1967), 575.

South," were equally adamant in welcoming "progress." Together these two perspectives created additional stress in an already disjointed society.

A deep conflict of values was inevitable.[24] The conflict was evident in economics and politics, as well as in literature, religion, and education. Moreover, the social and community issues signaled the deeper problems of personal and individual identity and development. For Faulkner, as for any artist who relies upon the value system of his society to measure or reaffirm his private value judgments, the problems were acute.

A major portion of the tensions during the period may be traced to the treatment and conception of the Negro, who, as Louis D. Rubin, Jr., maintains, had "the crucial role" as "index and cause of Southern attitudes."[25] As perhaps the central theme in southern life, the Negro was a significant factor in the transition from rural to urban life. Regarding this point, Thomas D. Clark has declared: "When the modern Southerner speaks so vehemently about maintaining the Southern way of life, he is not talking about old economic or regional folk patterns . . . he has in mind one specific subject—racial relations."[26]

The twenties and thirties continued the practices of the post-Reconstruction era, when the central tenet of white southern need was keeping "the Negro" in his place. Notions of his "place" were complicated by the general fluidity of the southern social system as

24 An interpretation of the conflict between the old ideals centering around the "Lost Cause" and the new proclaiming industrialism and progress appears in C. Vann Woodward's chapter, "The Divided Mind of the South," in his *Origins of the New South, 1877–1913* (Baton Rouge: Louisiana State University Press, 1951), 142–74.

25 Rubin, *The Faraway Country*, xi. Rubin is not alone in this interpretation. In the 1850s Frederick Law Olmstead made a similar conclusion after his travels throughout the South, and in 1929 Ulrich B. Phillips identified the slave or Negro influence as the central one in southern history. For a symposium of the various historical theories regarding the central themes distinguishing the South, see Monroe L. Billington (ed.), *The South: A Central Theme* (New York: Holt, Rinehart and Winston, 1969).

26 Clark, *The Emerging South*, 206–207; see also 176. In 1912 James Weldon Johnson pointed out that the white southerner is "impassably limited by the ever present 'Negro Question'; . . . it would be safe to wager that no group of Southern white men could get together and talk for sixty minutes without bringing up 'the race question.' If a Northern white man happened to be in the group, the time could be safely cut to thirty minutes." *The Autobiography of an Ex-Coloured Man* (1912; rpt. New York: Knopf, 1927), 76.

the individual's traditional relationship to the land changed. The enigmatic position of blacks, highly visible, yet outside the mainstream, sustained a tension-filled atmosphere and blurred visions of life. Because the society was so filled with tensions—varied, impersonal, obscure—"the Negro" became a scapegoat, a personified threat to long-cherished and conflicting values of white southerners: individualism, localism, family, and clan.

The years between the mid-twenties and the end of the thirties witnessed a literary Renascence; nevertheless, they were also years when racial segregation and white supremacy were not merely ingrained patterns of southern thought, but accepted civil institutions as well. Just as slavery had been rationalized as a charitable institution and justified by biblical interpretations, so was "Jim Crow" in the twentieth century. This segregationist strategy had been encouraged on the state and local levels by the official sanctions of Woodrow Wilson's administration.[27] In fact, the period following World War I brought about the "greatest stratification of the races and widespread enactment of 'Jim Crow' laws."[28] Lynchings, too, though declining, were not uncommon. By 1926 (the year Faulkner's first novel, a southern pastoral, was published), the new Ku Klux Klan had reached a peak of five million members nationally and was an active force in "inflaming prejudice, encouraging race violence, and strengthening segregation codes."[29] Here again, for the artist the quality and meaning of southern life in a positive sense could not be readily determined from these external activities.

In 1927 Faulkner's home state, Mississippi, dubbed "the worst American state" by H. L. Mencken after an exhaustive statistical survey,[30] became especially infamous for brutality in enforcing black subjugation through "Jim Crow" codes, lynchings, and economic exploitation (possibly because as of 1934 it was the last southern

27 For a useful discussion of the spread of segregation in Washington, D.C., and the departments of government under Wilson, see Lawrence J. Friedman, *The White Savage: Racial Fantasies in the Postbellum South* (Englewood Cliffs, N.J.: Prentice-Hall, 1970), 150–72.
28 C. Vann Woodward, *The Strange Career of Jim Crow* (2nd rev. ed.; New York: Oxford University Press, 1966), 115.
29 *Ibid.*
30 Charles Angoff and H. L. Mencken, "The Worst American State," *American Mercury*, XXIV (1931), 1–16, 175–88, 355–71.

state with over 50 percent black population).[31] Already known for violent resistance to change, it was the state most committed to the unabashed style and race-baiting of "redneck" politics.[32] Mississippians and demagogues James K. Vardaman and Theodore C. Bilbo have become synonymous with the racism of a political approach pitting poor-whites against blacks.

Not only did Mississippi have the highest illiteracy rate, but also as the most rural southern state, the highest unemployment, resulting from the collapse of the cotton market. Within the state the black population was, as a matter of course, hardest hit by the failure of both education and King Cotton. Even in his personal version of Mississippi history, Faulkner found the oppression of blacks pervasive:

> The lynching of Negroes not for the crimes they committed but because their skins were black (they were becoming fewer and fewer . . . soon there would be no more of them but the evil would have been done . . . irrevocable because there should never have been any); the inequality; the poor schools they had when they had any, the hovels they had to live in unless they wanted to live outdoors; who could worship the white man's God but not in the white man's church; pay taxes in the white man's courthouse but couldn't vote in it or for it; working by the white man's clock but having to take his pay by the white man's counting.[33]

At the same time Mississippi, more than any other state, proclaimed the myths of the Old South—elegance, grace, and order. There was a semblance of truth to the myths, for large plantations and rural folk mores and values remained more nearly intact in Mis-

---

31 W. T. Couch, "The Negro in the South," in *Culture in the South*, ed. W. T. Couch (Chapel Hill: University of North Carolina Press, 1934), 438.

32 Tindall, *The Emergence of the New South*, 233–34. See also Albert D. Kirwan's analysis of political conflict within Mississippi and between economic classes in *The Revolt of the Rednecks: Mississippi Politics, 1876–1925* (Lexington: University of Kentucky Press, 1951).

33 William Faulkner, "Mississippi" (*Holiday*, April, 1954), rpt. in James B. Meriwether (ed.), *Essays, Speeches, and Public Letters of William Faulkner* (New York: Random House, 1965), 37. The facts in Faulkner's account closely follow those in *Mississippi: A Guide to the Magnolia State*, Federal Writers' Project "American Guide Series" (New York: Knopf, 1937). His reworking of the *Guide* materials involves a shifting of emphasis to the role and position of the Negro in the history of the region, and to his personal experiences with blacks—particularly his recollections of his mammy, Caroline Barr. See, for instance, Faulkner, "Mississippi," 16–17, 19–20, 39–43.

sissippi than anywhere else. Louis D. Rubin, Jr., has concluded about the social milieu of Mississippi that "nowhere else in the South has the tension between tradition and change, between moral precept and animal instinct, between wealth and poverty, between order and disorder, between black and white, between aristocracy and redneck, been so sharply drawn, and so dramatically revelatory."[34] And Rubin's listing does not at all exaggerate the great dichotomies within the state. In general attitudes and specific conditions Mississippi was a microcosm of the southern condition.

By my concentration on the South, I do not mean to suggest that Faulkner's fiction is a mimetic treatment of "southern" reality. There is, after all, no "fact" or evidence that can be used to validate any of his fictional statements. As he pointed out, storytelling is a form of lying.[35] Moreover, his identification of himself as "sole owner and proprietor" of Yoknapatawpha is his way of emphasizing the author's complete authority over his people and events. My discussion of the transitional South is intended to indicate that the conflicting patterns of Mississippi and southern life during this period suggest an experience that was stimulating to the creative writer. And the Negro lies at the heart of that experience. As Nancy Tischler has remarked in a survey of black character in modern southern fiction, "The Southern writer has very little choice—if he is to write about the South, he must write about the Negro."[36]

For the artist inclined to explore "life," the Negro had a special appeal. By virtue of his enslavement and separation from his African homeland, the Negro is a dramatic representation of human struggle for survival in a world (especially in a modern, industrial world bereft of traditional customs and values). His African heritage also makes him particularly attractive as an exotic primitive offering a vicarious escape from mundane concerns. Because of his traditional position in southern life, the Negro evokes a wide range of associations and is capable of interaction with all levels of society. For instance, only the Negro has traditionally had contact with every pos-

---

34 Rubin, *The Faraway Country*, 68.
35 Gwynn and Blotner (eds.), *Faulkner in the University*, 277.
36 Nancy Tischler, *Black Masks: Negro Characters in Modern Southern Fiction* (University Park: Pennsylvania State University Press, 1969), 12.

sible caste and class in the South, from aristocrat to poor-white, from plantation owner to industrial worker. His presence alone can evoke myths of "blackness" as evil, damned, or mysterious; or it can recall theories of blacks as descendants of Ham and the progeny of Cain. The Negro can be used to suggest conceptual structures: slavery, sexuality, primitivism, fraternity, endurance, hope. He may symbolize historical contexts: the antebellum South, the Civil War, Reconstruction. Or he may represent change: the destruction of the cavalier and plantation myths; the failure of King Cotton; the conversion power of faith or love; the rise of the modern South.

Largely because of the Negro, the southern artist found a coherent locus of meaning in the South. By observing and synthesizing the Negro's experience, the artist saw that the tragedy and the comedy of fundamental human experience could be approached directly. Or, as in the case of works such as *Soldiers' Pay* and *The Sound and the Fury*, Negro experience could place the experience of southern life in wider perspectives and less parochial contexts. However, Negro life, even when considered superficially, made accessible to the artist (no matter the degree of his talent or powers of observation) the inner realities of southern culture. In addition, Negro life laid bare complex personal emotions and responses to the vicissitudes of existence. For both artist and average southerner, "the Negro" personified life's simpler functions and its serious problems; in a pseudo-theoretical sense he represented an attitude toward being that counteracted the more destructive conditions of industrialization and the breakdown of rural patterns.

Paradoxically, though the Negro became the South's metaphor for change, he remained the region's lone constant while traditions crumbled. He contributed much to the southerner's need for continuity and stability. Within a context of change and conflict, the Negro provided a central rallying point of order and meaning for the diverse ideologies about both "the Negro" and the "New South." There was much truth to an old saying about the Mississippi Delta region: "The variable factors are high water and the price of cotton; the constant is the Negro."[37]

37 Federal Writers' Project, *Mississippi*, 4.

The progress toward the literary exploitation of Negro life during the transition can be simply stated, though the actual process was much more complex. The general conditions of southern life gave rise to a literary concern with social issues and problems. The resulting efflorescence of the literature was termed the "new realism," which actually meant social criticism. And social criticism for the southerner invariably involves the Negro. The Negro provided a fresh symbol for analyzing man in society, as well as a familiar, generally agreed upon language system for that analysis. Perhaps a symbolic statement of the new trends in southern literary activity were the deaths between 1922 and 1925 of four of the major figures associated with the genteel tradition of the nineteenth-century South: Thomas Nelson Page, Mary Noailles Murfree, George Washington Cable, and James Lane Allen.

By 1922 with the publication of Hubert A. Shands's *White and Black*, T. S. Stribling's *Birthright*, and Clement Wood's *Nigger*, the cultural and literary Sahara delineated by Mencken had become a region reassessing itself in its literature, and to a large extent by making use of "the Negro," his folk life, and unique character.[38] Richard Wright's pronouncement that "the Negro is America's metaphor"[39] may elicit some dissent, but clearly at this point in time the Negro was the South's metaphor. At the end of the thirties, Shields McIlwaine could declare that "literature as well as trouble seems to start with the 'darky.' "[40] His observation is, in fact, historically accurate,

38 1922 was also the year of the publication of Ambrose Gonzales' *Black Border*. Between 1922 and the end of the decade writings by southern artists related to the Negro were so voluminous that even a list of the more important (artistically or historically) is lengthy: Jean Toomer, *Cane* (1923); Walter White, *The Fire and the Flint* (1924), *Flight* (1926); Dubose Heyward, *Porgy* (1925), *Mamba's Daughters* (1929); Elizabeth Madox Roberts, *My Heart and My Flesh* (1927); James Weldon Johnson, *God's Trombones* (1927); Julia Peterkin, *Black April* (1927), *Scarlet Sister Mary* (1928); E. C. L. Adams, *Congaree Sketches* (1927), *Nigger to Nigger* (1928); Roark Bradford, *Ol' Man Adam an' His Chillun* (1928), *Ol' King David and the Philistine Boys* (1929); Howard Odum, *Rainbow Round My Shoulder* (1928), *Wings on My Feet* (1929). And Faulkner's own *The Sound and the Fury* (1929) may be added to this list because its portrait of black humanity is central to the novel's meaning.

Howard Odum cites 800 nonfiction works on Negro life, 400 on nature and the folk, and 100 on socioeconomic studies during the first fifty years of this century. Odum, "On Southern Literature and Southern Culture," in Rubin and Jacobs (eds.) *Southern Renascence*, 85.

39 Richard Wright, *White Man, Listen!* (Garden City: Doubleday, 1957), 109.

40 Shields McIlwaine, *The Southern Poor-White: From Lubberland to Tobacco Road* (1939;

linking as it does the 1920s and 1930s to the 1880s (the rise of local color and genteel literature); during both periods black characters, their folklore and race relations, inspired, and to a degree dominated, much of the literary activity.

The popularity of the Negro as a fictional subject has been explained in terms of "his tragic evolutionary background, his stranger-than-fiction Southern story and his modern unprecedented quick entry into the total consciousness of a nation."[41] But these are the more comprehensive reasons which do not take into account the pervasive, superficial generalizations about the Negro's personality: his love of rhetoric, his ability to tell a good story, his enjoyment of life, his capacity for love and laughter, his harmony with the natural rhythms of life, his instinct for survival, his faith in God and belief in the supernatural. Various combinations of these stereotypes attracted white authors of the transitional South to the black experience. These same stereotypes led to gross distortions of blacks (primarily as amoral primitives) that cannot be overlooked in a consideration of the literary background affecting Faulkner and contributed to by him.

There are two main reasons for the attraction to "Negro-centered" subjects. The first has to do with the Negro's part in an abiding pattern of southern life, which W. J. Cash has summarized:

> And in this society in which the infant son . . . was commonly suckled by a black mammy, in which gray old men were his most loved story-tellers, in which black stalwarts were among the chiefest heroes and mentors of his boyhood, and in which his usual, often practically his only companions until he was past the age of puberty were the black boys (and girls) of the plantation—in this society in which by far the greater number of white boys of whatever degree were more or less shaped by such companion-

---

rpt. New York: Cooper Square, 1970), 70. McIlwaine's statement may even be extended to the 1960s, the period of another revival of literature in the South which relied heavily upon the Negro. Woodward calls the rediscovery of blacks in the sixties acculturation in reverse, *The Burden of Southern History*, 181.

Literary critics in the sixties also pointed to the significance of the Negro. See Lewis Lawson, "Portrait of a Culture in Crisis: Modern Southern Literature," *Texas Quarterly*, X (Spring, 1967), 143–55; and Louis D. Rubin, Jr., "Southern Local Color and the Black Man," *Southern Review*, n.s. IV (October, 1970), 1011–30.

41 Odum, "On Southern Literature and Southern Culture," 97.

ship, and in which nearly the whole body of whites, young and old, had constantly before their eyes the example, had constantly in their ears the accent, of the Negro, the relationship was by the second generation . . . nothing less than organic. Negro entered into white man as profoundly as white man entered into Negro— subtly influencing every gesture, every word, every emotion and idea, every attitude.[42]

Cash describes the nature of the nineteenth- and early twentieth-century relationships between blacks and whites which, judging from fictional representation, were still integral in the twenties and thirties. Moreover, Cash presents the pattern of life and thought that led to two conceptions of blacks deeply entrenched in southern white consciousness and literature of the period. The two are the inherent capacity of blacks to serve others and their innate ability to appreciate life—stereotypes basic to much southern white writing of this period.

The second reason for the gravitation toward the Negro in literature has to do with the artist himself. Because of the adaptability of the Negro as character and symbol, the artist whose talents allowed him only poor communication of his vision or whose vision was itself inadequate used images of the Negro as a crutch, a convenient convention. Even some of the better writers exploited the Negro as a safe, though provocative type. Elizabeth Madox Roberts and T. S. Stribling, for instance, presented "problem" novels relying on the question of "the Negro's place" in the culture. Others of the "new realists" were interested in colorful sociological accounts (Howard Odum and Ambrose Gonzales, for example), or in the folk adventures of the African in the South (E. C. L. Adams or R. Emmet Ken-

42 Wilbur J. Cash, *The Mind of the South* (New York: Knopf, 1941), 49–50. Although Cash's book has been called into question because of its historical relativism, it retains much of its usefulness. Cash's writing may come more out of his experiences and observation of his native Carolinas than the whole South, yet it is applicable to Faulkner's Deep South. For example, his analysis provides a background for understanding Faulkner's heritage regarding blacks and his creative use of that heritage in numerous works, such as *Go Down, Moses* and *Intruder in the Dust*. Note, in particular, Molly Beauchamp as Ross Edmonds' nurse, Sam Fathers as Ike McCaslin's mentor, and Aleck Sanders as Chick Mallison's companion; all of these relationships, in light of Cash's work, suggest concrete detail imaginatively conceived and articulated out of a remembered past. For a reassessment of Cash's *Mind*, see Woodward, "The Elusive Mind of the South," in *American Counterpoint*, 261–83.

nedy). Some depicted ingratiating primitives, such as Roark Bradford's characters and Julia Peterkin's Carolinians, who in many
respects rivaled earlier "noble savage" conceptions (George Washington Cable's Bras-Coupé is an example).

One reason for the often exotic pattern of their portrayals is that
many of these writers were preoccupied with exploring the progress
of their own revolt against puritanism. They saw their own emancipation from repression in terms of the primitivism of black life, and
the effect on their art was often stifling.[43] Nonetheless, the very nature of their personal rebellion demanded rejection of the more simplistic, sentimental, and romantic treatments associated with the
fawning plantation "darky" and the caricatures of minstrelsy, thereby breaking ground for more human and artistic depictions of
blacks. For example, despite the limitations of Peterkin's series of
new plantation novels, her treatment of blacks was a conscious
break with the old plantation tradition of Joel Chandler Harris and
Thomas Nelson Page. Her early work, and that of others such as
Paul Green, Stribling, and Dubose Heyward, helped to bring about
the modern acceptance of the Negro as a serious subject for the serious writer. Not without cause, one critic, in considering the period, states that "fiction devoted to the problem of the Negro was
the most remarkable development of the Renaissance,"[44] while another makes the prediction that "so long as the Negro remains and
history can speak with authority, the South will be a potent subject
for serious art."[45]

Faulkner's early career and his conception of "the Negro" are part
of this welter of activity in the South. Not long after the writing of
Sartoris, Faulkner voices a particularly meaningful awareness of his
South and his fiction:

> The long work I had had to create opened before me and I felt my-
> self surrounded by the limbo in which the shady visions, the hosts

43 Perhaps because Faulkner's outward revolt against the puritanism of southern life
found expression in his youthful identification with RAF hero and monocled aes-
thete, he did not find it necessary to identify outright with the Negro's "primitivism"
in order to assert a personal notion of freedom. Faulkner does, however, see the
Negro in primitive terms.
44 Bradbury, *Renaissance in the South*, 79.
45 Holman, "View from the Regency-Hyatt," 32.

which stretched half formed, waiting each with it's [sic] portion of
that verisimilitude which is to bind into a whole the world which
for some reason I believe should not pass utterly out of the memory of man, and I contemplated those shady but ingenious shapes
by reason of whose labor I might reaffirm the impulses of my ego
in this actual world without stability, with a lot of humbleness, and
I speculated on time and death and wondered if I had invented the
world to which I should give life or if it had invented me, giving me
an illusion of greatness.[46]

In the spontaneous visionary experience Faulkner recalls is his discovery of his subject, and in a sense the outline of its shape, in a
world he could not allow to "pass utterly out of the memory of
man." He perceives the necessity of synthesizing the diverse, often
discordant, materials of his private South into an artistic whole. That
perception suggests a reciprocity between the strength of individual
initiative in the artistic creation of life and the power of the aesthetic
experience in rearranging or affirming already existing relationships
(whether social, moral, or aesthetic). In his major novels, *The Sound
and the Fury*, *Light in August* and *Absalom, Absalom!*, Faulkner works
out the relationship between his "shady visions" and the impulses
of his ego; these novels illustrate the nurturing of an artist's own
imaginative powers by the materials of experience—the Negro, the
South, and Mississippi.

46 Joseph Blotner, "William Faulkner's Essay on the Composition of *Sartoris*," *Yale Library Gazette*, XLVII (January, 1973), 121–24.

CHAPTER II

Novel Beginnings

Anderson, New Orleans, *Dark Laughter,* and *Soldiers' Pay*

I learned more than that from him . . . I learned that, to be a writer, one has first got to be what he is, what he was born; that to be an American and a writer, one does not necessarily have to pay lip-service to any conventional American image such as his and Dreiser's own aching Indiana or Ohio or Iowa corn of Sandburg's stockyards or Mark Twain's frog. You had only to remember what you were. "You have to have somewhere to start from: then you begin to learn," he told me. "It dont matter where it was, just so you remember it and aint ashamed of it. Because one place to start from is just as important as any other."

"Sherwood Anderson: An Appreciation,"
Essays, Speeches and Public Letters, p. 8

Faulkner's earliest writings, his poetry and prose published at the University of Mississippi between 1916 and 1924, show no interest in the Negro, and very little in his cultural setting. His work during this period reflects a preoccupation with sophisticated postwar scenes and artificial worlds of nymphs and fauns. It seems that in subject and style Faulkner considered himself more Continental than American or Mississippian.[1]

1 See, for example, William Faulkner, *University Pieces,* ed. Carvel Collins, (Folcroft, Pa.: Folcroft Press, 1962), and Faulkner's two volumes of poetry, *The Marble Faun* (Boston: The Four Seas, 1924) and *The Green Bough* (New York: Harrison Smith and Robert Haas, 1933). For discussions of Faulkner's early writings, see Carvel Collins, "Faulkner at the University of Mississippi," *William Faulkner: Early Prose and Poetry* (Boston: Little, Brown, 1962), 3–33; H. Edward Richardson, *William Faulkner: The Jour-*

As a young, mainly derivative poet, Faulkner stated literary preferences that were far from the provincial. He admired Swinburne, Eliot, Pound, Shakespeare, Spenser, Keats, Shelley, Mallarmé, Gautier, and Verlaine.[2] But he had little regard for American writers. For example, he considered Mark Twain "a hack writer who would have been fourth rate in Europe, who tricked out a few of the old proven 'sure fire' literary skeletons with sufficient local color to intrigue the superficial and lazy."[3] His harsh evaluation of Mark Twain is characteristic of his attitude, before his 1925 sojourn in New Orleans, toward American literature in general and America herself as a "land possessing no tradition." In 1922, for instance, he had written of America as "aesthetically impossible"[4] and as having "no drama or literature worth the name, and hence no tradition."[5] In a review of Conrad Aiken's *Turns and Movies,* Faulkner refers to the "fog generated by the mental puberty of contemporary American versifiers while writing inferior Keats or sobbing over the middle west" and to "Mr. Vachel Lindsay with his tin-pan and iron spoon, Mr. Kreymborg with his lithographic water coloring, and Mr. Carl Sandburg with his sentimental Chicago propaganda" as "so many puppets fumbling in windy darkness."[6]

One reason for Faulkner's early literary affinities with Europeans rather than Americans is surely bound up in the matter of his personal inclinations and tastes; as Hugh Kenner has remarked, "Styles are not obliged, not by decorum, not by tradition. . . . Styles are *elected.*"[7] However, another factor may also have some bearing on

---

ney to Self-Discovery (Columbia: University of Missouri Press, 1969), 46–60, on *The Marble Faun;* 62–82 on the poems appearing in *The Mississippian.*
2 See Faulkner's essay, "Verse Old and Nascent: A Pilgrimage," *The Double Dealer* (April, 1925), in Collins (ed.), *William Faulkner: Early Prose and Poetry,* 114. See also Richard P. Adams, "Faulkner: The European Roots," in George H. Wolfe (ed.), *Faulkner: Fifty Years After "The Marble Faun"* (University: University of Alabama Press, 1976), 25.
3 Faulkner, "American Drama: Inhibitions," *The Mississippian* (March 17, 1922), in Collins (ed.), *William Faulkner: Early Prose and Poetry,* 94.
4 *Ibid.*
5 Faulkner, "American Drama: Eugene O'Neill," *The Mississippian* (February 3, 1922), in Collins (ed.), *William Faulkner: Early Prose and Poetry,* 87.
6 Faulkner, "Books and Things," in Collins (ed.), *William Faulkner: Early Prose and Poetry,* 74, 75.
7 Hugh Kenner, *A Homemade World: The American Modernist Writers* (New York: Knopf, 1975), 217. Kenner's italics.

Faulkner's directions prior to New Orleans. When Faulkner began to write novels in the twenties, the South was not then a region of which an intellectual studying it realistically might be proud. This South was still that place caricatured by Mencken in "The Sahara of the Bozart"; it was the South just before the full awakening of the Renascence.

It seems possible, then, that Faulkner like other southern artists of the time was sensitive to being identified with the South as a specified region of customs and ethics, which might result in charges of provincialism, and he specifically contrasted both the Midwest and New York to the South as regions hospitable to the artist.[8] Yet Soldiers' Pay (1926), his first novel, incorporates the Negro, a distinctly American type, into the very fabric of life in Charlestown, Georgia, the "southern" fictional setting. Blacks are present everywhere: on the streets and roads; in the white man's stores, gardens, and homes; and in their own shanty town's houses, school, and church. Throughout Soldiers' Pay, vignettes of Negro life function as lyrical counterpoint to Faulkner's main tonal composition. Blacks appear as a kind of musical refrain which reinforces the poetic design of the novel. Moreover, the conclusion of Soldiers' Pay depends directly upon the felt presence of the Negro as a community of faith and feeling. In the final chapter the earthy, religious blacks stand in thematic counterpoint to the post–World War I despair and disillusionment at the center of the novel.

Faulkner's progress from the concerns of his early poetry to those of Soldiers' Pay may appear, initially, to be a minimal transition, particularly because contemporary critics have carefully outlined the poetic influences.[9] Undeniably, the novel does depend greatly upon

8 Faulkner, "An Introduction to The Sound and the Fury," 410–11. In this essay and others from his early career, Faulkner expresses particular interest in the Midwest, which by the 1930s had gained nationwide recognition because of its prominent artists, such as Theodore Dreiser, Carl Sandburg, Edgar Lee Masters, Sherwood Anderson, Willa Cather, Carl Van Vechten, Vachel Lindsay, and Zona Gale. See Frederick Hoffman, The Twenties: American Writing in the Postwar Decade (rev. ed.; New York: The Free Press, 1962), 367–77; and Woodward, The Burden of Southern History, 30.
9 See Richard P. Adams, "The Apprenticeship of William Faulkner," Tulane Studies in English, XII (1962), 113–56; rpt. in Linda W. Wagner (ed.), Faulkner: Four Decades of Criticism (East Lansing: Michigan State University Press, 1973), 7–43; and also Richardson, "Soldiers' Pay: Detour Through Decadence," William Faulkner: The Journey to Self-Discovery, 139–63.

Faulkner's poetry and his European influences in terms of language and symbols. At the same time, the structure and the relationship between scene and reality make use of literary impressionism, which is characteristic of Sherwood Anderson's work from *Winesburg, Ohio* (1919) to *Dark Laughter* (1925). Moreover, *Soldiers' Pay* concludes with an aesthetic sensibility that is different from the *fin de siècle* tradition marking Faulkner's poetry. That sensibility is uniquely American, and it is most clearly evident in the use of the Negro in the final chapter. Apparently, during the time between Faulkner's inception of the work and his conclusion, he came to a different estimation of American literature generally, and his changed opinion freed him from imitative reliance upon European models.

Faulkner's use of the Negro reveals that *Soldiers' Pay* reflects, at least on one level, a turning to materials emanating more immediately from Faulkner's own heritage. Given the intensity of his later involvement with his region as a stimulant to his imagination and as raw material for his fiction, Faulkner's turning to the world he knew best seems inevitable. However, one explanation for his change in direction centers in his experiences during his 1925 stay in New Orleans and his friendship at that time with Sherwood Anderson.

Faulkner's extensive inclusion in *Soldiers' Pay* of blacks as a reflection of the psychological state of whites and as counterpoint to the sterility of contemporary life may well stem from the general literary climate of New Orleans during the twenties, and perhaps especially from Anderson, whose interest then in black people as expressive of American experience seems obsessive. It is clear that in 1925 Faulkner began to show different attitudes toward his own writing and toward American literature. Remarkably, in an April 26, 1925, essay on Anderson, Faulkner praised the older writer as a gifted, talented writer whose best feature was his "American" quality: "He is American, and more than that, a middle westerner, of the soil: he is as typical of Ohio in his way as Harding is of his. A field of corn with a story to tell and a tongue to tell it."[10] His opinion of Anderson

10 William Faulkner, "Sherwood Anderson," Dallas *Morning News* (Sunday, April 26, 1925), in Carvel Collins (ed.), *William Faulkner: New Orleans Sketches* (rev. ed.; New York: Random House, 1968), 139.

stands in marked contrast to his earlier view of American writers. Faulkner's statement about Anderson suggests a drastic ideological shift: increased respect for a uniquely American literary tradition and broadened critical base for judging American writing. This dramatic development in his assessment of an American author occurred three months after his January, 1925, arrival in New Orleans, the city he describes as "a courtesan whose hold is stronger upon the mature, to whose charm the young man must respond."[11]

Consequently, in considering the immediate literary background of Faulkner's treatment of the Negro, New Orleans marks an important awakening. "New Orleans was a mystery and a promise," contends Oliver La Farge, one of the artists who lived in the "crescent city" during the twenties: "Mystery and promise, the assurance that you could not walk those streets without adventure, the sense that anything might happen."[12] And for Faulkner New Orleans seems indeed to have been a mystery and a promise, because just as the South with its myriad tensions and possibilities ultimately helped to shape Faulkner's subject matter and his perception of that matter, so his New Orleans experiences were formative and consequential in moving him to a reconciliation with American literature and toward fiction as his primary genre. The intellectual and artistic life of the city that centered around *The Double Dealer*, a nationally known "little" magazine, contributed to his appreciation for Anderson's work and his reassessment of American literature.

Between Faulkner's arrival in January and the April publication of his review of Anderson's works for the Dallas *Morning News*, Faulkner associated with the local literati and with Anderson himself.[13] His experiences during this period seemingly helped him discern

---

11 Faulkner, "The Tourist" in "New Orleans," a series of sketches in *The Double Dealer* (January-February, 1925), In Collins (ed.), *William Faulkner: New Orleans Sketches*, 14.
12 Oliver La Farge, *The Copper Pot* (Boston: Houghton Mifflin, 1942), 1.
13 Sherwood Anderson with his third wife, Elizabeth Prall, lived in the New Orleans French Quarter between 1924 and 1927. See Anderson's fictional account of his first meeting with Faulkner, "A Meeting South," written near the end of 1924 and published in 1925, rpt. in *Sherwood Anderson's Notebook* (New York: Boni and Liveright, 1926), 103–21. For more detailed accounts of the Faulkner-Anderson friendship, see Richardson, "The View Carré: Anderson's Influence," *William Faulkner: The Journey to Self-Discovery*, 110–38; Collins, "Introduction," *William Faulkner: New Orleans Sketches*, xi–xxiv; and Joseph Blotner, "January-June, 1925," *Faulkner: A Biography* (2 vols.; New York: Random House, 1974), I, 385–431.

more accurately the value of American authors and showed him that meeting Mencken's challenge to the southerner did not necessitate a turning to European models as the only viable standard for American writers. Giving impetus to Faulkner's change, the literary group in New Orleans was, in general, a part of the post–World War I cultural phenomenon of growth in arts and letters and pronounced changes of life styles and values. These artists, concerned with the multifaceted appeal of America, were sympathetic to American literature and to a native American experience.

As artists they were aware of a substantial American tradition; at the same time, they saw change as a vital process among American "moderns." They were a part of a period that has been considered: "the first modern decade in American life, [with] changes so vast and so rapid as totally to reshape mores and patterns of human behavior, and changes of style in another sense—the change in literary forms and structures, the growth of a more modernist mode of writing, the shift of writers, toward bohemianism and toward a much more intense obsession both with their craft and with the distinctive and exposed moral condition of their generation."[14] As a result, they saw change as a twofold phenomenon: a transmutation of form and a change in subject matter. In particular, the literary people Faulkner met in New Orleans displayed a genuine preoccupation with the possibilities afforded by certain American types, especially the Negro, created and individualized by the American experience. They were active participants in the literary trends of the times, the "new" realism and the reconsideration of southern life.

Perhaps typical among those forming the intellectual core of the younger circle with which Faulkner became involved were Roark Bradford (short story writer and editor of the *Times Picayune* city desk) and Oliver La Farge (novelist and anthropologist at Tulane University).[15] Bradford was interested in southern black people— their language and idiom, their folk stories and beliefs as literary

14 Malcolm Bradbury and David Palmer, "Preface," *The American Novel and the Nineteen Twenties* (London: Edward Arnold, 1971), 7.
15 Their successful circle of artists also included Hamilton Basso (Tulane University student and novelist), John McClure (poet, newspaperman, and a founding editor of *The Double Dealer*), Lyle Saxon (novelist and feature writer for the New Orleans *Picayune*), and William Spratling (artist and teacher of architecture at Tulane).

materials. His collection of pseudo-black biblical tales in dialect, *Ol' Man Adam an' His Chillun* (1928), while not reflecting authentic religious concepts of blacks, formed the basis of the Pulitzer Prize drama *Green Pastures*. Bradford, according to Joseph Blotner, was "an expert mimic, particularly adept at Negro dialect," and was "like Anderson in that he loved to tell stories."[16]

On the other hand, La Farge, a New Englander and Harvard-trained ethnologist, sought out the American Indian as his subject. One of his works, a novel of Navajo life, *Laughing Boy* (1929), won a Pulitzer Prize and has become an American classic. But La Farge (who for a time shared cooking arrangements with Faulkner and Bill Spratling)[17] also highly regarded blacks as literary material. Both he and Bradford exemplify the younger artists who, in their concern with native American subjects for American writers, provided Faulkner with the intellectual stimulation that perhaps helped to raise his estimation of American literature.

The most visible artist among the New Orleans literati was, of course, Sherwood Anderson, whose reputation as a major writer was at its height primarily because of *Winesburg, Ohio* (1919), *The Triumph of the Egg* (1929), and *Horses and Men* (1923). Like the younger artists in the Vieux Carré (the old French Quarter of the city), he was aware of the new directions in form and subject. For instance, his main character in *Dark Laughter* (1925) reflects on a "consciousness of brown men, brown women coming more and more into American life—by that token coming into him too."[18] Anderson's own "consciousness of brown men, brown women" is revealed by his attempts to seek out the company of blacks in order to discover the meaning of their lives.[19]

---

16 Blotner, *Faulkner,* I, 394. Two other writers from this group later wrote novels treating the experience of blacks in the South. Basso, best known for *The View from Pompey's Head* (1954), wrote *Court House Square* (1936), a study of the prejudice and bigotry encountered by David Barondess and mulatto Alcide Fauget in a small southern town, and *Cinnamon Seed* (1934), a story of plantation life in Louisiana. Saxon's *Children of Bondage* (1937) is a novel with a mulatto heroine.

17 See Spratling's anecdotal account of Faulkner's New Orleans experiences, "Chronicle of a Friendship: William Faulkner in New Orleans," in the reprint of the 1926 work, William Spratling and William Faulkner, *Sherwood Anderson and Other Famous Creoles* (Austin: University of Texas Press, 1966), 11–16.

18 Sherwood Anderson, *Dark Laughter* (New York: Boni and Liveright, 1925), 74.

19 See the following essays in Ray Lewis White (ed.), *Sherwood Anderson's Memoirs: A*

During the twenties, Anderson valued blacks and common folks generally as a rich field for fiction. A champion of the little man, Anderson believed, as did the cultural primitivists, that ordinary people, the underprivileged, the poor, children, and blacks, are somehow better and nobler than others because they retain an elemental connection with the earth, with their own feelings and emotions. One of his "Notes Out of a Man's Life" is a typical expression of Anderson's belief in the promise of black life as subject matter: "If some white artist could go among the negroes and live with them much beautiful stuff might be got. The trouble is that no American white man could do it without self-consciousness. The best thing is to stand aside, listen and wait. If I can be impersonal in the presence of black laborers, watch the dance of bodies, hear the song, I may learn something."[20] While he lived in New Orleans, Anderson observed blacks; he frequented the docks where black men worked, and he strolled about the French Quarter where black women sat on their galleries or sold goods in the markets.

The appeal lay in what Anderson thought of as the Negro's mystical qualities—intuitive sensitivity to man's innermost life and instinctive perception of human nature. But Anderson's attraction to the Negro's "elemental exoticism" obscures the truth about his life, as Sterling Brown has observed; consequently, Anderson, who is "harassed by Puritanism and industrialism," finds in the life of the Negro "elements that bring him peace, rather than interpretation of a people."[21] Despite his imperfect understanding of blacks, Anderson seems obsessed by a vision of black life as a counterpoint to the sophisticated postwar society. And in the mid-twenties he was determined to share his vision with others by means of his writings.

Faulkner attributes his turning to the writing of novels to Sherwood Anderson's example, because Anderson projected the dual image of dedicated writer and affable man-about-town by working

Critical Edition (Chapel Hill: University of North Carolina Press, 1969): "We Whites and the Negroes," 471–85; "The Negro Woman," 507–13; "Bertrand Russell and the Negro Woman," 523–33.

20 *Sherwood Anderson's Notebook*, Note 23, p. 223. See also Note 4, pp. 64–65, in which Anderson relates his feelings about southern blacks.

21 Sterling Brown, *The Negro in American Fiction* (1937; New York: Atheneum, 1969), 151.

diligently on *Dark Laughter* yet reserving ample time for social activities and friends in and about the French Quarter. This combination greatly impressed Faulkner, appealing especially to his sense of a "good life."[22] While Anderson's daily pattern may well have attracted Faulkner, it seems more likely that a combination of Anderson's personality, his dedication to the art of writing, and his literary conversations prompted Faulkner to try writing a novel, even though Faulkner at this time considered himself a poet.

It seems, moreover, that Anderson's theories about writing were also a factor in Faulkner's decision, and they evidence the more serious side of Anderson's appeal. Although the extent of Anderson's influence may be arguable, the correspondence between his ideology and the direction that Faulkner's writing took in New Orleans is readily apparent. In his essay "The Modern Writer," for example, Anderson states:

> In a compact small country in which for hundreds of years the same people have lived, slowly building up traditions, telling old tales, singing old songs, the story teller or the poet has something in which he can rest. People grown old, as a people, on the same land, through which old rivers flow, looking out for new generations upon the same great plains and up into the same mountains, come to know each other in an intimate way. . . . The son following in the footsteps of his father dreams old dreams. The land itself whispers to him. Stories are in the very air about the writer. They spring up out of the soil on which for many hundreds of years people of one blood have been born, have lived, suffered, had moments of happiness and have died.[23]

Anderson's celebration of the land and the generations of people who live on it was a constant factor in his often changing career. He respected folk traditions and culture. Though he was a middle westerner, Anderson spoke of things familiar to the southerner, who

---

22 See Faulkner's humorous statements about Anderson's work and relaxation habits, Interview with Ralph Thompson, New York *Times* (November 7, 1948), and Interview with Jean Stein, in Meriwether and Millgate (eds.), *Lion in the Garden*, 62, 248–49.

23 Sherwood Anderson, "The Modern Writer" (1925), rpt. in Paul P. Appel (ed.), *Homage to Sherwood Anderson, 1876–1941* (Mamaroneck, N.Y.: Paul P. Appel, 1970), 173–74.

also grew up with traditions, with old tales and songs, and with generations rooted in the same soil.

Anderson took being an American writer seriously. He could say of himself in 1924: "I am the American man. . . . There is no doubt of it. I am just the mixture of the cold, moral man of the North into whose body has come the warm pagan blood of the South. I did not want to be merely a writer living in America, but wanted to be an American writer, wanted to make my tale telling fit me more snugly into the life about me."[24] He recognized an integral connection between the writer and his land. Anderson envisioned his materials as the lives of men and women:

> Consider . . . the materials of the prose writer, the teller of tales. His materials are human lives. To him these figures of his fancy, these people who live in his fancy, should be as real as living people. . . . To take the lives of these people and bend or twist them to suit the needs of some cleverly thought out plot to give your readers a false emotion is as mean and ignoble as to sell out living men and women. . . . The need of making a living may serve as an excuse but it will not save you as a craftsman. Nothing really will save you if you go cheap with tools and materials. Do cheap work and you yourself are cheap.[25]

In this passage Anderson expresses two notions about writing which are also central to Faulkner: "people" as the material of fiction and the writer (the "teller of tales") as craftsman (journeyman or skilled laborer). Faulkner, in discussing his writing, generally refers to his basic interest in people, his concern with creating "flesh and blood people that will stand up and cast a shadow."[26] In addition, one of Faulkner's characteristic metaphors for himself as artist is that of "craftsman" or carpenter-builder working with a set of tools.[27]

Anderson's assumptions about human lives as the basic material

24 Sherwood Anderson, *A Story Teller's Story* (1924), ed. Ray Lewis White (Cleveland: The Press of Case Western Reserve University, 1968), 22, 297.
25 Anderson, "The Modern Writer," 188.
26 Gwynn and Blotner (eds.), *Faulkner in the University*, 47. See also 48–50. In his interviews and conferences, Faulkner typically discusses his characters as though they were living people who continued to have adventures and misadventures long after the composition and publication of the work in which they appeared.
27 See Gwynn and Blotner (eds.), *Faulkner in the University*, 12, 48, 103, 257.

of the teller of tales anticipates Faulkner's own discovery of "people" as the starting point of his fiction, a discovery which he relates in discussing the composition of *Sartoris:*

> So I began to write, without much purpose, until I realized (that to make it . . . truely [*sic*] evocative it must be personal. . . .) . . . So I got some people, some I invented, others I created out of tales that I learned of nigger cooks and stable boys (of all ages between one-armed Joby, . . . 18, who taught me to write my name in red ink on the linen duster he wore for some reason we both have forgotten, to . . . old Louvinia who remarked when the stars "fell" and who called my grandfather and my father by their Christian names until she died) in the long drowsy afternoons. Created I say, because they are partly composed from what they were in actual life and partly from what they should have been and were not.[28]

Significantly, Faulkner recounts here more than just his turning to real "people" in order to create personal tales. This shift in direction becomes important because his early poetry is so obviously concerned with artificial worlds. He reveals a conscious decision to mine the unique regional tales (whether in subject or method) of the black storytellers from his youth. Along with a preoccupation with people, then, the passage reflects Faulkner's acceptance of folk culture and his specific southern heritage.

In fact, years after their New Orleans days, Faulkner recalls that Anderson advised him to explore his Mississippi homeland as material for his fiction. In retelling the advice, Faulkner captures the cadence and style of Anderson's speech: " 'You have to have somewhere to start from: then you begin to learn,' he told me. 'It dont matter where it was just so you remember it and aint ashamed of it. Because one place to start from is just as important as any other. You're a country boy; all you know is that little patch up there in Mississippi where you started from. But that's all right too. It's America too; pull it out, as little and unknown as it is, and the whole thing will collapse, like when you prize a brick out of a wall.' "[29] The lesson

---

28 Blotner, "William Faulkner's Essay on the Composition of *Sartoris*," 123.
29 William Faulkner, "Sherwood Anderson: An Appreciation," in Ray Lewis White (ed.), *The Achievement of Sherwood Anderson: Essays in Criticism* (Chapel Hill: University of North Carolina Press, 1966), 197–98. James B. Meriwether rightly maintains that in his essay on Anderson, Faulkner's major concern is with instructing young writers by

is one of respect for Faulkner's Mississippi homeland, his America that he had avoided in his poetry. The important message in Faulkner's account nearly thirty years after his contact with Anderson is that Faulkner intended to place his art within the specific context of its relationship to Mississippi. Whether Anderson verbally directed Faulkner to his piece of America or whether Faulkner interpreted Anderson's example to suit his own needs is not precisely evident. However, Faulkner presents at length what he claims is Anderson's advice about the *American* writer:

> "America aint cemented and plastered yet. They're still building it. . . . That's why ignorant unschooled fellows like you and me not only have a chance to write, they must write. All America asks is to look at it and listen to it and understand it, and then try to tell it, put it down. It won't ever be quite right, but there is always next time; there's always more ink and paper and something else to try to understand and tell. And probably wont be exactly right either, but there is a next time to that one, too. Because tomorrow America is going to be something different, something more and new to watch and listen to and try to understand; and, even if you cant understand, believe."[30]

Though Faulkner here mimics Anderson, his intention is to praise the older writer, not to ridicule him. Certainly, Faulkner's tribute is a restatement of his own enduring refrain about his writing—his compulsion to try over and over again to capture some truth about the world he knew. His account indicates that the decision to use his native territory as a realistic basis for his fiction is a conscious aesthetic choice for unlimited imaginative resources and a full range of artistic possibilities.

Exposure to Anderson's positive ideas and his personal achievements led to a reversal of Faulkner's early literary notions.[31] Perhaps

---

sharing an "unfactual" account of his own development. See Meriwether, "Faulkner's Essays on Sherwood Anderson," in Wolfe (ed.), *Faulkner: Fifty Years After "The Marble Faun,"* 178. A point not developed by Meriwether is Faulkner's concern with communicating to younger writers the necessity of understanding their American roots and of accepting the validity of their materials, which is the larger lesson Faulkner learned from Anderson's example.

30 Faulkner, "Sherwood Anderson: An Appreciation," 198.

31 Other commentators have observed Anderson's influence on Faulkner, but they have failed to notice that at the base of Faulkner's acceptance of Anderson is a recon-

such a reversal was inevitable, but the Anderson friendship seems to have hastened it. In one of his longest interviews, Faulkner made a crucial appraisal of Anderson as an American writer connected both to Mark Twain and to Faulkner himself. "He was the father of my generation of American writers and the tradition of American writing which our successors will carry on. He has never received his proper evaluation. Dreiser is his older brother and Mark Twain is the father of them both."[32] Anderson, in Faulkner's analysis, becomes the "father" of his writing, and Mark Twain, the "hack writer" of his earlier evaluation, becomes the "grandfather" of their American tradition. Anderson, then, is the key to Faulkner's reappraisal of American literature, while Mark Twain becomes "the first that grew up in the belief that there is an American literature."[33]

Faulkner's revised opinion of American literature persisted throughout his career. As late in his lifetime as April 20, 1962, Faulkner linked Anderson (as well as Dreiser and Sinclair Lewis) with Shakespeare, Tolstoy, Dostoevsky, Balzac, and Gautier when he pointed out the authors whose works portray the feelings and emotions of the human heart.[34] Perhaps the most pertinent of Faulkner's evaluations of Anderson is one made in Japan: "I think he was the father of all my works, of Hemingway, Fitzgerald, etc., all of them—we were influenced by him. He showed us the way, because up to that time the American writer had been an easterner—he looked across the Atlantic to England, to France, but only at Anderson's time had we an American who was primarily an American. He lived in the big central part of the Mississippi valley, and wrote what he found there."[35] Without his apprenticeship in New Orleans, Faulkner may well have taken much longer to arrive at his appreciation for the ma-

---

sideration of the quality and potential of American literature. See Adams, "The Apprenticeship of William Faulkner," 113–56, and Richardson, *William Faulkner: The Journey to Self-Discovery,* 110–38.

32 Interview with Jean Stein, Meriwether and Millgate (eds.), *Lion in the Garden,* 249.

33 Interview in Japan, *Lion in the Garden,* 137. During this same series of interviews in Japan, Faulkner listed Mark Twain among the five greatest American novelists.

34 Joseph L. Fant and Robert Ashley (eds.), *Faulkner at West Point* (New York: Random House, 1964), 114.

35 Interview in Japan, Meriwether and Millgate (eds.), *Lion in the Garden,* 101.

terials of his specific American homeland and culture, especially the Negro and the folk in that culture.

Soldiers' Pay is a culmination of the first portion of Faulkner's literary career. It is a culmination of both his immediate New Orleans experiences and his early concerns with poetry. Consequently, the novel is a pastiche which moves unevenly in several unreconciled directions. Set in April and May of 1919, *Soldiers' Pay* initially treats returning World War I veterans and their adjustments to civilian life. What there is of a plot centers on Donald Mahon, a wounded flyer who returns home to die. Two strangers, Joe Gilligan and Margaret Powers, sympathize with his condition and accompany him to Charlestown, Georgia, his hometown. But Faulkner has myriad characters and a variety of narrative threads which he struggles to keep in a recognizable relationship to one another. He attempts an intricate, lyrical story pattern which avoids traditional plot disclosures. As a result, there is no single main event, or series of events, that would cause plot complications or tensions to be resolved in the course of the novel. Accordingly, *Soldiers' Pay* is an innovative "modern" novel developed around the private emotional lives of individual characters.

Faulkner uses the Negro to establish the basic rhythm of life that has been lost to the modern, postwar world. His Charlestown blacks provide a combination of music and feeling as a backdrop for the action. The sound of their voices is a musical accompaniment which is also the embodiment of feeling.

Black voice as emotion itself is a major part of Anderson's *Dark Laughter,* the novel which occupied so much of Anderson's time during his association with Faulkner. The voices of blacks echo throughout *Dark Laughter,* and the symbolism depends upon a conception of black voice as mysterious, powerful, and intuitive. Anderson's protagonist, Bruce Dudley, remembers the sound of river workers heard in his youth:

> From the throats of the ragged black men as they trotted up and down the landing stage, strange haunting notes. Words were caught up, tossed about, held in the throat. Word-lovers, sound-

lovers—the blacks seemed to hold a tone in some warm place, under their red tongues perhaps. Their thick lips were walls under which the tone hid. Unconscious love of inanimate things lost to the whites—skies, the river, a moving boat—black mysticism—never expressed except in song or in the movements of their bodies. The bodies of the black workers belonged to each other as the sky belonged to the river. Far off now, down river, where the sky was splashed with red, it touched the face of the river. The tones from the throats of black workers touched each other, caressed each other. (DL, 106)

As this passage suggests, and as Anderson pointed out to his friends, *Dark Laughter* evidences, behind the action and the reflections of characters, the deeply penetrating sound of blacks and the meaning that sound has for his characters. The sound of the black river worker is especially meaningful to Bruce Dudley because, dissatisfied with his life as John Stockton (Chicago newspaperman), he escapes, like Huck Finn, by drifting down the Mississippi River in search of fulfillment.

Anderson uses "the Negro" to provide thematic counterpoint to the sterile lives of his whites. His blacks stand as ironic comment on the activities central to the novel. He wrote to Horace Liveright, his publisher, that his subject was "the neuroticism, the hurry and self-consciousness of modern life and back of it the easy, strange laughter of the Blacks. . . . the dark earthy laughter."[36] The Negro voice becomes a metaphor for an uncomplicated existence that is still close to nature and in touch with man's buried life of feeling. In using blacks to exemplify this notion and as counterpoint to whites, Anderson emphasizes a drive toward the renewal of innocence and the search for simplicity common to modern man. He uses the sound of two black housekeepers to reflect the secret longings of Aline Grey, a woman who had been a promising student in Paris during the Armistice, but who is trapped in a loveless marriage:

> Negroes sing——
> An' the Lord said . . .
> Hurry, hurry.

36 Howard Mumford Jones (ed.), *The Letters of Sherwood Anderson* (Boston: Little, Brown, 1969), 142.

Negroes singing had sometimes a way of getting at the ultimate truth of things. Two negro women sang in the kitchen of the house as Aline sat by the window upstairs watching her husband go down the path, watching the man Bruce digging in the garden. (DL, 248–49)

The voices remind Aline that she is barren and that her husband is too involved in the complicated world of business to care. She suffers from a private emptiness comparable to that of Bruce Dudley.

Anderson's underlying conception is of blacks as fecund primitives whose life style evidences the fact that the unity of all human life with nature is still possible in the modern world, which "had got out of touch with things—stones lying in fields, the fields themselves, houses, trees, rivers, factory walls, tools, women's bodies, sidewalks, people on the sidewalks" (DL, 62–63). Blacks can, according to Anderson, still "get life more clearly" (DL, 96). They remain in touch with primordial longings and feelings, an ability missing in the confused mainstream of postwar life: "They would think as their natures led them to think, feel as their natures led them to feel" (DL, 266).

Anderson uses blacks as counterpoint to the stultification of feeling and impulse at the root of the problems encountered by his whites. In particular, the two black women in the Grey household reflect his interest in black people as primitives, in tune with their sexual desires and wiser than their white employers in this respect. The two women are described in simple terms that portray an uncomplicated response to the senses: "Negro women have an instinctive understanding. They say nothing, being wise in women-lore. What they can get they take. That is understood" (DL, 233). Their laughter comments upon the activities in the Grey household. The two seem to know intuitively that something is wrong between Aline and her husband, Fred: "The two negro women . . . watched and waited. Often they looked at each other and giggled. The air on the hilltop was filled with laughter—dark laughter. 'Oh, Lord! Oh, Lord! . . .' one of them cried to the other. She laughed—a high pitched negro laugh" (DL, 253). The laughter of the childlike and earthy blacks is a means of bringing into focus an entire spectrum of contrasted central ideas: sterility and fertility, intuition and reason, industrialization and craftsmanship, freedom and repression (especially as related to the sexual life and the expression of love).

Similar to Anderson in *Dark Laughter,* Faulkner assumes the significance of the laughter of blacks in *Soldiers' Pay.* But the laughter of his blacks is edged with sadness, instead of with the irony Anderson employs. Laughter in *Soldiers' Pay* most often is the "soft meaningless laughter" of "slow unemphatic voices cheerful yet somehow filled with the old despairs of time and breath."[37] Faulkner frequently repeats this same idea with slight variations; for example, "the slow unemphasis of their talk and laughter" (146). Or he expands upon the idea, such as when a pair of whites who are aware of the incongruous elements of modern life walk through the town and hear "the voices of the negroes raised in bursts of meaningless laughter or snatches of song in a sorrowful minor . . . and the slow reverberations . . . smote at measured intervals"(157–58).

The sadness in the laughing voices of Negroes is a notion that persists into *Sartoris* (1929). In that novel Faulkner uses the sounds and music of Negroes as a counterpoint to the malady of his lost-generation hero, Bayard Sartoris. Bayard watches the movement of country blacks through the town at noon: "—negroes slow and aimless as figures of a dark, placid dream, with an animal odor, murmuring and laughing among themselves; there was in their constantless murmuring something ready with mirth, in their laughter something grave and sad."[38] In both of these early novels, Faulkner shows an awareness of the historical condition of the southern Negro, and he intimates the hidden reality of Negro life.

However, laughter is only one part of Faulkner's use of Negro voices in *Soldiers' Pay.* Unlike Anderson, he does much more with the sounds of blacks. Charles Nilon has simplified Faulkner's use of blacks in *Soldiers' Pay, Sartoris,* and *Sanctuary* (1939) to four functions: "They give verisimilitude to the scenes, illustrate the social thesis, establish tone, atmosphere, and place, and provide choric comment on the behavior of the white characters."[39] But Nilon's gen-

37 William Faulkner, *Soldiers' Pay* (New York: Horace Liveright, 1926), 312.
38 William Faulkner, *Sartoris* (New York: Harcourt, Brace, 1929), 119–20.
39 Charles Nilon, *Faulkner and the Negro* (1962; rpt. New York: Citadel Press, 1965), 67.

eralization, accurate though it may be, does not tell us nearly enough about the Negro in the first novel.

Faulkner associates the Negro with music and feeling in order to establish the rhythm, tone, and mood of Soldiers' Pay. He does so in two ways. One is by means of presenting the actual sound, secular or sacred, created by the voices of black people as the emotional context of individual scenes. The other way is by means of presenting black figures and their activities as a metaphor for the essential, harmonious rhythm of life itself.

In using the Negro as a lyrical leitmotif establishing the rhythm of life in Charlestown, Faulkner relies primarily on brief pictures of black people in the background of the central action. The Negro functions either in response to the needs of major figures or in contrast to their vision of life. Here, in an embryonic form, Faulkner makes use of the divided world of the South. He assumes that blacks are inherently associated with nature and natural processes, and as such are psychologically simple and childlike.[40] His blacks, then, are loyal, humble, and docile figures who, in their simplicity, do not reflect the complexity and diversity of rounded, modern human beings. They represent for Faulkner a viable folk culture. One result of his limited vision of blacks is that Faulkner frequently relies on animal imagery, especially an analogy between "niggers and mules," in order to create a cultural context for his fiction.

In a series of impressionistic passages which create the atmosphere of the southern afternoon, Faulkner uses "niggers and mules" to form the scene. The first one describes the square: "Wagons tethered to slumbering mules and horses were motionless in the square. They were lapped, surrounded, submerged by the frank odor of unwashed negroes . . . their slow, unemphatic voices and careless, ready laughter which has also somehow beneath it something elemental and sorrowful and unresisting, lay drowsily upon the noon" (144). The Negroes and their "slow," "elemental" voices

40 While Faulkner as a primitivist is no longer a significant critical question, his use of the concepts and methods of the primitivists remains pertinent to a study of his characterizations of blacks. For an early discussion of regression to a simpler cultural life and various modes or cults of primitivism, see Harry M. Campbell and Ruel Foster, William Faulkner: A Critical Appraisal (Norman: University of Oklahoma Press, 1951), 140–58.

are intricately related to the noon. It is during moments such as this one that Charlestown becomes unequivocably "southern."

In the second, and more lyrical, "niggers and mules" passage, Faulkner reinforces the dreamlike state of the novel:

> Niggers and mules. Afternoon lay in a coma in the street, like a woman recently loved. Quiet and warm. . . . Leaves were like a green liquid arrested in mid-flow . . . leaves were as cut through with scissors from green paper and pasted flat on the afternoon: someone dreamed them and then forgot his dream. Niggers and mules.
> Monotonous wagons drawn by long-eared beasts crawled past. Negroes humped with sleep, spontaneous upon each wagon and in the wagon bed itself sat other negroes upon chairs: a pagan catafalque under the afternoon. Rigid, as though carved in Egypt ten thousand years ago. Slow dust rising veiled their passing like Time; the necks of mules limber as rubber hose swayed their heads from side to side, looking behind them always. But the mules were asleep also. "Ketch me sleep, he kill me. But I got mule blood in me: when he sleep, I sleep; when he wake, I wake." (151).

Faulkner links the Negro to an ancient past and to a ritual of survival. His impressionistic rendering of a slow, suspended life is juxtaposed to the fast, nervous rhythms of sophisticated modern existence symbolized by the war through the novel. Cleanth Brooks's evaluation of the general function of blacks in *Soldiers' Pay* seems especially appropriate in relation to the "niggers and mules" sequence: "[Faulkner] consistently presents the Negro as calmer, wiser, still strong in the religious faith, and thus less shaken by the War than are the disaffected whites who have been tossed by the winds of change blowing out of the great world beyond Charlestown. But except for the Negroes, Charlestown, Georgia, might just as well have been Charlestown, New Hampshire, or Charlestown, Indiana."[41] Faulkner's South in this novel is a representative landscape created by the presence of the Negro.

The last of the "niggers and mules" passages moves from the dream sequence into the reality of the troubled world of the whites:

41 Cleanth Brooks, "Faulkner's First Novel," *Southern Review*, VI (Autumn, 1970), 1056–74.

"The afternoon dreamed on toward sunset. Niggers and mules. . . . At last Gilligan broke the silence" (152). While Gilligan and the other characters have been affected by the war and changing times, "niggers and mules" represent the continuity and the acceptance of time.

Late in the novel Faulkner again uses animal imagery to equate the Negro to primitive wellsprings which link him to the intuitive aspects of life.

> He looked about, then beckoned to a negro youth reclining miraculously on a steel cable that angles up to a telephone pole. "Here, son."
>
> The negro said Suh? without moving. "Git up dar, boy. Dat white man talkin' to you," said a companion, squatting on his heels against the wall. The lad rose and a coin spun arching from Gilligan's hands.
>
> "Keep your eyes on them bags till I come back, will you?"
>
> "Awright, cap'm." The boy slouched over to the bags and became restfully and easily static beside them, going to sleep immediately like a horse.
>
> "Damn 'em, they do what you say, but they make you feel so— so——"
>
> "Immature, don't they?" she suggested.
>
> "That's it. Like you was a kid or something and that they'd look after you even if you don't know exactly what you want." (302)

Neither Faulkner's thinking nor his analogy is insightful. He depends upon stereotypes of blacks, and he thinks in clichés. However, his attempt is to capitalize on the difference between blacks and whites and to use that difference to forward his theme.

Another recurrent image is that of a Negro mowing grass, which appears in order to reinforce both the dreamlike passage of time and the rhythm of life itself. The repetition of the man and mower throughout *Soldiers' Pay* suggests the passage of only one day and the slowed motion of Charlestown life. In the first reference, it is morning: "the lawn sloping fenceward was gray with dew, and a negro informal in undershirt and overalls passed a lawn mower over the grass, leaving behind his machine a darker green stripe like an unrolling carpet" (104). Later a sense of the languid Charlestown afternoon is provided partially by another scene with the gardener:

"The lawn mower was long since stilled and beneath a tree she could see the recumbent form and one propped knee of its languid conductor lapped in slumber" (115). Charlestown at midday is a still, motionless place. And again in a descriptive passage the black man and the lawn mower recur: "The same negro in the same undershirt droned up and down the lawn with his mower, an occasional vehicle passed slumbrous and creaking behind the twitching mules, or moving more swiftly and leaving a fretful odor of gasoline to die beneath the afternoon" (155). This description captures the monotony of life in the town. In another brief glimpse of the Negro and the mower, the function is to authenticate the place and time: "The afternoon dreamed on, unbroken. A negro, informal in an undershirt, restrained his lawn mower, and stood beneath a tree, talking to a woman across the fence" (182). The final view of the Negro and his incessant mowing is even more revealing; the black man seems to orchestrate nature itself with his mowing: "Leaves grew larger and greener until all rumor of azure and silver and pink had gone from them; birds sang and made love and married and built houses in them and in the tree at the corner of the house that yet swirled its white-bellied leaves in never-escaping skyward ecstasies; bees broke clover upon the lawn interrupted at intervals by the lawn mower and its informal languid conductor. The mode of life had not changed" (281).

This last description clearly suggests a concern with showing a certain sameness and almost timeless quality about Charlestown and its inhabitants. Despite the activities in the outside world (the war and its effects), Charlestown remains suspended (much as Donald, the wounded pilot, is physically and Margaret, the war widow, is emotionally—suspended in a dreamlike, sleeping state). Time passes, yet simultaneously time remains the same. The figure of the Negro and his mower recurs over a major portion of the novel; nevertheless, the time sequence of his appearances suggests a period of one calendar day. The various images of the man and his mower constitute a subtle leitmotif establishing a time-locked, constant factor in an otherwise changing world.

The second way in which Faulkner associates the Negro with music and feeling to establish mood and tone is by means of the secular and sacred music of blacks. References throughout *Soldiers' Pay* represent the Negro in relation to music. Some are clumsy; for example, in describing a kindly, grinning porter, Faulkner uses the phrase, "white teeth were like a suddenly opened piano" (16). The more effective, and significant, of these references, however, link a specific mood or emotion contrapuntally to the white world; for instance, "A negro woman passing crooned a religious song, mellow and passionless and sad" (286). Statements such as this one occur mainly near the conclusion. The echoes of song heard in the final sections are all of the Negro's sacred music, the spirituals, whereas in the earlier portions of the novel and particularly in the climactic fifth chapter the music heard is secular, specifically jazz, the most irreverent of the new music.

A dance party, the central event in the fifth chapter, unites the elements of the novel and interconnects the characters. The dance sequence is the focal center which brings together all the major and minor characters in a miniature reflection of the world of isolation created in large part by the war. The chapter is experimental in tone and concept; its elaborate narrative strategy is more poetic than prosaic, but it relies heavily upon jazz, that modern music of American origin. Internal feelings are rendered by means of lyrical, metaphorical language. Impressionistic scene painting forwards the plot and creates an intense mood.

As the central characters approach the party, they hear "a rhythmic thumping soon to become music" (187). With this statement suggesting the rhythmic beating of the heart, the dance begins a microcosm of human life. Snatches of songs and their beats become an integral part of the chapter: "Uncle Joe, Sister Kate, all shimmy like jelly on a plate" (192); or "Uncle Bud, ninety-two, shook his cane and shimmied too" (193); or "Shake it and break it, don't let it fall" (197); or "oh, oh, I wonder where my rider's gone" (198). The rhythms syncopate throughout the dance scene: "The syncopation pulsed about them, a reiteration of wind and strings and troubling as water" (197). The sequence renders the isolation of the whole spectrum of characters from each other and from themselves by showing just how far removed their inner thoughts are from what they say or do. The syncopation of the jazz rhythms suggests the ways in which the dance vignettes fit together in order to form a larger picture of human life.

Four statements relate a black cornetist, whose music enlivens the dance, to Faulkner's vision of the Negro as reflecting the rhythm of life. Described as more of a general than a musician, the cornet player aggressively leads his band. The first instance contains a provocative figure of speech: "The negro cornetist stayed his sweating crew and the assault arrested withdrew, leaving the walls of silence peopled by the unconquered defenders of talk" (190). The second description suggests the musician's consciousness as a southern black man: "The negro cornetist, having learned in his thirty years a century of the white man's lust, blinked his dispassionate eye, leading his crew in a fresh assault" (192). The cornetist ignores a white girl pulling up her stocking. In the next instance, he "restrained his men and removed them temporarily and the porch was deserted save for the group sitting on the balustrade" (201–202). And then finally, "The negro cornetist unleashed his indefatigable pack anew and the veranda broke again into clasped couples" (210).

These descriptive phrases establish the Negro's "new" music as the backdrop for a modern sexual warfare being conducted among the dancers. Like the opening of the chapter, the dance scenes dwell upon war and fornication.[42] For example: "The [dancing] couple slid and poised, losing the syncopation deliberately, seeking and finding it, losing it again. . . . Her limbs elude his, anticipated his: the breath of a touch and an escape, which he, too, was quick to assist. Touch and retreat: no satiety. 'Wow, if that tune ever stops!'" (197). The new music and its new rhythm have sexual connotations: "Locked together they poised and slid and poised, feeling the beat of the music, toying with eluding it, seeking it again, drifting like a broken dream" (195). The black band's jazz also strengthens an analogy between the party-dance and the dance of life: "He [George Farr] heard the rhythmic troubling obscenities of saxophones, he

---

42 The relationship between war and sex gives meaning to the cryptic remark of the Negro driver who, in response to Joe Gilligan's comment that "You can see right through her [Cecily's dress]," states, "'Dat's the war'" (208, 209). The suggestion is that the war, once World War I, has become a war between the sexes, a new war abetted by the modern, provocative style of dress.

saw vague shapes in the darkness and he smelled the earth and things growing in it" (195).

Another paragraph especially expresses the excitement and the admixture of times (war and postwar): "' . . . throw it on the wall. Oh, oh, oh, oh . . . ' ' . . . wont never forget his expression when he said, Jack, mine's got syph. Had her . . .' 'Shake it and break it, shake it . . .' 'First night in Paris . . . then the other one. . . .' '. . . don't let it fall. . . .' ' . . . with a gun . . . twenty dollars in gold pinned to my. . . .' 'I wonder where my easy, easy rider's'" (200). Here Faulkner fuses the lyrics and rhythms of jazz emanating from the black musicians with snatches of sophisticated conversation by the returned soldiers. He echoes the tone, mood, and method of Anderson's New Orleans sequences in *Dark Laughter*. While Faulkner's chapter is a finer conception than Anderson's, it contains, nonetheless, related aspects of style and literary technique.

In a short chapter near the beginning of *Dark Laughter*, Anderson introduces the metaphor, "Dance life! Awake and dance!" (DL, 65). Throughout the novel he employs this phrase as a refrain orchestrating a dance of life: "Dance life! Catch the swing of the dance if you can" (68). Anderson's Chapter 10, which makes up Book Four, continues the use of "dance life" in the lyrical impressions and portraits of New Orleans (especially of blacks in that city). References to dance are interspersed throughout the chapter. Anderson speaks of the consciousness of brown men and women coming more into American life: "Standing laughing—coming by the back door—with shuffling feet, a laugh—a dance in the body" (74). The dance motif is used to paint a scene depicting the wide variety of people around the New Orleans docks: "Niggers on the docks, niggers in the city street, niggers laughing. A slow dance always going on. German sea-captains, French, American, Swedish, Japanese, English, Scotch. . . . Clean ships, dirty tramp ships, half-naked niggers—a shadow dance" (75). Anderson's "slow dance of life" unites all nationalities, and all human beings by extension.

Ultimately Anderson's use of the dance motif becomes obsessive and life seems phantasmagoric. One long passage suggests the relationship of Faulkner's work as well as the difference in Anderson's handling of the metaphor:

> They dance south—out of doors—whites in a pavilion in one field,
> blacks, browns, high browns, velvet-browns in a pavilion in the
> next field—but one.
> We've got to have more earnest men in this country.
> Grass growing in a field between.
> Oh, ma banjo dog!
> Song in the air, a slow dance. (DL, 76)

Here Anderson presents multifaceted concerns and layers of thoughts, all loosely held together. He employs jazz rhythms as the basis of his prose line, and he includes song ("Oh, ma banjo dog!"), varying the normal cadence of speech. His intention in the juxtaposition of elements seems to be the portrayal of the buried life beneath the surface, the internal life of feeling and expression located below the exterior mask. In a letter to Alfred Stieglitz dated September 13, 1925, he describes *Dark Laughter* in these terms: "I tried to make it dance along, jazzed it a little at the first where the theme fitted the mood. I wanted to give the sense of a dancing, shifting world of facts, moods, thoughts, impulses."[43] Anderson utilizes "dance" literally in terms of the flowing of sundry activities and various movements of life.

On the other hand, Faulkner's use of jazz and dance is more sophisticated because it combines the literal and symbolic in one metaphor. But both men rely upon their personal experiences in New Orleans (a city even then synonymous with the new music) to enrich the language, themes, and form of their work by means of the jazz motif. Faulkner's dance sequence ends with the fading sound of music: "Music came faint as a troubling rumor beneath the spring night, sweetened by distance: a longing knowing no ease" (SP, 212). The sound of the music carries Faulkner's thematic idea: trouble and longing distilled through space. The tone of this final statement of Chapter 5 anticipates the more subdued tone of the concluding chapter, which emphasizes the sound and rhythm of the Negro's religious songs as the emotional counterpoint to the tensions of modern life.

The first of these representations of black life in Chapter 9, the last

43 Jones (ed.), *The Letters of Sherwood Anderson*, 147.

chapter of *Soldiers' Pay*, presents a mammy figure, whose song and physical presence offer comfort to a white boy experiencing the reality of loss and grief. The incident is brief and traumatic:

> How strange everything looked! This street, these familiar trees—was this his home, where his mother and father were, where Sis lived, where he ate and slept, lapped closely around with safety and solidarity, where darkness was kind and sweet for sleeping? He mounted the steps and entered wanting his mother. But, of course, she hadn't got back from— He found himself running suddenly through the hall toward a voice raised in comforting, crooning song. Here was a friend mountainous in blue calico, her elephantine thighs undulating gracious as the wake of a ferry boat as she moved between table and stove.
>
> She broke off her mellow, passionless song, exclaiming: "Bless yo' heart, honey, what is it?"
>
> But he did not know. He only clung to her comforting, voluminous skirt in a gust of uncontrollable sorrow, while she wiped biscuit dough from her hands on a towel. Then she picked him up and sat upon a stiff-backed chair, rocking back and forth and holding him against her balloon-like breast until his fit of weeping shuddered away. (298–99)

The boy hears his "friend" before he sees her; her voice is raised in "comforting, crooning song." Her song is "mellow, passionless," and the sound itself offers sympathy.

The sentiment and posture of the cook are reminiscent of Elnora, the black housekeeper in *Sartoris* and *Flags in the Dust*. In *Flags in the Dust*, for example, Elnora cooks while "crooning one of her mellow endless songs."[44] Additionally, "in the kitchen Elnora crooned melody as she labored; her voice became rich and plaintful and sad along the sunny reaches of the air" (205). Both of these women seem to sing out of an awareness of man's difficulty in life.

The nameless cook offers the boy a reassurance based on her knowledge of life and pain. Her gesture is one of love and understanding. She is an embryonic Dilsey, the romanticized servant in *The Sound and the Fury*, who gives not merely her labor but herself to nurture and sustain a white family. Her description, like Dilsey's,

---

44 William Faulkner, *Flags in the Dust*, ed. Douglas Day (New York: Random House, 1973), 204.

mixes adulation with the grotesque ("a friend mountainous in blue calico, her elephantine thighs undulating gracious as the wake of a ferry boat"). She is a person of grossly exaggerated proportions, "mountainous and elephantine" with a "balloon-like breast." Yet, the portrait is not totally offensive because the woman's size becomes some measure of the heart, her propensity to sympathize with another human being. Her size, in essence, is a reflection of her humanity and the implicit possibility of retaining humanity in the modern world. The scene, then, evokes a sense of pathos and hope in spite of the exaggeration, which under other circumstances would be comic.

Beginning with this brief scene involving the cook, Faulkner moves toward a surer representation, in the last chapter, of the Negro as possessing emotional and spiritual resources unavailable to whites. He recognizes the singing of blacks as touched with sadness and hope. Consequently, in his first novel Faulkner reveals a sensitivity to blacks as people capable of more than the laughter and buffoonery common to many conventional portraits.

The last chapter of *Soldiers' Pay* brings into clearer perspective the fabric of the entire novel. Its meaning relies primarily upon the presence of the Negro. Faulkner fuses the symbolic meaning of his Negroes with the sound of their voices. Intricate in construction, the chapter is made up of numerous subdivisions which are separate, distinct units, having little interdependency. Each unit reveals an individual's response to some very personal feeling or emotion related to sex (longing, frustration) or death (loss, deprivation, separation). Each section provides an interpretation of the total accumulated action. Faulkner redefines the intent and the limits of his novel. He erases some of the preceding confusions and ambivalence regarding character and motivation. The ending suggests more realistic concerns—the breaking with the dream sequence and rousing to work for a more viable and vital reality. For the first time in the novel, Faulkner exercises tight authorial or narrative control; he assigns the final point of view to an omniscient narrator rather than to one of the characters.

Rector Mahon and Joe Gilligan, who have experienced the action of the novel, remain to make sense of it all. The two men walk together, feeling the death of Mahon's son, Donald, and the departure of Margaret. They share the common human experience of loss and loneliness. Their fragmentary perceptions juxtaposed to the simple conceptions of the Negro point to a level of meaning heretofore merely implied by the impressionistic descriptions. During their walk, Joe has a moment of vision in which he knows "suddenly all the old sorrows of the race, black or yellow or white" (317). Similarly the rector perceives that he and Gilligan are kindred spirits, suffering from "the facts of division and death" (318).

The ending contrasts the angles of vision symbolized by the two separately sustained worlds—the one that of agnostic and cerebral whites (exemplified by Gilligan and Dr. Mahon), and the other that of religious and earthy blacks. Symbolic of this mutually exclusive condition, the two suffering white men hear "a pure quivering chord of music wordless and far away" (318). They are drawn in the direction of the sound:

> "They are holding service. Negroes," the rector explained. They walked on in the dust passing neat tidy houses, dark with slumber. An occasional group of negroes passed them, bearing lighted lanterns that jetted vain little flames futilely into the moonlight. "No one knows why they do that," the divine replied to Gilligan's question. "Perhaps it is to light their churches with." (318–19)

This passage introduces the Negro church service for reasons other than providing "local color."[45] Faulkner combines *dusk, dark,* and *slumber* with *lanterns, flames,* and *light;* the contrast emphasizes the duality of human life, its dark and light. That the lanterns "jetted vain little flames futilely in the moonlight" suggests both the insignificance of the lights and the harmony of the artificial lights with the natural moonlight. Despite the difficulty involved, the blacks at least make an effort to find harmony with the world in which they live. Even this initial description of the Negro churchgoers portrays the dominance of voice and light symbolism. Something of the mystery of religion is implied by the rector's statement, "No one knows why they do that" (that is, carry lighted lanterns to church). The

---

45 Richardson, *William Faulkner: The Journey to Self-Discovery,* 151, cites the Negro church as an example of "local color" inspired imagery.

blacks perform a ritual that is an external manifestation of their faith. They have found a way (no matter how inexplicable) of holding their own in the world. The statement also emphasizes the division that exists between the white and black worlds by suggesting that the Negro is unknowable, that his consciousness cannot be penetrated by whites. In a sense Mahon's observation (and Faulkner's) is a perceptive acknowledgment of the masked part of black American life—the part not subject to facile generalizations about the simplicity of blacks and folk culture. The insight implied here occurs again in *The Sound and the Fury,* in which Faulkner actually shows the pluralistic pattern of Negro life when the Reverend Shegog begins his sermon in standard speech, but shifts almost imperceptibly into folk dialect.

The scene on the road outside the church contrasts the themes of personal and spiritual isolation (personal for Gilligan and spiritual for Mahon) with that of community (the Negro churchgoers). Suffering has fragmented white society and united the black. These themes are dramatized as Dr. Mahon and Gilligan crouch among the trees in order to observe the blacks:

> They saw the shabby church with its canting travesty of a spire. Within it was a soft glow of kerosene serving only to make the darkness and the heat thicker, making thicker the imminence of sex after harsh labor along the mooned land; and from it welled the crooning submerged passion of the dark race. It was nothing, it was everything; then it swelled to an ecstasy, taking the white man's words as readily as it took his remote God and made a personal Father of Him. (319)

The passage links light ("a soft glow of kerosene") and heat in a sensual atmosphere. The scene combines physical immediacy and the Negro's relationship to his God, who is neither indifferent nor distant.

In pointing out that the blacks have taken the white man's "remote God and made a personal Father of Him," the narrator reiterates an idea stated earlier: "Under the moon, quavering with the passion of spring and flesh, among whitewashed walls papered inwardly with old newspapers, something pagan using the white man's conventions as it used his clothing, hushed and powerful, not knowing its own power: 'Sweet chariot . . . comin' fer to ca'y me home'" (312–13). The sound of the spiritual, "Swing Low, Sweet Chariot," integrates the example of the Negro's past with his present realities. Both passages suggest the ability of blacks to take what they need from alien conventions and customs, to refashion them into something (different in kind or intent from the original) that is serviceable to their peculiar needs and ends. Essentially, the blacks have assumed a stance toward existence that the whites in a changing, postwar society need to incorporate into their own lives. In the hymn of the church people, "Feed Thy Sheep, O Jesus," the two onlookers perceive "All the longing of mankind for a Oneness with Something, somewhere" (319). In this moment, Faulkner unites his image of Negro voice as an emotional sound and of black presence as symbolic of harmony and rhythm with nature. This image has its climactic expression in the Easter sermon of *The Sound and the Fury*.

Gilligan and Mahon stand outside the church, beyond the reach of whatever comfort it may have to offer them. Their plight is emphasized by the picture of their standing "side by side in the dusty road. The road went on under the moon, vaguely dissolving without perspective" (319). Neither man has a clear perspective on life or death, much less a positive notion of spiritual significance; yet both continue to follow the road. Despite Dr. Mahon's position as an Episcopal priest, he is as remote from consolation as is Joe. He is certainly less representative of simple, functional Christianity than Callie, Donald's mammy, whose religious faith fosters a clarity of vision. It is her abrupt comment that we hear as Donald's funeral cars pass through the black section: "'Well, Jesus! we all gwine dat way, some day. All roads leads to de graveyard'" (296).

For Dr. Mahon and his companion, Joe, the church looms as a symbol of spiritual comfort, albeit inaccessible to them. In a moment of vision, each man feels the disparity of his own life more acutely in wake of the sound emanating from the church:

> Feed Thy Sheep, O Jesus. The voices rose full and soft. There was no organ; no organ was needed as above the harmonic passion of bass and baritone soared a clear soprano of women's voices like a flight of gold and heavenly birds. They stood together in the dust, the rector in his shapeless black, and Gilligan in his new hard

serge, listening, seeing the shabby church become beautiful with mellow longing, passionate and sad. Then the singing died, fading away along the mooned land inevitable with tomorrow and sweat, with sex and death and damnation; and they turned townward under the moon, feeling dust in their shoes. (319)

The congregation has instinctively accepted life with the inevitability of pleasure and pain as intrinsically interwoven into the fabric of man's existence. In spite of the fact that the two men stand in marked contrast to each other, they are inextricably linked in their isolation. They can listen and see the poor, shabby church become beautiful by dint of the welter of emotional feeling pouring from it in the song "Feed Thy Sheep, O Jesus," but they cannot become part of that beauty, because (according to the logic of the novel) they have moved too far away from simplistic notions of self, life, and religion. And so there is sadness and dejection in the final image of their turning toward the town, poignantly feeling their loss and their mortality, "feeling dust in their shoes." Faulkner's images in this final passage are effective (though his relentless pursuing of a mood of despair contrasted with one of hope seems too contrived). This final scene with its two separate visions of life, one black and the other white, anticipates the ending of *The Sound and the Fury,* which also juxtaposes the religious faith of blacks and the despair of whites. This scene presents the basic contours of the divided southern world which mark all of Faulkner's fiction, and the scene establishes the essential meaning of that world which underlies much of Faulkner's thinking.

The use of the Negro community in the concluding section provides Faulkner with a way of imposing a sense of meaning and order upon various elements and isolated units of his novel. Throughout *Soldiers' Pay* he uses the Negro to elicit responses to his main characters and situations. His method is no different in the last chapter. The few glimpses of the Negro in the concluding chapter serve to dramatize a sense of community and consolidation; finally, the Negro evokes a sense of thematic unity. Faulkner orders his fiction so that the actual placement of incidents involving the Negro (the lighted torch procession, for instance) tangential to those involving the more developed white characters (specifically Dr. Mahon and Joe

Gilligan) suggests that a comparison ought to be made and that emerging out of that comparison may be a pattern of meaning. Juxtaposition encourages the drawing of associations and connections, relating both to thematic statements and character development. This method of juxtaposition, too, becomes characteristic of Faulkner's subsequent novels. The suggestion here is that the Negro congregation has taken an idealization (Christianity) and turned it into a practical way of life.

What is ultimately most significant about the ending of *Soldiers' Pay* is not that thematically the black church offers some measure of faith or spiritual reassurance inaccessible to whites of the lost generation, but rather that at the beginning of his career as a novelist, Faulkner seized upon the strength of the Negro in the South in order to unify the experience of life and the experience of words which are central to his work. Perhaps the treatment of the Negro emerging in the final section is only loosely developed from the rest of the novel, but it is the strongest restatement of the style and subject in the whole work. It suggests Faulkner's growing awareness of the inherent symbolic value of the Negro community. In the final pages, he does not strive to achieve a record of quaint folk customs, as did Bradford or Saxon in the New Orleans group; instead he renders moral certainty in simple faith and external nature.

Faulkner exploits the Negro as a symbol of moral certainty much as religious painters exploit children in representing the angelic. It is not necessarily truth in reality but aesthetic truth that is the object of such representations. Thus, a moral ambiguity or confusion lies at the heart of *Soldiers' Pay*, because the practical religious faith of the Negro is merely a technical device superimposed upon the ending to provide a strong unifying focus where there has been none. Ultimately, the last pages of the novel have to be accounted for in terms of the message of Faulkner's art wrought from the racial organization of his culture. Specifically, within these pages Faulkner recognizes the technical and thematic possibilities inherent in the lives of the southern Negro. The Negro church service functioning as a mood piece with lights and voices concludes the novel, although logically the novel ends when Gilligan runs after the train carrying Margaret to Atlanta. The final tableau cannot be explained in terms

of tying up the loose ends involving the main figures because no further information is provided concerning any of the major characters.

Although a first reading of *Soldiers' Pay* may suggest that black
character is not a central consideration, analysis of the Negro in the
novel reveals the direction of future work. Whereas *The Sound and
the Fury, Light in August,* and *Absalom, Absalom!* do not contain major
incorporations of the actual music of the Negro, each of these later
major novels depends significantly upon notions of blacks as counterpoint to whites, a counterpoint which the sound and feeling of
Negro voice and the natural rhythm of Negro life in *Soldiers' Pay* ultimately suggest. From the beginning of his career as a novelist, then,
Faulkner evidences an artistic dependency upon the Negro in order
to enrich his fiction, to add a measure of complexity and ambiguity,
to suggest the dimensions (depths or shallowness) of his white characters' humanity, and to give structure to his conclusion. In an artistic sense, he is obsessed not with the Negro as a rounded character
or as part of the world of humankind, but with the Negro as an idea
which impinges upon the white man's internal world of thought and
feeling, and upon the artist's own imaginative world. Faulkner's
achievement in a first novel is, of course, singular, but it emerges out
of the intellectual and artistic milieu of New Orleans and out of
Sherwood Anderson's tutelage and example. Moreover, his achievement charts the course followed with skill in his major novels.

CHAPTER III

The Sound and the Fury

> She still remained one of my earliest recollections, not only as a person, but as a fount of authority over my conduct and of security for my physical welfare, and of active and constant affection and love. She was an active and constant precept for decent behavior. From her I learned to tell the truth, to refrain from waste, to be considerate of the weak and respectful of age. I saw fidelity to a family which was not hers, devotion and love for people she had not born.
>
> "Funeral Sermon for Mammy Caroline Barr:
> Delivered at Oxford, Mississippi—February 1940,"
> *Essays, Speeches and Public Letters,* p. 118.

Faulkner recognizes the value of the Negro in grounding *Soldiers' Pay* in a practical realism, but his Negro is a type still closely linked to a personal sense of cultural actuality and dependent upon literary treatments by other writers. The result is a stereotyped rendering of a mode of existence. Blacks remain in the background of both plot and structure, even though they emerge in the conclusion as a major thematic idea. Faulkner has not yet fully grasped the artistic importance of either his heritage as a white Mississippian or the Negro in his culture.

His third novel, *Flags in the Dust,* accepted by Harcourt, Brace under the condition that it be condensed, marks a departure from his overt concerns in *Soldiers' Pay* and *Mosquitoes* (1927) with the post–World War I malaise of veterans and artists. Completed during the fall of 1927, but not published as *Sartoris* until January, 1929, this novel initiates Faulkner's immersion in the milieu he knew best— the racially divided, parochial world of the Deep South. Written after his return to Oxford early in 1927, *Flags in the Dust* begins Faulkner's serious attempt to understand characters and motivations within the context of a particular physical environment and against the protracted background of familial heritage. Though no less intrigued by psychological responses to modern conditions, he seems more familiar with his characters, black and white, and more comfortable with their emotions and actions. As a result, Faulkner plausibly develops the people and situations introducing Yoknapatawpha County. However, his unsuccessful struggle to integrate vision and technique shows in his unwieldy narrative.

In *Flags in the Dust* Faulkner extends his treatment and conception of the Negro as contrapuntal to his primary thematic concerns. He establishes the singing of the yellow Negro cook, Elnora, as accompaniment to her housework and the activities within the Sartoris household. ("Elnora's endless minor ebbed and flowed. . . . *'Sinner riz fum de moaner's bench,/Sinner jump to de penance bench,'*" 20–21; "Elnora's voice welled in mellow falling suspense. *All folks talkin' 'bout heaven aint gwine dere,*" 36.) Her voice, a serious undercurrent heard mainly during the early chapters, is a reminder that a constant faith exists simultaneously with the despair experienced by her white employers.

Despite his sketching of Elnora, Faulkner relies heavily upon the comic value of blacks as relief from the central tensions of white life. Simon Strother, Elnora's father, and Isom, her son, are creations suggestive of plantation fiction. Old Simon, "with his race's fine feeling for theatrics" (7), longs for an irretrievable past in which "'Sartorises set de quality in dis country'" (103). A loyal family retainer whose comic foibles are tolerated by his masters because he represents a nostalgic link to their past, Simon has a weakness for younger women and for getting into debt. He sees himself as a Sartoris and above "de commonality" (22). His presence assures old Bayard Sartoris and Aunt Jenny that the twentieth-century world has not changed drastically from their familiar nineteenth-century one.

His grandson, Isom, is a sixteen-year-old youth whom the Sartorises treat as an incompetent fool. He takes the blame for Aunt Jenny's poorly executed garden because he cannot tell his right hand from his left. Jenny watches Isom perform "his deprecatory effacing movement behind the slow equanimity of his ivory grin" (41), and she avows, "'Now, how can anybody keep a decent garden, with a fool like that'" (50). Isom's antics and his description as a "negro lad lean and fluid as a hound, lounging richly static" (20) are similar to Faulkner's treatment of the Negro in *Soldiers' Pay.*

Faulkner's comic depictions of the Negro in *Flags in the Dust* often seem inappropriate. For example, Caspey, Simon's son, returns from the war a different man—no longer content with his place in the traditional southern world. He is insolent and rebellious, but his discontent is well-motivated by the disparity between his position at home and his experiences in France. While he exaggerates his heroics abroad for the benefit of his relatives, Caspey has witnessed the world overseas and can thus recognize the inequitable treatment of American blacks who "'saved France and America bofe'" (53). He argues quite reasonably: "'I dont take nothin' f'um no white folks no mo'. . . . War done changed all dat. If us colored folks is good enough to save France f'um de Germans, den us is good enough to have de same rights de Germans has. French folks thinks so, anyhow, and if America dont, dey's ways of learnin' 'um'" (53). But Caspey's argument isolates him from the conservative blacks in the Sartoris household who interpret his response to second-class citizenship as destructive. Faulkner does not pursue his development of Caspey's rebellion and changed attitudes; instead he lapses into ridiculing the youth's militancy by having the aged white patriarch, Bayard Sartoris, beat him into submission to his former status. In spite of the brief delineation and the reversion to type, Caspey's loss of faith in the old mores and his desire for change are harbingers not only of Faulkner's increased awareness that the tensions between past and present affect blacks as well as whites, but also of his inability to portray the sensibilities of modern blacks.

Nonetheless, *Flags in the Dust* is a germinal, transitional work because in it Faulkner conceives the artistic use of the Negro which becomes central as his career progresses. In shifting the location of the despair and longing of white characters from isolated postwar experiences to southern history and familial inheritance, Faulkner discovers that the Negro is a viable means of relating his major concerns to the past, of supplying an additional perspective upon the meaning of that past, and of increasing dramatic tensions between the past and present. He places a family of black servants within the household of his major protagonists. These blacks provide access to added information about the private and public lives of the protagonists. While this inclusion may not seem to be a fictional innovation, it does allow for a more natural and sustained alternative perspective, unlike the artificial shifts to black scenes in *Soldiers' Pay*, which, though representing the Mahons as southerners, does not involve blacks in conventional servant roles within the Mahon house. Because Faulkner is interested in various possibilities for interpreting experience within a nexus of complex relationships, his narratives require methods of encompassing inherently different, but authoritative, points of view. The Negro operating as a member of the household can unobtrusively provide one of these points of view.

For instance, in *Flags in the Dust* five generations of Strothers, from Simon's grandfather Toby to his grandson Isom, have served the Sartorises. They emphasize the personal and social history of their white employers, as well as the continuity and alteration of their condition in the modern world. Because the Strothers are still unindividualized types from earlier literary traditions, they exist amicably as extensions of the white family, rather than as distinct people who, by virtue of their differences, can illuminate the dominant white society. Although, in connecting the Strothers to the Sartorises, Faulkner has not yet found an effective method of integrating his conception of blacks with his primary ideas about whites, he has come to an understanding of a basic contribution the black family can make to his vision.

Faulkner's technique of contrasting white and black life—not from two separate, insular positions (such as at the end of *Soldiers' Pay*), but from a degree of intimacy—is more fully realized near the end of *Flags in the Dust* when a nameless black family accentuates and partly relieves the problems endemic to the Sartorises. Young Bayard, suffering from having caused his grandfather's death and grieving for the loss of his twin brother, feels responsible for the demise of the Sartoris family. He flees out of guilt, but loses his way during a storm. Bayard seeks refuge with a rural black family. His arrival coincides with Christmas, which he spends sharing the generosity of the poor. Even though he consistently labels their smells, appearances, food, and shelter "Negro," Bayard experiences the warmth of a family surviving together:

> The stale, airtight room dulled him; the warmth was insidious to his bones wearied and stiff after the chill night. The negroes moved about in the single room, the woman busy at the hearth with her cooking, the pickaninnies with their frugal and sorry gewgaws and filthy candy. Bayard . . . dozed the morning away. Not asleep, but time was lost in a timeless region where he lingered unawake and into which he realized after a long while that something was trying to penetrate; watched the vain attempts with peaceful detachment. (336)

Within the room, Bayard senses communal effort and security. The fire for heating and cooking on their broken hearth reflects not merely the simplicity of their lives, but also their bond of love. Bayard acknowledges the family's humanity, yet can view it only in sharp contrast to his own. He and they are "two opposed concepts antipathetic by race, blood, nature and environment, touching for a moment and fused within the illusion of a contradiction" (336). The moment is a frieze, rich with potential that goes unrealized because it cannot be included in the larger picture of Bayard's life as Faulkner presents it in this novel.

Bayard's Christmas with the black family and other unsustained glimpses of black humanity in *Flags in the Dust* enrich Faulkner's portrayal of a particular South and establish intrinsic connections between blacks and whites; however, they are inadequately related to the main focus of the work. Faulkner achieves a synthesis of the Negro with the primary concerns of his art in *The Sound and the Fury*.

The process of developing the Negro as an integral part of his artistic vision leads Faulkner to a technical breakthrough in his fourth novel. Although he accents the social actuality of the Negro's place and role in the white southerner's world, he does so innovatively and respectfully. He escapes the tyranny of stereotypes by acknowledging, as no earlier novelist had, the humanity of individual black people within the family and the church—the major institutions affecting their lives. *The Sound and the Fury* clearly indicates that Faulkner's interest is in the external manifestations of the Negro's inner resources, of which he apparently was firmly convinced. While his literal understanding of blacks is largely shaped by his particular heritage and place in the white world, his artistic development of their presence in plot, structure, themes, and symbols transcends the limitations of his personal perspective.

In *The Sound and the Fury* Faulkner divides the southern world into black and white. He uses the black world, as he perceives it from the outside, in order to characterize the weaknesses or, more rarely, the strengths of the white world and its inhabitants. He draws extensively upon a family of black servants, the Gibsons, who are in close contact with the white Compson family. His strategy, however, depends upon the blacks and whites maintaining different attitudes and values. His blacks (primarily, but not exclusively, the Gibsons) contribute to the contrapuntal design of the novel, because their voices and actions create a meaningful contrast to the disintegrating Compsons and add greater dimension to the symbolism, themes, and narrative form.

Roskus and Dilsey Gibson are patriarch and matriarch of the black family in *The Sound and the Fury*. Their children, Versh, Frony, and T. P., and grandson, Luster, progress with the younger Compsons over the pages of the novel and history. The Gibsons take care of the Compson place and family. They play strong, supportive roles and frequently dominate the action (particularly in the first and fourth sections, in which Luster and Dilsey are central figures in the narrative present). The Gibsons function to foreshadow events, as well as to reiterate motifs. They are integral to Faulkner's formal ordering principles, and they are touchstones by which those principles become familiar to the reader.

Representing opposition to the sterility and decay evidenced by the white family, the Gibsons project a vital creativity, an inventiveness in looking at life and a spiritedness in confronting it all. Frony, for example, wears her new clothes on the climactic Easter morning even if it means getting wet, because as she states, "'I aint never stopped no rain yit.'"[1] Like the rest of the family, she accepts the natural course of things, but does not relinquish her individual will. Frony's older brother Versh also has a level-headed approach to himself and to life. He tells Benjy, the retarded Compson son: "'You aint had to be out in the rain like I is. You's born lucky and dont know it'" (85). In other words, Benjy is born white in a region where those of his race have all the advantages. Versh quite simply places Benjy within a frame of reference that, while realistic, may be overlooked because of Benjy's idiocy. As Versh suggests, even the life of a retarded white man seems easier than that of a normal black man, because in their world blacks are circumscribed by racial restrictions to lives of hard, unrewarding work. Juxtaposed to the various kinds of lunacy demonstrated by the Compsons are the Gibsons—practical, "common-sense variety" blacks whose individual and collective voices create an eloquent contrast to the white world and form, on a level of emotion and reason, a more viable approach to life.

In the Gibson family Faulkner succeeds in capturing the symbolic and spiritual significance of a whole generation of southern blacks as they are understood by the white South. He explores the artistic possibilities inherent in traditional black life, thought, and expression. His treatment of black community suggests that the simple bonds of faith and love embodied in that community's daily relationships are ignored by the modern southerner in his search for meaning in a changing, complex society. For example, Roskus, Versh, T. P., and Luster, depicted as interchangeable elements, are present to insure the smooth operation of the place (tending the stock, driving the carriage, and caring for Benjy), but their presence also creates a sense of fused generations in a closely knit family, and of the flux of individuality bending to a stable historical community. In their closeness they represent a continuity of family that is vital to a traditional society. Dilsey at one point in Benjy's narrative remarks to the aging, arthritic Roskus, "'T. P. getting big enough to take your place'" (34). The son's carrying on for the father, assuming his responsibilities and position, is what no Compson son is able to do, and the white family is the weaker for it.

1 William Faulkner, *The Sound and the Fury* (New York: Jonathan Cape and Harrison Smith, 1929), 361.

By means of the Gibsons, Faulkner examines the experience of traditional black characters and their major institutions—the family and the church—for what that experience can reveal about interpreting life and mediating the forces of time and history. Frony, for instance, as a child interacting in family relationships (with both Compsons and Gibsons) and as an adult attending Easter services is a younger version of her mother in applying a black-centered experience to the larger white world and in instinctively recognizing the shortcomings of both. In his use of the black family and church, Faulkner realizes the significance of the Negro as the South's indigenous symbol, and he treats that symbol creatively and seriously as one pervasive influence on the imaginative life of the southern artist.

Not enough critical attention has been paid to the significance of the Gibsons as a family group adding another dimension to the contrapuntal design by framing the disintegration of a white southern family with the survival of a black family. Roskus, his sons and daughter, and even Luster have all been overshadowed by the figure of Dilsey, whose gaunt, silent presence dominates the fourth section. Dilsey is the major focus, but even on that Easter Sunday three generations of the black family make the pilgrimage together to attend the climactic Easter service. Moreover, both parents and all the children have meaningful places in the memories and action of section one and in Quentin's mind in section two. Quentin, for instance, on the train heading back south from Cambridge, suddenly realizes that he has missed "Roskus and Dilsey and them" (106). He misses not only Dilsey but the whole family. And in Benjy's section, Dilsey admonishes Roskus: "'Your bad luck talk got them Memphis notions into Versh. That ought to satisfy you'" (37). She voices her displeasure not so much with her husband's talk of bad luck on the Compsons' place, but with such talk as being responsible for dividing her family.

Structurally the pattern of development in which "Roskus and Dilsey and them" act as counterpoint to the Compsons is a reflection of the social order of two southern classes. The interaction between the Gibsons and the Compsons is a ritual of survival enacted by the black servant class and the southern white gentility: service and loyalty in exchange for material goods and protection. The two groups, Compsons and Gibsons, occupy the same physical space, the old Compson place, yet are of two different worlds—each one impelled by its own values and priorities. Each group retains an orientation to life that, though familiar to its own peers, is private and inaccessible to the outside group. "'I knows what I knows,'" young Frony emphatically states about Damuddy's funeral (43, 46). But Caddy protests, "'That's niggers. White folks dont have funerals'" (39). As young as they are, the two girls symbolically echo attitudes derived from distinctly different orientations. However, in the relations between the two groups, it is the "place" and function of the blacks to sustain the whites and reinforce their world—a fact which Dilsey's question regarding the baby girl, Quentin, ironically reiterates: "'Who else gwine raise her 'cep me? Aint I raised eve'y one of y'all?'" (246).

It seems no coincidence that the two families are symmetrical. Both fathers, Jason Compson and Roskus Gibson, are philosophers of sorts. Roskus is a homespun philosopher who voices folk beliefs gleaned from signs and omens. He senses the deaths of the Compsons: "'They been two, now. . . . Going to be one more. I seen the sign'" (34). Roskus is also somewhat fatalistic: "'They aint no luck on this place. . . . I seen it at first but when they changed his name I knowed it'" (35). Though more learned and sophisticated, Mr. Compson is, like Roskus, fatalistic. His pessimistic philosophy encompasses the entire species: "All men are just accumulations of dolls stuffed with sawdust swept up from the trash heaps where all previous dolls had been thrown away" (218); "Man [is] the sum of his climatic experiences. . . . A problem in impure properties carried tediously to an unvarying nil: stalemate of dust and desire" (153). Both Mr. Compson and Roskus become relatively helpless prior to their deaths. Roskus is crippled by "rheumatism," and periodically "'cant lift his arms'" (9). Mr. Compson is crippled by alcoholism, and becomes totally dependent upon drinking (154, 29). When they die, the two men leave wives to bear the family's burden in the narrative present.

Though their personalities and strengths are at variance, Caroline Compson and Dilsey Gibson are corresponding figures. Caroline envisions herself as a long-suffering mother and talks about her all-important role. Dilsey dispenses with Caroline's empty rhetoric and acts out the more significant mother function. Caroline says of herself, "'At least I can do my best to shield her [Quentin]'" (247). But it is Dilsey who physically shields Quentin from Jason and a beating by stepping in front of the girl. "'I aint gwine let him tech you,'" she comforts Quentin (230). She also tells Jason, "'Hit me, den . . . ef nothin else but hittin somebody wont do you. Hit me'" (229–30). Caroline's feeble laments, always outside an active context of doing, are paltry in comparison: "'But it's my place to suffer for my children. . . . I can bear it'" (274). Her words, "At least I can do my best," are more meaningfully restated by Dilsey in the final section: "'I does de bes I kin . . . Lord knows dat'" (396). Dilsey's statement underscores the ironical correspondence and the tension between the two women.

The symmetry of the families also extends to the children. The Compsons have two "normal" sons and a daughter, and so do the Gibsons. Jason Compson and T. P. Gibson stay on in Jefferson; Quentin Compson commits suicide in Cambridge, Massachusetts, and Versh leaves for Memphis. Caddy Compson and Frony Gibson, the daughters, attain their greatest significance in the remembered sequences, with Caddy's role being not only the more important of the two, but the pivotal one of the novel as well.

Benjy, the third Compson son, is associated with Luster (Frony's son) throughout the novel. Thus, Benjy, "three years old thirty years" (19), and Luster, who remains a youth, complete the symmetrical design suggested by the two families.

Luster occupies a position in the opening paragraph of the novel which symbolically represents a contrapuntal relationship between the Compsons and the Gibsons:

> Through the fence, between the curling flower spaces, I could see them hitting. They were coming toward where the flag was and I went along the fence. Luster was hunting in the grass by the flower tree. They took the flag out, and they were hitting. Then they put the flag back and they went to the table, and he hit and the other hit. Then they went on, and I went along the fence. Luster came away from the flower tree and we went along the fence and they

stopped and I looked through the fence while Luster was hunting
in the grass.

One Compson, the narrator, and one "Gibson,"[2] Luster, the only
two characters who sustain the experience of childhood throughout
the novel, are present and actively involved in the scene. Each is
aware of the other and tied to him, as the sequence of events suggests: "they went on and I went along the fence. Luster came
away from the flower tree and we went along the fence and they
stopped." The fence separates the two from the larger outside
world, and it confines them to the Compson place. Yet, each pursues an independent activity which almost totally absorbs his attention and which connects him to the world on the other side of the
fence. Benjy, the teller, watches the men play golf on what had been
his pasture; Luster searches for a lost quarter that will admit him to a
traveling show. Benjy sees the present but evokes the past; Luster
searches in the present but with anticipation of the future. These
two outlooks, toward the past for the Compsons and for the blacks
toward the future (ultimately the Christian afterlife as the Easter
Sunday section makes clear), pervade the novel and are central to its
resolution.

"Luster's search for the lost quarter, whose mandala shape suggests wholeness, coherence, and order," as Sally R. Page points out,
"is paralleled by Benjy's wandering search for the security, wholeness, and order wrought by the love of Caddy."[3] An equally important observation is that the two searches, one physical and the other
symbolic, demonstrate the thematic and structural significance of
Luster, whose lost quarter provokes his current impatience with
Benjy and provides a logical introduction to memories of Caddy's
kindness. Faulkner's handling of Luster makes clear his control over
content and form in the first section and illustrates his reliance upon
the Negro in the technical development of *The Sound and the Fury*.

2 The lack of detail regarding Frony's marriage and husband suggests that Faulkner
sees Luster as an extension of the Gibson family. Frony's own presence and position
as Luster's mother are played down. Dilsey, for all practical purposes, is both mammy
and mother to Luster; she almost completely overshadows Frony as Luster's mother.
3 Sally R. Page, *Faulkner's Women: Characterization and Meaning* (Deland, Fla.: Everett/
Edwards, 1972), 53.

The structure of Benjy's narrative is partially dependent upon the contrast between Luster's and Caddy's treatment of Benjy. The arrangement of details stresses the difference between Luster's (the present) and Caddy's (the past) approaches to Benjy. This contrast forms one pattern whereby fragmentary scenes are interwoven and the experiences of the novel ordered. Luster, a child himself, has charge of Benjy during 1928, the narrative present. His pairing with Benjy (particularly their passing through the broken place in the fence) recalls Caddy, who had assumed much of the responsibility for Benjy in the past.

Caddy's words, " 'He's not too heavy. . . . I can carry him'" (77), are expressive of her total relationship with Benjy; she assumes not only his physical weight, but also the emotional burden of a retarded brother. Caddy is the one character who is solicitous of both Benjy's comfort and his emotional well-being. Even Dilsey, the other character showing a genuine concern for Benjy, is unlike Caddy, because she attempts to keep Benjy quiet rather than happy: " 'Git in, now, and set still until your maw come.' Dilsey said. She shoved me into the carriage" (9). Dilsey's words, and her disciplinary activity, fail to approach Caddy's level of sensitive, maternal concern. Caddy's actions, because they are measured against Luster's, are all the more warm, affectionate, and selfless.

In his treatment of Benjy, Luster is a foil to Caddy. He emphasizes the actual difficulty and the normal frustrations of looking after a thirty-three-year-old idiot ("'I aint going to follow him around day and night both,'" Luster declares, 69). His brash and teasing manner is typically childlike, whereas Caddy's gentle, patient, and loving manner is altogether mature and responsible. The presentation of the lumbering adult Benjy under Luster's care justifies the transition to Caddy's past attention to the child Benjy as a means of defining both the deterioration of the Compsons and the personality of the absent sister.

Luster considers Benjy an unwanted burden. The first time he speaks Luster makes his attitude toward Benjy plain: " 'Listen at you, now,' Luster said. 'Ain't you something, thirty-three years old, going on that way. After I done went all the way to town to buy you that cake. Hush up that moaning. Aint you going to help me find that quarter so I can go to the show tonight'" (1–2). Luster cares little about Benjy's comfort. He is self-centered, as the average youth might be. He is, after all, saddled with a constant responsibility beyond his years. Many of his actions and statements reflect an irritability resulting from the drudgery of his charge. For instance, Luster, upset over his lost quarter, the physical representation of his opportunity to attend the show, tells Benjy: "'Now you aint got nothing to moan about. . . . Hush up. I the one got something to moan over, you aint'" (66).

Just as he claims, Luster has "something to moan over." He knows that his loss of the quarter may be translated directly into another loss—his chance to see the show. For Luster there is an immediate association of cause with effect, while the Compsons recognize effects but not causes. Luster's loss is an extension of the obsessive sense of loss dominating all three Compson narrators, who are incapable of truly understanding their loss either emotionally or intellectually. Each of the three brothers is particularly out of touch with his emotions. It is not that Benjy cannot articulate what motivates his moanings, but that as an idiot he simply does not know. Similarly Quentin and Jason, while seeing, however imperfectly, the manifestations of their own predicaments, cannot express what drives one into a quiet retreat from life and the other into angry confrontation with it, because neither can construct a meaningful tandem of feeling and thought. Quentin never has any insight regarding his feelings for Caddy; he remains as emotionally infantile as Benjy. Jason, too, is unaware of the emotional causes underlying his behavior. For example, twice he looks upon his father's coffin and "feels funny" (250, 252), but at neither time does he make logical connections or comprehend his feelings. He reacts, instead, by moving away—his method of handling all such emotional situations. All three brothers are united by blood (and their relationship to Caddy), by their position as narrators, and by their inability to understand or interpret casually the emotional core of familial interaction.

In contrast, Luster's loss immediately increases his impatience with Benjy, perhaps rightly so, because it accentuates his position as a working man[4] who receives neither wages nor an allowance. His position, something else for him to moan about, is that of a bondsman, body servant, or family slave, rather than that of a modern employee. His insistent search suggests the difficulty of obtaining another quarter, despite his confident boast to the boys at the branch ("'Plenty more where that one come from,'" 16).

When Jason offers to sell Luster a show ticket for only five cents, he ironically draws attention to the traditional nature of the relationship between the two families. Jason reveals more than that his brother's full-time attendant does not receive a penny for his trouble; he reveals that the question of payment for Luster's services is completely foreign to Jason's conception of the black boy and his own responsibility. It never occurs to Jason that he should be ashamed, not, as Dilsey suggests, for his blatant disrespect for Luster's feelings (that is, Jason burns two tickets while Luster watches), but for his failure to compensate Luster for his man-size job. The normalcy of Luster's frustration with Benjy is reiterated by these economic considerations.

In overall effect, Luster's treatment of Benjy denies the stereotype of blacks as inherently kind, loving, and submissive due to a "peculiar disposition." However, Luster does superficially resemble a comic minstrelsy figure in action, and a pickaninny or Sambo in appearance. His portrait seems to be a more fully developed version of young Isom (*Flags in the Dust*), who is a one-dimensional humorous figure. The comic exchange between Luster and the other two black youths at the branch evokes the minstrel tradition. Their dialogue is a series of fast-paced quips, akin to folk humor:

> "Where'd you get a quarter, boy. Find it in white folks' pockets while they aint looking."
> "Got it at the getting place." Luster said. "Plenty more where that one come from. Only I got to find that one. Is you all found it yet."

---

4 Faulkner himself later terms Luster "a man." In the 1946 appendix for *The Sound and the Fury*, he identifies Luster as: "A man aged 14. Who was not only capable of the complete care of an idiot twice his age and three times his size but could keep him entertained."

"I aint studying no quarter. I got my own business to tend to."
"Come on here." Luster said. "Help me look for it."
"He wouldn't know a quarter if he was to see it, would he." (16)

Their extended repartee contains the exaggerations of a minstrel
show, but it is as well Faulkner's attempt to establish early in the
novel a special oral quality and a cohesion between memory and activity, which mark *The Sound and the Fury* as a unique achievement.
This initial concentration on the animation, color, and rhythms of
black speech builds toward the black folk sermon delivered by the
minister, an expert showman, the Reverend Shegog.

The description of Luster in his Easter finery, a new straw hat, implies the Sambo or pickaninny stereotype: "The hat seemed to isolate Luster's skull, in the beholder's eye as a spotlight would, in all its
individual planes and angles. So peculiarly individual was its shape
that at first glance the hat appeared to be on the head of someone
standing immediately behind Luster" (360). This portrait relies upon
the conventions of the Sambo figure for its humor, so that not only
the black boy's appearance (the shape of his head), but also his dress
(the straw hat) are ridiculed.

On the other hand, Luster's attitude toward his white charge overshadows the minstrelsy and pickaninny overtones. In his treatment
of Benjy, Luster inverts the relationship traditionally depicted between blacks and whites in the South. Luster is neither overly sympathetic nor solicitous. He is obviously not endowed with the ster-
eotypical temperament suited to serving whites. His repeated threat
to whip Benjy openly defies the tradition of white supremacy which
has, not infrequently, been maintained by violence. In answer to the
question, "'What does you do when he start bellering,'" Luster declares, "'I whips him'" (17). And he follows his claim with the warning to Benjy, "'Hush up. . . . You old loony. You want me to whip
you'" (19). Luster flouts the tradition; his threat, accordingly, is
radical for a black in 1928 (whether in fact or in fiction). It is significant that Luster does not ever actually strike Benjy. The threat itself
is sacrilegious enough to create an impression of his high-handed
treatment of Benjy and to indicate the individual bent of his character. Though even his companions do not believe that he would

dare strike Benjy, they are sufficiently impressed by his forceful statements.

Luster's grandmother, Dilsey, recognizes the danger in this side of his personality: "'You bound fer de chain gang'" (398). She attempts to curb Luster's conduct because, in the traditional order of things in the South, such conduct can only lead to suffering or perhaps even death. Luster is bright and creative; examples are his witty replies to the boys at the branch and his makeshift replica of golf equipment. He is also gutsy, as he manages to hold his own against the two most forceful characters, Dilsey and Jason. Precisely because of these qualities, Luster may face difficulties with the system. Critical interpretations of Luster as "indolent, careless, traditional"[5] are incomplete, because they seem to be based upon an unstated premise that Luster ought, by virtue of a natural law, to care for a full-grown idiot both day and night, and what is more that he should enjoy his work. Luster's position underscores the danger of taking Faulkner's situations at face value.

Luster's relationship with Benjy goes beyond the traditional. Representing the white man as idiot-child and the black child as guardian-man is a bold innovation both literally and symbolically in fictional black-white relationships, because the Compsons resemble in some ways the whites of nineteenth-century plantation fiction. Mrs. Compson, for instance, refers to the blacks on the place as "darkies" (348), an appellation out of the world of James Lane Allen or Thomas Nelson Page. The white man-idiot and the black child-guardian reiterate the themes of the disintegration of an aristocratic southern family in the modern world. Even more provocative is the subtle announcement of a resulting change in the status of blacks; the black boy is given the upper hand, precarious though it may be. Luster's portrait contains the suggestion of the psychological emancipation of the coming generation of blacks from white dominance, or at the very least, the uneasy relationship of the younger generation of blacks to the racial patterns governing southern life and thought (and accepted by former slaves and first-generation free

5 John Longley, *The Tragic Mask: A Study of Faulkner's Heroes* (Chapel Hill: University of North Carolina Press, 1963), 232.

men). Only Jason's physical violence against Luster's person in the final scene of the novel asserts Benjy's order, and by extension the traditional order of white authority over blacks which, following Reconstruction, generally hinged upon violence or the open, public threat of it.

The sequences involving Luster are significant, too, because they help to clarify Faulkner's technique in constructing the first monologue. Faulkner's inclusion of materials relating to Luster's search for the lost quarter, his desire to go to the show, and Benjy's age and birthday is, according to Michael Millgate,[6] one of the substantial revisions from the manuscript to the typescript and then to the published text. Faulkner's revisions and additions to Benjy's monologue suggest the importance he attached to Luster in the total scheme of the chapter and also his careful attention to detail in writing the first section. The implication is that Faulkner's rationale for changes may have more to do with artistic considerations than with the provision of assistance to the perplexed reader. For example, the italicized passages have generally been considered primarily as a device to assist the reader in recognizing time shifts.[7] However, the italics, as the sections with Luster juxtaposed to those involving Caddy suggest, are also used to stress personal qualities of characters by juxtaposing them to contrary characteristics of others. Faulkner's use of italics, then, is both a method of characterization and a thematic design.[8] In

6 Michael Millgate, *The Achievement of William Faulkner* (New York: Random House, 1966), 93. Millgate, for the most part, merely presents his findings from the unpublished work. Therefore, for detailed examples of Faulkner's additions, see Emily K. Izsak, "The Manuscript of *The Sound and the Fury:* The Revisions in the First Section," *Studies in Bibliography,* XX (1967), 189–202.

7 For example, Lawrance Thompson's annotation of the changes in type is quite accurate, but his assessment seems tied to a preconception that they are mainly indications of time shifts. *William Faulkner: An Introduction and Interpretation* (New York: Holt, Rinehart and Winston, 1967), 35. Curiously, Thompson also discusses "Ben's tension of interest" in the monologue without once referring to Luster. See 33. Thompson is much more cautious in his questioning of Faulkner's use of italics than are George R. Stewart and Joseph M. Backus. After extensive work on the time sequence and italicized passages, they conclude that "the actual method of printing [italics] causes greater confusion than if Faulkner had used no 'gimmick' at all." See "'Each in Its Ordered Place': Structure and Narrative in Benjy's Section of *The Sound and the Fury,*" *American Literature,* XXIX (January, 1958), 440–56.

8 That Faulkner did not consider his use of italics as simply a device to help the reader avoid difficulties with time changes is implicit in his defense of the italics

the early part of the monologue, the italicized sections frame and highlight Caddy's treatment of Benjy, and they establish her centrality. Two passages illustrate Faulkner's method.

Early in Benjy's monologue, the narrative moves directly from Caddy's kindness to Benjy on her return from school to Luster's brusque treatment of him on his thirty-third birthday. The section reads:

> "Did you come to meet Caddy." she said, rubbing my hands. "What is it. What are you trying to tell Caddy." Caddy smelled like trees and like when she says we were asleep.
> *What are you moaning about, Luster said. You can watch them again when we get to the branch. Here's you a jimson weed. He gave me the flower. We went through the fence, into the lot.*
> "What is it." Caddy said. "What are you trying to tell Caddy. Did they send him out, Versh." (5)

Following the italicized section involving Benjy and Luster, the narrative returns to Caddy and Benjy at the iron gate outside the Compson house; it does not proceed with the incidents of April 7, 1928, Benjy's birthday. The italicized segment, then, is not a transition indicative of a time shift. It emphasizes the difference between Caddy's reaction to Benjy and Luster's reaction to him and, by means of the contrast, characterizes Caddy.

A second passage supports this reading:

> Caddy knelt and put her arms around me and her cold bright face against mine. She smelled like trees.
> "You're not a poor baby. Are you. You've got your Caddy. Haven't you got your Caddy."

---

against Ben Wasson's charges that they did not differentiate all the separate time periods and so were unnecessary. In a letter to Wasson (early summer, 1929), Faulkner wrote: "I think italics are necessary to establish for the reader Benjy's confusion; that unbroken-surface confusion of an idiot which is outwardly a dynamic and logical coherence." At the end of the letter, Faulkner urged Wasson to delete his editorial changes and restore the section to its original form: "I purposely used italics for both actual scenes and remembered scenes for the reason, not to indicate the different dates of happenings, but merely to permit the reader to anticipate thought-transference, letting the recollection postulate its own date. Surely you see this." Joseph Blotner (ed.), *Selected Letters of William Faulkner* (New York: Random House, 1977), 44–45.

> *Cant you shut up that moaning and slobbering, Luster said. Aint you shamed of yourself, making all this racket. We passed the carriage house, where the carriage was. It had a new wheel.* (8)

The italicized paragraph is used associatively by Faulkner in his ordering process and by Benjy in his telling. It leads into another time period, one before Roskus' death but after Mr. Compson's death and the girl Quentin's arrival. However, the italicized segment is not present merely to introduce a different chronological period. This passage, like the preceding example, suggests that the incidents involving Luster, while differentiating past from present, also underscore Caddy's affection and concern for Benjy as being more sensitive and sympathetic than the attitudes of the others (Compsons or Gibsons, children or adults). At the same time, the passage establishes memory as equal in importance to physical activity. In addition, the sections involving Luster and Benjy, because they trace the movements of the two across the Compson place, give a sense of the spatial organization and content of the Compson's physical world.

Although I have concentrated on Luster in the early segments as evidence of Faulkner's extensive use of the Negro in his creative process, I believe that throughout the novel all of the Gibsons serve structural, thematic, and symbolic functions. The Gibsons represent a picture of the Negro in the early years of the South's transition to modernity—the Negro as consciously in the shadow of the Civil War as his white counterpart and still held in a tenuous relationship to the South's cultural past and aristocratic values. Dilsey can refer as matter-of-factly to "white trash" (362) as she can to Luster's "Compson devilment" (344). The servant's sense of belonging to his "people" (his white family) evolves from a historical condition of long, close association. Even the youngest servant readily develops the traditional attitude toward his "people" and himself. Luster, for example, while driving Benjy to the graveyard, decides, "'Les show dem niggers how quality does, Benjy'" (399). Whether or not his statement is intended as an ironic reference to Benjy as "quality," Luster includes himself in the description (as exalted driver of a surrey while "dem niggers" are walking).

On the other side, the white family assumes an attitude of paternal duty and responsibility toward servants of long standing. Faulkner manipulates this pattern in *The Sound and the Fury* to reflect a specific historical and cultural place. He extends the meaning of his fiction outward from an individual family to a larger society by drawing upon the responses of white characters to blacks, particularly those whose lives over several generations carry the social history of the whites. Faulkner achieves this perspective most effectively in "April Sixth 1928," Jason's monologue, by placing Jason in open conflict with his present world and his family's legacies. Faulkner uses the Gibsons as faithful family retainers in order to shape the cultural background to which Jason reacts. Although he assigns the blacks conventional roles, Faulkner adapts them to elicit Jason's determining attitudes and his controlling patterns of action.

One of Jason's bitter harangues touches upon the relationship that normally developed between black servants and whites: "That's the trouble with nigger servants, when they've been with you for a long time they get so full of self importance that they're not worth a damn. Think they run the whole family" (257–58). Jason's sense of his own manhood does not allow him to admit that, at least in the case of his family, not only do the servants think they run the whole family, they actually do run it. Although his mother retains the household keys, she assumes none of the responsibility for the house. Dilsey, the black cook and housekeeper, has taken charge. Accommodations, accordingly, are made on both sides so that the household operates with some semblance of expected order. For the most part, Dilsey and Jason avoid each other because, for them, contact becomes confrontation, with authority hanging in the balance. The state of the Compson household establishes the reality of Jason's world and undermines his assertions of power and control.

Ironically, although Jason accuses the blacks of "self importance," his relationship with the Gibsons enhances his own sense of importance. His repeated references to "a whole kitchen full of niggers" reflect his personal commitment to the connection between the Gibsons and his own place in the social hierarchy. In the opening of his monologue, Jason calls attention to his "six niggers that cant even stand up out of a chair unless they've got a pan full of bread and meat to balance them" (223). This idea forms a recurrent motif. Jason adheres to old class values; he sees himself as the master who should be catered to in every way. He tells Luster, " 'I feed a whole damn kitchen full of niggers to follow around after him [Benjy], but if I want an automobile tire changed, I have to do it myself' " (231). Explicitly a complaint, this statement also contains an implicit boast: that at a time when the status of the Compson males is at its lowest, Jason Compson retains servants and provides their food.

When Jason claims, "I haven't got much pride, I can't afford it with a kitchen full of niggers to feed" (286), his statement is loaded with double meanings. His disclaimer carries with it an assertion of pride in both individual and familial accomplishment. He declares his family's past connections and its continued rank. It is a way of saying that the Compsons are still important enough to maintain "six niggers." Servants, especially those inherited from a previous generation (in spite of Emancipation), validate a family's standing. Jason suggests class status in his observation of Dilsey's advancing age: "She was so old she couldn't do any more than move hardly. But that's all right: we need somebody in the kitchen to eat up the grub the young ones cant tote off" (229). Because the Compsons are "quality," they can maintain their lifelong servants even after they are too old to work. For Jason, Dilsey and the current household workers are a continuation of his family's history as landed slaveholders. He admits that this particular heritage distinguishes him and his family from most of the residents of Jefferson: "I says my people owned slaves here when you all were running little shirt tail country stores and farming land no nigger would look at on shares" (298). In light of his admission, his "kitchen full of niggers" may be interpreted as a reminder lest someone fail to comprehend his true station.

Jason emphasizes his position to whoever will listen. " 'You ought to be working for me,' " he remarks to Job, a black who works for Jason's employer. " 'Every other no-count nigger in town eats in my kitchen' " (235). The bragging is disguised in complaints: "I have to work ten hours a day to support a kitchen full of niggers in the style they're accustomed to and send them to the show with every other nigger in the county" (298). While he may well work ten hours a day, he burns two tickets to the show rather than give one away to Luster. The fact is that Jason continues to "feed" his blacks because for him there is no viable alternative. He has inherited, and accepted, membership (physical and psychological) in a social order once based upon wealth and class, but degenerated into empty rituals and manners—the external trappings of an old order.

Jason needs a place of his own. He desires recognition for his value and strength, because throughout his life he has been denied approval by his family and even the Gibsons. His childhood shows his exclusion from the family's affection,[9] as well as from the servants' concern. His mother insists that he is a Bascomb, but her family is of a lower class status than the Compsons, and its lone male representative, Maury, lacks economic independence, personal valor, and physical strength—character traits considered masculine in their culture. Jason's father gives him little evidence of love; in fact, whereas Mr. Compson sacrifices a portion of his land to send Quentin to Harvard and to pay for Caddy's wedding, he makes no comparable display of affection for Jason or concern for his future. As a result of his treatment, Jason is driven to prove his virility and his superiority. While his entire monologue turns upon his assertion that he is a better man than anyone else, especially his alcoholic father and suicidal brother, his protestations of superiority stem from his actual insecurity: his feeling that he has to prove his position among the other Compsons. Unfortunately, the changing society in which he lives provides no opportunity for Jason to become a man of action. His stylized reactions and invectives are the consequences of a decayed gentility that has left intact only forms, which are rendered irrational upon analysis, either because they originate in myth, prejudice, and superstition or because they have outlived the social contexts which gave them meaning.

His dwelling upon feeding so many mouths builds his self-esteem. "I'm a man, I can stand it," Jason insists (307). Nonetheless, his personal insecurities[10] about his manhood cause his vituperative

9 Linda W. Wagner, "Jason Compson: The Demands of Honor," *Sewanee Review*, LX-XIX (Fall, 1971), 560. Wagner's attempt to redeem Jason is more successful in its analysis of his childhood than in its conclusions about his generosity and kindness.
10 John Hunt points out that throughout Jason's narrative, "'like I say,' 'what I say,'

attacks upon everyone around him—especially the Gibsons, who are more vulnerable as members of a lower caste and servant class. "Let these damn trifling niggers starve for a couple of years," Jason states, "then they'd see what a soft thing they have" (237). He measures his own value and manhood by his ability to feed others. He inflates his own ego ("At least I'm man enough to keep the flour barrel full," 286), and receives reinforcement from his mother, who warns her granddaughter: "'He is the nearest thing to a father you've had. . . . It's his bread you and I eat'" (324). Both Jason and Mrs. Compson allude to the cultural meaning attached to the head of a southern family.

Traditionally, one job expected of patriarchs of aristocratic or well-connected families was the provision of food, not just for blood kin, but also for members of the extended family—the numbers (large or small) of slaves and later free servants who lived on the "family place." The bounty of the table indicated economic and social status. However, beginning with the Civil War, many upper-class men lost the means of fulfilling traditional obligations. One of the small crises of Reconstruction was the inability of the family provider to continue feeding either relatives or the black inhabitants of the family's land. Indeed, some of these ex-slaves fed their former masters from small vegetable gardens. Because of the massive failure of crops in the twenties (cotton destroyed by the boll weevil, and food stuff by several disastrous floods),[11] many heads of modern households could not provide for their own children and kin, let alone for the blacks. The severity of the problem is suggested by Job: "'Aint nobody works much in dis country cep de boll-weevil, nowadays'" (235).

Jason is connected to Faulkner's image of the southern patriarch,

---

and 'I always say' drop steadily into monologue to butress his tenuous self-confidence." *William Faulkner: Art in Theological Tension* (Syracuse: Syracuse University Press, 1965), 71.
11 Faulkner is cognizant of the boll weevil and the floods as important elements of the setting and atmosphere. Both are synonymous with failure and precarious fortune. Job, the black man whom Jason chides about his work, makes several references to the effects of boll weevils on the Yoknapatawpha community (235). Louis Hatcher (in Quentin's monologue, 141–42) talks about an earlier flood affecting Mississippi, but Faulkner may well have been drawing upon the devastating floods of 1927.

which is generally sympathetic, but satirical as well. For example, Jason is reminiscent of Bayard Sartoris, the aged aristocrat and gentleman banker in *Sartoris* and *Flags in the Dust*. Bayard maintains a family of black servants after World War I, and he threatens them in terms similar to Jason's: "'I'll be damned . . . if I haven't got the triflingest set of folks to make a living for God ever made. There's one thing about it: when I finally have to go to the poorhouse, every damned one of you'll be there when I come'" (*Flags in the Dust*, 77). Bayard's cantankerous remarks suggest that Faulkner uses him as one model not only for Jason's paternalism toward blacks, but also for his relationship to a particular past which his attitude conveys.

Jason's own, more accessible, model is his father who, according to Quentin, said: "why should Uncle Maury work if he father could support five or six niggers that did nothing at all but sit with their feet in the oven he certainly could board Uncle Maury now and then lend him a little money who kept his Father's belief in the celestial derivation of his own species at such a fine heat" (218). Mr. Compson expresses in his wry way a personal satisfaction in accepting Maury Bascomb's freeloading and in supporting idle blacks. Jason, who is incapable of thinking or acting creatively, imitates his father's convictions about lazy blacks and parasitic relatives.[12] Neither father nor son is in control of his life. Traditional notions trap Mr. Compson and Jason in the pretentiousness and racism of a paternalistic system.

Jason's conduct, however, is more complexly motivated than that of his father or earlier Faulkner characters, because he exists marginally in both the family and the community and cannot reconcile his public image with his private sense of self. He feels vulnerable to

12 For a discussion of Jason's relationship to his father, see Duncan Aswell, "The Recollection and the Blood: Jason's Role in *The Sound and the Fury*," *Mississippi Quarterly*, XXI (Summer, 1968), 211–18. Faulkner apparently based Jason's use of language on his own father, Murry Falkner. His mother, Maude Falkner, has reported that Jason "talks just like my husband did. . . . His way of talking was just like Jason's, same words and same style. All those 'you know's.' He also had an old 'nigrah' named Jobus. . . . He was always after Jobus for not working hard enough, just like in the story." See James Dahl, "A Faulkner Reminiscence: Conversations with Mrs. Maude Falkner," *Journal of Modern Literature*, III (April, 1974), 1028. However, because Jason echoes Mr. Compson in many ways, he may be a subtle autobiographical link to Faulkner himself, as well as to Murry Falkner.

public opinion ("All the time I could see them watching me like a hawk, waiting for a chance to say Well I'm not surprised I expected it all the time the whole family's crazy," 290), and obligated to maintain a public image based upon his sense of social place. The signals are his references to having gained "position in this town" (234) and those to his family's good name. In the heat of chasing his niece Quentin and the showman down alleys, Jason lets his mind wander to "Mother's health and the position I try to uphold to have her with no more respect for what I try to do for her than to make her name and my name and my Mother's name a byword in the town" (291). For all his seeming indifference to others, Jason has more than a slight regard for his standing in the community.

It takes the old family servant to give Jason his comeuppance. "'You's a cold man, Jason, if man you is,'" Dilsey judges from her privileged vantage point (258). She is unafraid to stand up to Jason. She chastises him for his behavior in general and for his treatment of Quentin in particular: "'Whyn't you let her alone? Cant you live in de same house wid you own blood niece widout quoilin?'" (316). Dilsey's long years of service allow her to take certain liberties with Jason; she freely expresses her moral indignation because of her position as a servant and surrogate mother in the household. In fact, she addresses him at times as though he were still a child ("'Go on in dar now and behave yoself twell I git supper on,'" 317). Dilsey's response to Jason is based upon familiarity. She knows him, perhaps better than he knows himself.

For such an old woman, Dilsey is a remarkably strong force. She stands firm against Jason's cruelty, though she complies with Mrs. Compson's whims. Dilsey may be enfeebled, but when necessary she confronts Jason head on: "'I dont put no devilment beyond you'" (230); "'I thank de Lawd I got mo heart dan dat, even ef hit is black'" (258). She proves to be both a restraining force and a verbal match for Jason. He, in turn, acknowledges her refusal to cower to him, and at one point he admits as much to her: "'I know you wont pay me any mind, but I reckon you'll do what Mother says'" (258). Because Dilsey has moral strength, she refuses to compromise her beliefs to satisfy Jason. Her presence in the Compson house deflates Jason's verbal assessment of his stature.

Cleanth Brooks has concluded that Jason "is bound to nothing. He repudiates any traditional tie. He means to be on his own and he rejects every community. The fact shows up plainly in the way he conducts himself not only in his own household but also in the town of Jefferson."[13] But nothing shows up plainly about Jason, as his remarks about the Gibsons make evident. If anything at all is known about Jason Compson, it is that he is not trustworthy. "Dont you trust me?" Jason asks Caddy after their father's funeral. "'No,' she says, 'I know you. I grew up with you'" (253). Jason is a master of deception, even of deceiving himself. He cannot be taken at his word. His vehement statements against family and tradition are his chief misrepresentations of the truth.

Old Job, a character comparable to the Gibsons in displaying folk wisdom, penetrates Jason's masks: "'Aint a man in dis town kin keep up wid you fer smartness. You fools a man whut so smart he cant even keep up wid hisself. . . . Dat's Mr Jason Compson'" (311–12). Undeceived by Jason's pretenses because he is an astute observer, Job extends the traditional intimacy and polarity between servants and masters from Jason's homelife to his work place.

Jason asserts that he is on his own even while evidencing his need for tradition. His reference to "his niggers," to his mother as a lady of quality, his treatment of his Bascomb uncle and everyone with whom he comes in contact (especially Job and blacks, Earl and his customers), all suggest Jason's conception of himself as an aristocrat—a position which would carry automatic validation of his worth. Moreover, what Jason vocally repudiates is any personal *need* for traditional ties, but not the ties themselves. Ironically, even his repudiation of the need is self-deceptive. Like others of his class in Faulkner's novels, Jason holds on to the memories of the past (298), and he does not relinquish what the past represents to those with similar memories. He hates the South, his family, and tradition a good deal less than he thinks. Even Jason's speculation on the cotton market, although suggesting Snopesism, northern materialism, and the New South, links him to the past in which gentlemen (and po-

13 Cleanth Brooks, *William Faulkner: The Yoknapatawpha Country* (New Haven: Yale University Press, 1963), 342.

tential leaders) of the Deep South had only cotton and politics as "professions" from which to amass respectable fortunes. Unlike his older brother Quentin, who searches for meaning in the tradition, Jason reveals a desperate struggle for a *place* in the tradition, because his precise relationship to his family, community, and himself is tortured and complex.

Far from being "the least 'Southern' of the sections," as Michael Millgate claims,[14] Jason's section is based precisely on the importance of women and family, as well as the Negro, to the southerner's sense of self and physical well-being. His monologue is intensely "southern" in its obsessions with feeding his blacks, upholding his place, protecting his mother, and cursing his victimization by his family (his father, brother, sister, and niece). Because "place" and "family" are traditionally important ways of defining self, the absence or erosion of the two precipitates an identity crisis. Jason, a constant malcontent, is not so insulated from his heritage as he would have others believe. His uncertainty about his rightful place in the Compson family, for which he does deserve measured sympathy, is magnified by the obvious deterioration of what family he has left to claim—a hypochondriac, an idiot, and "a hot one" (Quentin). Jason attempts by means of his paranoid cruelty (to Dilsey, Luster, Quentin, Mrs. Compson, and himself), his boasting lies, and his authoritative demands to negate the meaning that place and family have acquired in his culture and his personal existence. But he is unsuccessful.

The conclusion of his monologue, which occurs, appropriately, during supper, links money to the table (family position) in Jason's individual quest for place and personal status: "I just want an even chance to get my money back. And once I've done that they can bring all Beale Street and all bedlam in here and two of them can sleep in my bed and another one can have my place at the table too" (329). "Beale Street" and "bedlam" connect blacks and idiots to the

14 Millgate, *The Achievement of William Faulkner*, 98. Jason is certainly as "southern" as his brother Quentin, and is not "anti-traditional," as Millgate contends, because Jason depends upon the survival of tradition to give meaning to his damaged life. For an extended analysis of Jason as southerner, see André Bleikasten, *The Most Splendid Failure: Faulkner's "The Sound and the Fury"* (Bloomington: Indiana University Press, 1976), 169.

complete downfall of the house and to the usurpation of Jason's position as family head. He believes that retrieving the money from his niece will redefine his status and create a place for him. But Jason Compson has no "even chance"; the contradictions in his own psychological makeup and the social reality of a changing culture combine to assure his failure.

At the center of Jason's portrait, and his dilemma, is a complex problem regarding perception of self and others that is intrinsic to Faulkner's art: the intellectual and emotional duality of southerners which is most forcefully revealed in the double standards of race. Having its historical origins in slavery, in postbellum society this duality pertains directly to the spread of "Jim Crow" which insured that the two already existing societies, one white and the other black, would be opposed to each other. Faulkner's fiction relies upon differences between values, attitudes, beliefs, or hopes of white and black life. His characters who most avidly uphold racial distinctions cannot acknowledge a common humanity. Jason, for example, voices one of the commonplace assumptions resulting from this view: "When people act like niggers, no matter who they are the only thing to do is to treat them like a nigger" (225). Jason uses "people" as a synonym for whites. A "nigger," according to Jason's logic, is not a person and so cannot behave as "people."

   Because of this fragmented condition, Faulkner's white and black characters develop the ability to live mutually exclusive lives, which acknowledge the existence but not the validity of the other. As a result, they are suspended in moral and intellectual contradictions. They learn to live with a false sense of harmony by partially blinding themselves to reality. Although their separate worlds sometimes show signs of consolidation beyond superficial contact, such signs prove misleading. Faulkner's whites especially are rivetted to rituals and manners; their relationships remain fixed and static. Change is frustrated by impotency and fear—outgrowths of an isolation dictated by historical division. In *The Sound and the Fury,* Faulkner presents the Gibsons seemingly within reach of the Compsons, who need new models for saving themselves; however, he maintains implicitly that the Gibsons are inaccessible to the whites. He suggests that the Compsons cannot learn from the example of the Negro because they do not see the example. The partitioning of their society distorts their vision of life and themselves.

The girl Quentin in her relationship with Dilsey is Faulkner's most dramatic rendering of duality in a divided world. Her contradictory feelings toward the black servant prevent her from receiving the maternal comfort she seeks. In Benjy's section, Dilsey defends Quentin against Jason's insinuations: "*Hush your mouth, Jason, Dilsey said. She went and put her arm around Quentin. Sit down, honey, Dilsey said. He ought to be shamed of hisself, throwing what aint your fault up to you*" (87). But Quentin responds by pushing Dilsey away. And in Jason's monologue, Quentin, stung by Jason's taunt ("You damn little slut"), calls out to Dilsey for comfort: " 'Dilsey,' she says, 'Dilsey I want my mother.' Dilsey went to her. 'Now, now,' she says, 'He aint gwine so much as lay his hand on you while Ise here'" (230). Yet when Dilsey touches Quentin, she is immediately rebuffed. Quentin knocks her hand down and cries out, " 'You damn old nigger'" (230).

Simultaneously, the white girl reaches out for Dilsey as a mother substitute and rejects "the nigger" who could never be her mother. Some part of Quentin is cut off from her immediate emotional response to Dilsey by a detached stereotype of "nigger." Her rebuke reflects the stratification of the world she lives in. The girl is at once strongly attracted to Dilsey's kind support and repulsed by the "old nigger." Despite her adolescent rebelliousness and need for love, Quentin is locked into acceptance of a divided world, which encourages and condones keeping Dilsey in a "nigger's place."

Even more than the other Compsons, Quentin, narrator of "June Second 1910," exemplifies the stultifying results of a fractured world, because in the process of learning to live in that world, he suffers an irreparable fragmentation of self. Quentin is an exaggeration of the southern gentleman, whose mind, no longer creative, is locked into sterile types and kinds, codes and manners. His unfailing attention to details of stylized behavior and custom, even when they lack meaning in social interaction, illustrates the extent of his division. His slavery to social conduct blocks off reality, particularly at the end of his monologue when he brushes his teeth and looks for a freshman hat before going to drown himself. His actions point to an evasion of reality by sacrificing clear perception and honest thinking.

Quentin's thoughts about blacks, however, most clearly reveal that his personality, his pattern of thought and behavior are rigidly shaped by an escape mechanism involving the fragmentation of self. Throughout his monologue Quentin returns time and again to "niggers": Deacon, bootblacks, nigger sayings, anonymous niggers, Louis Hatcher, the Gibsons. Even in the simple matter of getting on northern street cars, he notices immediately whether or not "niggers" are aboard (116). Despite his dwelling on blacks and his seeming awareness of them, Quentin still observes, "I used to think that a Southerner had to be always conscious of niggers" (106). He believes that he is not, and the irony lies in the discrepancy between what he believes about himself, and his world, and what his thoughts and actions reveal. Quentin's preoccupation with blacks represents his unacknowledged awareness of the other, alternative possibility for life in a divided world—the world which Quentin as southerner transposes to Massachusetts. The Negro populating Quentin's monologue becomes a strategic figure for what is missing in Quentin's white world and a subtle projection of his own internal state.

Because Faulkner sets the narrative present in this monologue during Quentin's year away from home, he does not rely upon the Gibsons as much as in the other sections. Whereas the black family remains crucial to Quentin's memories of the South, a new black character, the Deacon, achieves prominence in his activities and thoughts in Cambridge. Deacon serves functions similar to those of the Gibsons, but, more importantly, he is Quentin's double. Rather than bearing the youth's social and familial history as the Gibsons do, Deacon carries Quentin's psychological history. He forwards the exposition of Quentin's psyche and the tensions within his self-revelations. With the introduction of Deacon, Faulkner begins an exploration of the Negro as a dark presence creating tensions in the minds of his white characters that attains its greatest significance in later works, particularly *Absalom, Absalom!*[15] and *Go Down, Moses.*

15 John Irwin illustrates that Charles Bon in *Absalom, Absalom!* is "an unconscious projection of Quentin's psychic history." *Doubling and Incest/Repetition and Revenge: A Speculative Reading of Faulkner* (Baltimore: Johns Hopkins University Press, 1975), 35.

It is thematically and structurally appropriate that Quentin seeks out Deacon on the last day of his life. Deacon emerges directly out of Quentin's troubled thoughts about his father (*"Father behind me beyond the rasping darkness,"* 119). The black man appears in military regalia and offers Quentin a "salute, a very superior-officerish kind" (119), both of which link him to General Compson, Quentin's grandfather. Deacon seems to be a projection of Quentin's cultural past. His allusive figure, all that Quentin has left for farewells, is representative of Quentin's lack of immediate connection with any meaningful present world and his nostalgia for a romanticized past.

Despite his disclaimer of involvement in what Deacon is, Quentin is figuratively bound to Deacon, who knowingly observes, "'You and me's the same folks'" (122). Deacon is a manifestation of a side of Quentin's subconscious mind which both attracts and repels the white youth. The meeting of the two men establishes the darker, unconscious part of Quentin and makes concrete the burden of his personal and cultural past. Deacon's presence assures Quentin of immortality, because Deacon has mastered adaptation as a method of survival. At the same time, Deacon announces Quentin's suicide by symbolically replacing the chimes and shadows as pronouncements of death. Their meeting is an imaginative restatement of Faulkner's union of blacks and whites: "two opposed concepts antipathetic by race, blood, nature and environment, touching for a moment and fused within the illusion of a contradiction" (*Flags in the Dust*, 336). But in this meeting "the illusion of a contradiction" prevails, because Quentin fails to recognize Deacon's place in his life.

Quentin rightly calls Deacon a natural psychologist (119). Like the black southerner, Deacon understands the white man's need for the Negro to "see after" him. And because the white southerner's world in Faulkner's fiction depends upon a black presence, Quentin especially seeks out reminders of home and familiar things in that strange, antagonistic setting, "the North." Deacon extorts the maximum dividends from this condition; "he could pick out a Southerner with one glance . . . never missed and once he had heard you speak he could name your state" (119). He skillfully plays to the southerners' assumptions about reality. He greets them in "a sort of Uncle Tom's cabin outfit, patches and all" (120), and he uses the corresponding dialect: "'Yes, suh. Right dis way, young marster, hyer

we is'" (120). Deacon astutely recognizes a need and so fills it without qualms about prostituting himself. He appears to be the loyal,
fawning darky servant at first, and he is—but only for his own ends.
The one suspect part of his initial performance is that he loads the
luggage onto a fifteen-year-old white youth, who is actually Deacon's pack animal and delivery boy. The white boy should be the
southerners' clue that all is not what it appears to be with Deacon,
but their training has not been to examine the Negro closely. And so
for forty years, each new group continues to be duped upon arrival:
"he had you completely subjugated he was always in or out of your
room, ubiquitous and garrulous, though his manner gradually
moved northward as his raiment improved, until at last when he
had bled you until you began to learn better he was calling you
Quentin or whatever, and when you saw him next he'd be wearing a
cast-off Brooks suit" (120).

Despite his observation of the gradual change in Deacon's manner
and appearance, Quentin is not prompted to revaluate himself and
his southernness in relationship to the ritual drama Deacon insti-
gates. Deacon stands for the stubborn unreality of Quentin's world
and his approach to life. For Quentin, Deacon recalls the "reality" of
the South for which he is about to commit suicide. Deacon is hollow
and substanceless like that reality; he is not only illusive, but also a
successful perpetrator of "chicanery" and "hypocrisy" (terms Quentin applies to Deacon, 121). Yet, importantly, Deacon is a man who
knows how to cope with life. He chooses life over death, even if life
involves compromise.

Just as Gerald Bland and his mother, the wealthy Kentuckians
who constantly evoke the Old South in anecdotes of "Gerald's
horses and Gerald's niggers and Gerald's women" (112), are conventional types of southern characters, so is Deacon, the trickster, with
his multiple costumes and guises. Deacon seems to be an extension
of the black fugitive slave in antislavery fiction who, under various
disguises, hides his "true identity" in order to escape the South and
survive. He prefigures the modern hustler-trickster, such as Ralph
Ellison's Rinehart, a northern black of many guises in *Invisible Man*
(1952). Deacon's message is adaptation: take what is useful from the
old and transform it into the new.

However, Deacon is as incomprehensible to Quentin as the rest of the North and South, at least partly because Quentin's mental training in a divided world has been in terms of blacks being like other blacks and whites being like other whites. He can view Deacon's devices for survival only as objectionably "Negro." Thus Quentin makes an inevitable mistake; he looks at Deacon and sees, not himself, but Roskus: "His eyes were soft and irisless and brown, suddenly I saw Roskus watching me from behind all his whitefolks' claptrap of uniforms and politics and Harvard manner; diffident, secret, inarticulate and sad" (123). Quentin does not recognize the basis for his closeness to Deacon. He lacks the ability to be meaningfully self-critical, because as a southerner drawn to the old order of the South, Quentin suffers from the inability to identify himself with the Negro or to analyze himself in terms of what he finds there. Deacon symbolizes the lost, or missed, opportunity for personal integration in Quentin himself. Quentin fails, therefore, to see his own reflection ("diffident, secret, inarticulate and sad") in Deacon, even though he recognizes in another instant: "Roskus was gone. Once more he was the self he had long since taught himself to wear in the world's eye, pompous, spurious, not quite gross" (123). Quentin has also taught himself to wear in the world's eye a romantic self that is "pompous, spurious," a somewhat Byronic self that is as well "not quite gross."

Quentin and Deacon are linked by their pretenses and self-deceptions. Both men wear masks and play absurd roles; Quentin's is foisted upon him by his southern past; Deacon chooses his, though its archetype is found in the past. Both characters live lies, shape their existences to them, and believe in them in spite of themselves. Quentin desires to go beyond this position and force others to believe the lie too; Deacon is content merely to have others tolerate it. Quentin's failure makes death attractive because death captures the essence of an existence he has felt compelled to make actual in life. Such convoluted reasoning becomes another reflection of Quentin's confusion and his fragmentation.

At the same time, Quentin makes the seemingly penetrating observation "that a nigger is not a person so much as a form of behavior; a sort of obverse reflection of the white people he lives among" (106). That "nigger" is a social creation is insightful, but Quentin's generalization does not suggest that "nigger" is the white man's way of seeing the black man. The white southerner is subject to the same set of social mandates out of which he creates "nigger," and he becomes himself a form of behavior. Any such rote adherence purely to form, as opposed to substantive concerns, operates to negate individual identity. Quentin functions almost solely in relation to traditional forms of behavior. He seems unaware that Deacon, in his public posturing, his uniforms and manners, reflects Quentin's own movement in a behavioral pattern that is equally as stylized, if less flagrant.

Neither does Quentin read himself into Deacon's observation, " 'I draw no petty social lines. A man is to me a man, wherever I find him' " (123). Quentin does draw such lines; even in his search for Deacon, he does not see that a man is a man. But Deacon seems to intimate that there is indeed a possibility for Quentin to become a man; for certainly Deacon accepts Quentin in much the same way as does Louis Hatcher, a black farmer in Mississippi, who accepts Quentin as a hunter—a member of the fraternity of virile southern men.

Louis Hatcher, like Deacon, is a man prepared for living. In a comic scene that has serious resonances for Deacon's meeting with Quentin, Louis attributes his survival of a devastating flood to cleaning his lantern and keeping it ready. Quentin responds to the story in disbelief, but he receives a serious answer from a black perspective: " 'Yes, suh. You do you way en I do mine' " (142). Louis is a poor, uneducated black man, who has achieved a certain prepared "light" in his existence. In cleaning his lamp, Louis has prepared for living, even if living is dangerous. He knows how to adapt, to survive with dignity and grace. He displays a personal integration of self and harmony with the world, as his clear, mellow voice ("a part of darkness and silence, coiling out of it, coiling into it again," 142) and his ever-ready lantern suggest. Louis is akin to Deacon and the Gibsons; their lives are as resilient as Louis' voice. But, Louis Hatcher, like Deacon and the Gibsons, is black, and his model for living is incomprehensible to the white youth, who cannot recognize those pragmatic elements in blacks that would be useful guides for his choosing life over death.

Quentin, because he is so out of touch with self and world, does not see the disparity between his actions and reality, though he can

spot obvious contradictions in others. For example, he reflects, specifically on the question of southerners' awareness of "niggers" in
the North: "I learned that the best way to take all people, black or
white, is to take them for what they think they are, then leave them
alone" (106). But Quentin is unable to translate his words into positive action, particularly in terms of his family and his sister Caddy.

When Quentin takes a train back to the South during the Christmas holidays, he has an experience that allows for the expression of
the sentiment underlying his relationship with Deacon. After the
train has stopped in Virginia, Quentin looks out the window and
sees: "a nigger on a mule in the middle of the stiff ruts, waiting for
the train to move. . . . he sat straddle of the mule his head wrapped
in a piece of blanket, as if they had been built there with the fence
and the road, or with the hill, carved of the hill itself, like a sign put
there saying You are home again" (106). The single image of the
black man at home in the southern landscape carries Quentin's
thoughts to the familiar environs of Jefferson and home as no other
single figure or impression could have. A Negro on a mule is a traditional figure extending backwards into the southern past, and it is a
recurring image from Faulkner's first novel.

Immediately Quentin begins to act out a ritual exchange with the
man on the mule by playing "Christmas gift."[16] The man's ready response, "'Sho comin, boss. You done caught me, aint you?'" (107),
asserts what is for Quentin the natural order of things. Both know
from habit, and perhaps instinct, what the ritual entails:

> "I'll let you off this time." I dragged my pants out of the little
> hammock and got a quarter out. "But look out next time. I'll be
> coming back through here two days after New Year, and look out
> then." I threw the quarter out the window. "Buy yourself some
> Santy Claus."
>
> "Yes, suh," he said. He got down and picked up the quarter and
> rubbed it on his leg. "Thanky, young marster. Thanky." (107)

16. Charles D. Peavy points out that "Christmas gift" is an old tradition practiced by
blacks in the South. The game was to say "Christmas gift" first, "whether the game
was between Negro and Massa (or Missus), or between whites, adults or children. At
one time when Negroes said it to white children they may have expected nothing in
return—it was said in kindness. The game was to become ritualistic." "Faulkner's Use
of Folklore in *The Sound and the Fury*," *Journal of American Folklore*, LXXIX (July–
September, 1966), 437–47.

Quentin feels a need for the game and encourages the mechanical participation of the black man, because it confirms for him the reality of traditional relationships.

This incident is comparable to Mrs. Bland's telling "how Gerald throws his nigger downstairs and how the nigger plead to be allowed to matriculate in the divinity school to be near marster marse gerald and How he ran all the way to the station beside the carriage with tears in his eyes when marse gerald rid away" (132). The two incidents reveal the tendency of distorted perceptions to exaggerate the meaning of the Negro to suit an image of the aristocratic master, gallantly inspiring devotion. "Quentin attempts," Olga Vickery maintains, "to coerce experience into conformity with his system."[17] He sees himself as a gentleman of the Old South, and the Negro functions in accordance with his preconceptions. Mrs. Bland's story of Gerald's Negro is only a more extreme example of the same phenomenon. Neither Mrs. Bland nor Quentin sees the Negro as a person, and in reenacting rigid conventions, neither allows for individual self-development.

Ultimately, the meaning that Quentin distills from the Christmas gift incident is predictably disappointing, especially if he is to be considered a perceptive, sensitive youth:

> I leaned out the window . . . looking back. He stood there beside the gaunt rabbit of a mule, the two of them shabby and motionless and unimpatient. . . . they passed smoothly from sight that way, with that quality about them of shabby and timeless patience, of static serenity: that blending of childlike and ready incompetence and paradoxical reliability that tends and protects them it loves out of all reason and robs them steadily and evades responsibility and obligations by means too barefaced to be called subterfuge even and is taken in theft or evasion with only that frank and spontaneous admiration for the victor which a gentleman feels for anyone who beats him in a fair contest, and withal a fond and unflagging tolerance for white folks' vagaries like that of a grandparent for unpredictable and troublesome children, which I had forgotten. (107–108).

The Negro and mule standing "motionless and unimpatient" is a metaphor characterizing Jefferson and home, the way Quentin would like them to be. This scene of "static serenity" provides

17 Vickery, *The Novels of William Faulkner,* 38.

Quentin with a comforting image of a familiar, fixed world. The existence of man and mule confirms the reality of Quentin's sense of home. If "the greatest enemy of Quentin's ethical system is time,"[18] then the Negro on the mule is reassuring because of his timelessness. Poised in a substantial, enduring natural setting, he is the age-old conception of the South's "nigger." Frozen with his mule into a portrait simultaneously then and now, the Negro is literally the closest the southerner can come to a tangible configuration of continuity and permanence.

Quentin's thoughts, however, evidence a duality that is not simply a matter of praising the Negro in spite of his shortcoming; it appears more to be a praising him for faults which magnify the white man's difference and assure him of a special place in his world. His thinking about the Negro relieves the pressure of evaluating his family, home, and himself as they exist in actuality. Quentin's experience of life is shallow and his thoughts reflect as much. Richard P. Adams aptly terms this passage a "collection of condescending clichés."[19] These clichés expose Quentin's inability to work imaginatively within a given context of human interaction, as well as his lack of creative images or ideas. They reveal that his emotional and psychological dilemma will go unresolved. He may have an artist's sensibilities, but he is an extremely sterile and derivative artist. His thoughts disclose a mind that is already dead, smothered by a tradition in which he wholeheartedly believes.[20]

---

18 *Ibid.*, 39.

19 Richard P. Adams, *Faulkner: Myth and Motion* (Princeton: Princeton University Press, 1968), 247. Adams observes, too, that Quentin's understanding of blacks is "not really better than Jason's, the only significant difference is that Quentin thinks he likes them. Both regard Negroes as being static, only because they themselves are static" (247).

20 Quentin's age and his station in life make one question whether he would be in a position to make his judgment of blacks independently; his observations also cause one to wonder what range of personal experiences would lead him to his conclusions. Certainly none that the reader is privy to presents cause for the authoritative tone of his observations. Clearly Quentin's ideas are derivative; they are rooted in traditional paternalistic ideology that at once praises and chastises the Negro. They reflect an authorial intrusion, perhaps a subtle one but an intrusion nonetheless. Specifically, Quentin's words, "and withal a fond and unflagging tolerance for white folks' vagaries," echo the sentiment of Simon, the black servant in *Flags in the Dust*, of whom the narrator states: "for time and much absorbing experience had taught him a fine tolerance of white folks' vagaries" (*Flags in the Dust*, 22). Faulkner reassigns these words to Quentin, and by so doing he makes the white youth a mouthpiece for ideas already formulated in an earlier novel and by an older, conventional black character.

In Quentin's monologue, Faulkner experiments with a more complex method of incorporating the Negro into his fiction. He mirrors
and manifests the white youth's fragmentation by means of a subtle
handling of the Negro's presence in a divided world. His strategy
involves the larger metaphorical value of the Negro. He uses Deacon and the other blacks literally and figuratively to delineate an illusive reality and to render emotional stasis. His method, a symbolic
extension of the relationship between the Gibsons and Compsons,
widens the juxtaposition of blacks and whites to include sympathetic and antagonistic psychological relationships. Although in this
section, and in the novel as a whole, Faulkner implies but does not
fully develop the antagonism between the races, he seems much
more aware of its literary potential, particularly in his use of Deacon
to delineate Quentin's cultural conditioning as a cause of mental
stress and psychical division.

Faulkner's method of handling blacks is similar to an observation
Quentin makes about blacks coming "into white people's lives . . .
in sudden sharp black trickles that isolate white facts for an instant
in unarguable truth like under a microscope; the rest of the time
[blacks are] just voices that laugh when you see nothing to laugh at,
tears when no reason for tears" (211). Quentin perceives two separate realities for whites and blacks; his "white facts," for example, assume black facts as a corollary, an assumption which Faulkner uses for making ideological distinctions between his fictional
worlds. Whereas Quentin observes that blacks penetrate white consciousness suddenly and thereafter have no discernible meaning for
whites, Faulkner utilizes blacks to illuminate or magnify aspects of
his white characters and afterwards confines them to the background as an actual or symbolic presence responding to a reality incomprehensible to whites. Both Quentin's conception and Faulkner's method lead directly to the idea and technique of the final
section.

In "April Eighth 1928," Faulkner draws upon the distinctions, already established in the first three monologues, between his white
and black worlds as one basis for a shift in narrative style. He enlarges the meaning of his contrapuntal development of the Gibsons

and Compsons by articulating in comprehensible detail the reality of the blacks. By his attention to black life not only does he make the black world intelligible, but he also makes the fractured experiences of the white world coherent. Faulkner reenters the white world for a fourth time, but not from the subjective perspective of a Compson. He aligns a third-person narrator with the Gibsons' angle of vision. The Gibsons, as household servants, allow an intimate, yet relatively objective, access to the Compson's story; at the same time, as blacks they define that story from an antithetical perspective. Faulkner depends, then, upon the blacks' difference in thought, language, and emotion to conclude his novel.

In shaping the blacks to serve the technical demands of the fourth part of his novel, Faulkner works through cultural and literary images. He describes the Gibsons in conventional terms, but he transmutes traditional meanings by placing his emphasis on the specific ways in which familiar images of blacks operate symbolically, structurally, and thematically to create a fictional reality that is more compelling and vital than the Compsons'. By focusing on the positive values, faith and feeling, that he associates with blacks, Faulkner extricates his narrative from the distortions characterizing the whites in the three preceding sections and frees his vision of blacks from the debilitating effects of stereotypes.

The final section opens immediately with a contrast between an image of disintegration, rain recalling the Compsons, and one of survival, Dilsey Gibson beginning her day. The sensory description of a rainy morning restates symbolically the theme of human fragmentation: "The day dawned bleak and chill, a moving wall of grey light out of the northeast which, instead of dissolving into moisture, seemed to disintegrate into minute and venomous particles, like dust that, when Dilsey opened the door . . . and emerged, needled laterally into her flesh, precipitating not so much a moisture as a substance partaking of the quality of . . . oil" (330). A sense of the ominous overshadows the start of the day and sets the tone for the entire section; however, Dilsey appears to oppose the effects of the dismal weather.

Dilsey wears the colors and materials of royalty: " a maroon velvet cape," "a dress of purple silk" (330). She is regal and also weathered, as her "myriad and sunken face" (330) suggests. The description places her in opposition to the grey bleakness (figuratively her bright clothing) and to the image of disintegration (survival mirrored in her aged face). Faulkner builds upon Dilsey's majestic presence in establishing her position of authority in this section.

However, he attempts to substantiate Dilsey's credibility by describing her in realistic detail, seemingly based upon the appearance of older black women in his culture. For example, the richly colored cape has a border of fur that is "anonymous" and "mangy"; a "stiff black straw hat" is "perched upon her turban" (330). The result is a mixture of comic and serious modes of description. The comic mode exaggerates Dilsey's grotesque appearance ("her skeleton rose, draped loosely in unpadded skin that tightened upon a paunch almost dropsical," 331), while the serious mode emphasizes the heroic connotations ("as though muscle and tissue had been courage or fortitude," 331). The overall effect depends upon an acceptance of essentially unattractive terms for describing an admirable, aged woman: "The indomitable skeleton was left rising like a ruin or a landmark above the somnolent and impervious guts, and . . . the collapsed face that gave the impression of the bones themselves being outside the flesh" (331). Faulkner's intermingling of different elements, and perhaps even different attitudes toward Dilsey, culminates in the depiction of her expression as "at once fatalistic and of a child's astonished disappointment" (331), which, along with her dress and physical bearing, connects Dilsey to a long line of actual and fictional portraits of "mammy," the loving black servant praised for her service to a white family but often ridiculed because of her appearance.[21]

21 For general discussions of "the mammy" in fiction, see Catherine Juanita Starke's chapter, "Archetypal Patterns," in *Black Portraiture in American Fiction: Stock Characters, Archetypes and Individuals* (New York: Basic Books, 1971), 125–37; and Tischler's chapter on "Faithful and Faithless Retainers," *Black Masks*, 29–49. Faulkner's brother, Murry C. Falkner, provides a personal definition of a "mammy" out of the experiences of Faulkner's family. *The Falkners of Mississippi. A Memoir* (Baton Rouge: Louisiana State University Press, 1967), 13. Murry's image is based primarily upon Caroline Barr, who remained with the Falkners for over forty years. She figures in Dilsey's portrait not in physical appearance but in personal characteristics, faults, and virtues. Like Dilsey, Mammy Callie was, according to Faulkner's brother John, a combination of "shepherdess and avenging angel," "who was faithful" and "who endured." John Faulkner, *My Brother Bill, An Affectionate Reminiscence* (New York: Trident Press, 1963), 48.

Faulkner's description of Dilsey as a mammy in voluminous skirts and headgear may rely generally upon conventional types and specifically upon his own mammy, Caroline Barr; nevertheless, his imaginative portrait transcends symbol or stylized type. His use of Dilsey is much more complex than adherence to the traditional type would allow. She is not merely a "memorial to the Negro servant" as Charles Nilon maintains.[22] Neither is she simply a matter of creating a human being as opposed to a stereotype; for instance, Vickery sees Dilsey as emerging "not only as a Negro servant in the Compson household but as a human being."[23] The implication is that a Negro servant is somehow *not* a human being.

In the fourth section, Dilsey becomes a positive representative of clear vision, just as in Benjy's section it is her husband, Roskus, who possesses clarity of vision. She embodies the cohesion of memory and activity that is vital to the work as a whole. She functions as a medium of memory, through which Faulkner filters the experience of the past. On one level, the experience of the past is that of the Compson family, while on another level, the experience is that of the three preceding narratives, with all their events and relationships distilled through one character, Dilsey. The section may not be told from inside Dilsey's consciousness, but it is told from an angle of vision which places her in the central position.

On that Easter Sunday Dilsey moves slowly; her motion is both deliberate and painful. She continues her life even though she seems distant from all those around her. Roskus is dead, and her sons do not figure in the action of Easter Sunday. Luster's age and interests separate him from his grandmother. Frony, by virtue of her position as daughter, is not Dilsey's confidante. Even the other blacks whom the Gibsons meet going to church do not seem especially close to Dilsey: "And steadily the older people speaking to Dilsey, though, unless they were quite old, Dilsey permitted Frony to respond" (364). All of these details seem to imply that Dilsey has transcended many of the ordinary aspects of social interaction.

Dilsey's isolation points to a possible reason for a third-person narrator in this section. The use of the third-person narrator does

22 Nilon, *Faulkner and the Negro*, 101.
23 Vickery, *The Novels of William Faulkner*, 47.

not suggest that Faulkner is incapable of presenting a sense of Dilsey's immediate impressions and thoughts; neither does it suggest that he considers the entering of a black person's consciousness condescending.[24] It appears, rather, that one technical function of the section is the creation of the perspective of time. Faulkner creates a sense of the passing of an era, and within that perspective he presents the destruction of one family and the endurance of another.

If left still working through the immediacy of an "I" perspective in the final section, the reader would not have a sense of either the magnitude of the action or the slow, inevitable movement of time and humanity. Dilsey lends decorum and distance. Her position is a complicated one; she is a participant in the action, yet she remains outside it. She exists as a kind of sacred vessel, suggesting an experience that is both visionary and tragic. Her role on Easter is to help the reader feel the way back through the labyrinths that Dilsey's being recognizes in the Compsons' fall, but does not accept as unavoidable. Dilsey takes the reader from the level of intellectual exercise necessary to decipher and experience aesthetically the three preceding sections of the novel. Her function suggests that Faulkner envisions Dilsey (and his other blacks by extension) as existing on an intuitive, emotional level, but, at the same time, he ascribes to her a major aesthetic function.

Dilsey belongs to a dimension that assumes larger-than-life proportions quite distinct from caricature because its function has to do with the magnitude of an all-encompassing vision. Dilsey (whether or not her station in life is compatible with the burden of meaning Faulkner places on her characterization) is about vision; she does not merely stand for her own vision as an intuitive, sympathetic character, for she is also the medium for the vision of the reader. Through her the reader remembers and re-creates the novel. In effect, memory becomes a creative aesthetic process in which the reader is forced (as in *Absalom, Absalom!*) to participate in creating the experience of the novel.

24 Tischler, for example, notices "that it is a standard critical commentary of *The Sound and the Fury* that Faulkner fails to give Dilsey a stream-of-consciousness section parallel with that of each of the other main characters. Apparently he felt incapable of putting himself in the place of the Negro, although he chanced identifying with a woman and an idiot—a striking commentary on his belief in the remoteness of Negro psychology." *Black Masks*, 16.

Dilsey cannot emerge as a character having great psychological depth, which is the main charge made in labeling her a stereotype.[25] The reader does not know her thoughts. Nonetheless, Dilsey suggests the limitations of verbal patterns as conveyors of thought. The immediacy of thoughts and impressions properly belongs not to any character in this section but to the reader, who has Dilsey's painfully deliberate activity to help assimilate the passing of an historical moment and incorporate the perspective of time and the aging process into a total conception of meaning in the novel. Dilsey's inner life is not revealed through speech or thought, yet the reader obtains an immediate sense of the quality of her inward state. Her actions are shrouded in mystery; her motivations never clearly revealed. Therefore, if Dilsey ultimately becomes a positive, cohesive force in the novel, she accomplishes this feat as much by means of what her presence encourages the reader to feel, as by the activities she performs.

In her humanity, Dilsey is responsible for emphasizing that reality is ultimately subjective and that individual meaning is noncommunicable. She also shows how in this novel reflection becomes the most valid, perhaps the only possible, means of communication. In reflecting upon Dilsey, the reader comes to terms with the external events revealed through the process of internal monologue in the first three sections. The reader abstracts meanings from the flow of events by using Dilsey as a gauge to interpret the action. Because of the introspective movement of the work, there is no fusion into objectivity without Dilsey. She makes objectivity possible by exposing the contradictory forces of the Compsons' life and suggesting the possibility of counteracting them. The funereal focus on Dilsey revives the past in the novel and the reality of the aesthetic work.

Faulkner has revealed that before he began the Easter Sunday segment of *The Sound and the Fury* he realized that he would have to get completely out of the book: "that there would be compensations, that in a sense I could then give a final turn to the screw and extract some ultimate distillation."[26] Dilsey is a vital part of that "ultimate

25 See, for instance, Irene Edmonds, "Faulkner and the Black Shadow," in Rubin and Jacobs (eds.), *The Southern Renascence*, 194.
26 Faulkner, "An Introduction to *The Sound and the Fury*," 415.

distillation." Faulkner presents Dilsey's vision and perception as a creative center, because as Negro and other, she provides him with a way out of an artistic dilemma. Clearly, there is no resolution that Faulkner, a white southerner, could face in rendering the disintegration of the white world. Had he remained locked within the Compsons' world, he would have ended his novel in despair and nihilism, a conclusion which he could not accept. Dilsey, the embodiment of the blacks' alternative vision, rescues Faulkner from the conclusion of his own logic and the novel from fragmentation and stasis.

Faulkner specifically states, "There was Dilsey to be the future, to stand above the fallen ruins of the family like a ruined chimney, gaunt, patient and indomitable."[27] Though he speaks of Dilsey as representing the future, he compares her to "a ruined chimney," essentially a failed chimney that evokes associations with the past since it no longer serves its intended purpose. Yet that chimney is also "gaunt, patient and indomitable," certainly admirable and even virtuous because of its endurance, its ability to survive the past. By analogy, then, Dilsey may not have succeeded in holding the Compson family together, but she is the lone standard bearer of the attempt. Her tears reassure the reader that a system of morality is at work which encompasses both rewards and punishment. It is primarily an aesthetic reassurance. Dilsey's morality provides sustenance not for the white world Faulkner creates in *The Sound and the Fury*, but for the reader vicariously experiencing that world in juxtaposition to that of the imagined Negro.

Dilsey's experience on Easter morning emerges as singularly profound in the midst of the guilt-ridden, self-centered world of the Compsons. She, as Cleanth Brooks maintains, "affirms the ideal of wholeness in a family which shows in every other member splintering and disintegration."[28] She undergoes the "annealment" extended to her by the communal religious experience. Her prophetic words, "'I've seed de first en de last. . . . I seed the beginnin and now I sees de endin'" (371), seem irrefutable because she has be-

27 *Ibid.*, 414.
28 Cleanth Brooks, "Faulkner's Vision of Good and Evil," *The Hidden God* (New Haven: Yale University Press, 1963), 22–43; rpt. in J. Robert Barth (ed.), *Religious Perspectives in Faulkner's Fiction: Yoknapatawpha and Beyond* (Notre Dame, Ind.: University of Notre Dame Press, 1972), 72. Brooks treats Dilsey as a member of the Compson family.

come, through her odyssey to church, an absolutely venerable character. In church she reveals that she possesses the faith only implied previously; there she assumes an attitude of prayer which has been persistently used in narrative to reveal thought and character with unquestionable validity.[29] Dilsey's participation in the religious service helps to establish firmly that death and disintegration need not overcome the positive forces of existence, and that the erosion of morals, values, and meaning is not universal in modern life.

Importantly, Faulkner's presentation of the Easter service assumes (and acknowledges as few writers have previously) the innate significance of the Negro's faith, which in Faulkner's version presupposes an understanding of human motivation in its simplest form. He presents a picture of right moral conduct emanating from the basic recognition of human need. He does not explore Dilsey's motivation and, consequently, exposes his acceptance of the simplicity of ethical human conduct as well as his faith in the intuitive emergence of positive moral action. Faulkner relies directly upon the Easter service and the blacks to coalesce the fragmented visions of life issuing from the various monologues and to present dramatically the thematic possibility of community, harmony, and love. In working his way out of the quandary and despair of the Compson world, Faulkner turns to his preconceived notions of the black world. He brings to his fiction a belief in black religion as a spiritual experience unifying individuals into a oneness of emotion and purpose. He sees the congregation transformed in *The Sound and the Fury:* "Their hearts were speaking to one another in chanting measures beyond the need for words" (367).

Faulkner envisions his Negro as a homogeneous, coherent social group. His picture of the Easter service prefigures his statement that Christianity shows man "how to discover himself, evolve for himself a moral code and standard within his capacities and aspirations, by giving him a matchless example of suffering and sacrifice and the promise of hope. Writers have always drawn, and always will, on the allegories of moral consciousness."[30] In the example of the

29 Robert Scholes and Robert Kellogg, *The Nature of Narrative* (New York: Oxford University Press, 1966), 200–201.
30 Interview with Jean Stein, in Meriwether and Millgate (eds.), *Lion in the Garden*, 247.

Negro's Christianity, Faulkner finds a meaningful allegory of moral consciousness.

Nevertheless, that allegory is meaningful in this novel only if the tenets of Christian faith in everlasting life can be extended to the Compsons, and they are not. Because the Reverend Shegog and his black congregation are so far removed from the white world, there is no possibility that their experience of resurrection and life can have meaning and value for Jason, Quentin, or Mrs. Compson. The Compsons lack the simplicity which Faulkner stresses as fundamental to the blacks, and to Christian faith as well. Faulkner's vision falters because he is unable to show how the Negro's experience might have meaning or bearing on the white-centered world that is his subject. The church service occurs in isolation, and it cannot be superimposed upon the fragmented Compsons. The Christian vision of the Negro is inadequate because, in its isolation, that vision is ultimately no less private (for the blacks whom it encompasses) than the visions revealed in the three monologues.

Dilsey, though she sees clearly all the actions of the past and understands their implications for the present and future, does not share her intensely private vision with anyone. It does not appear to be a matter of her inability to articulate her vision; rather Faulkner refuses to allow her to make the attempt. Even Frony, who asks, "'First en last whut?'" does not receive an answer from Dilsey. Whatever is her knowledge remains hers alone and goes untranslated for the larger world. Frony's statement to her mother, who is crying silently, suggests that what blacks experience in the privacy of their church is not to be revealed to the other world: "'Whyn't you quit dat, mammy? . . . Wid all dese people lookin. We be passin white folks soon'" (371). Dilsey initially responds, "'Never you mind. . . . I seed de beginnin, en now I sees de endin.'" However, Dilsey apparently agrees with Frony, as the narrative suggests: "Before they reached the street, though, she stopped and lifted her skirt and dried her eyes on the hem of her topmost underskirt" (371). The white world will not even see her tears—the external manifestation of her vision of tragedy.

Despite the claim by John Hunt that the Compsons could have made the same response to their condition that Dilsey makes (that is, "love, self-sacrifice, compassion, pity"),[31] the central point is that they cannot in fact make the kind of response so natural for Dilsey. Dilsey's motivation and her reactions are connected first to the relatively rudimentary or primitive Negro world that Faulkner constructs, and only after that are they connected to a larger reality. Even that reality has been refracted by Dilsey's experiences and existence as a black southerner. The Compsons react out of an orientation to life that is white, southern, and basically aristocratic; they cannot accept the simplicity of emotion or philosophy that Dilsey does. A part of their tragedy, of course, is precisely that they cannot, that they are so alienated from a world of meaning and value. The Compsons do not experience and then reject Dilsey's faith and world; there exists for them an actual inability to accept Dilsey's approach to life because her world with the black religious experience at its very center is largely unknown to them. Thus, the world of faith is inaccessible as much because its representative activity is beneath their notice as it is because of its doctrine.

No institution reflects the fragmentation of the South more than the black church, because within the black community it is the place farthest removed from the mundane white world. From its inception, the southern black church has been responsive to the particular needs of its members, providing them with a place to exist in individual and communal meaning independent of their usual subjugation and definition by white southerners. As Grace Sims Holt observes, "A primary function of the church was to nourish and maintain the souls of black folks by equating them with the essence of humanness"; consequently, the black church developed as the institution which promoted "self-worth and dignity, a viable identity," and "help in overcoming fear."[32] More than a metaphorical promise

31 Hunt, *William Faulkner: Art in Theological Tension*, 98.
32 Grace Sims Holt, "Rappin' and Stylin' outta the Black Pulpit," in Thomas Kockman (ed.), *Rappin' and Stylin' Out: Communication in Urban Black America* (Urbana: University of Illinois Press, 1972), 189. See also Newbell Niles Puckett's discussion of the secular functions of Christianity in the lives of southern blacks in *The Folk Beliefs of the Southern Negro* (Chapel Hill: University of North Carolina Press, 1926), 526; and John Dollard's reporting of the psychological and emotional impact of religion on southern blacks in *Caste and Class in a Southern Town* (1937; rpt. New York: Doubleday, Anchor, 1957), 226, 249.

of an afterlife, the black church extended a way of living in the world. This church is primarily, then, an institution developed by blacks to meet not just the spiritual needs of displaced Africans, but also the secular needs of an oppressed people.

Faulkner's treatment of the black church service attended by the Gibsons shows an awareness of the special role of religious experience in the lives of traditional blacks. An anonymous church-goer, for example, responds to Frony's statement that "'Mammy aint feelin well dis mawnin'" (364), with assurance: "'Dat's too bad. But Rev'un Shegog'll cure dat. He'll give her de comfort en de unburdenin'" (364). The sentiment expresses a conviction that religion offers an actual haven in which the congregation could lay down their physical and emotionl burdens.

Faulkner uses a particular conception of black religious experience as the paradigm for Dilsey's faith. The religion he portrays helps perpetuate strength and community by inspiring a sense of freedom from any lasting pain and by offering an emotional comfort, which together reaffirm spiritual peace and purge psychological tensions. It serves a utilitarian function which stresses redemption and deemphasizes the vengeful, remote God of white Protestant theology and puritan morality. Because the lives of its participants are difficult and precarious, this religion, according to Benjamin Mays, rests upon a God "able to help . . . bridge the chasm existing between the actual and the ideal."[33] Practical faith in a concerned, loving God provides solace, absolution, and security. The resulting religious services counterbalance the dominant white atmosphere of sin, guilt, repression, and isolation. Faulkner accepts the reality of the redemption from the burdens of suffering and the expiation of personal guilt intrinsic to the black church service. He recognizes that no comparable freeing experience is available to whites in general and to the Compsons in particular, who, unlike the blacks, remain psychologically entrapped by their individual guilt and historical problems.

Although the religious service is significant in assisting blacks to interpret the meaning of life and mediate its negative forces, Faulkner's achievement in the last section is not his message of faith,

33 Benjamin E. Mays, *The Negro's God as Reflected in His Literature* (Boston: Chapman & Grimes, 1938), 255.

but his stylistic method. The Easter sermon delivered in the language of the black community recapitulates the oral narrative patterns of the novel. The voice of the Rev. Shegog becomes the instrument for one collective black voice literally freeing the congregation from the pressures of self and symbolically consolidating the narrative styles.

One important technical experiment in *The Sound and the Fury* has to do with "voice." Each of the four sections relies upon voice for creating a sense of the speakers and their perceptions of the world. From the opening section through the Easter Sunday section, the resonances of voices are crucial to the structure and meaning. In an introduction to the novel, Faulkner writes, "We [southern writers] need to talk, to tell, since oratory is our heritage."[34] *The Sound and the Fury* is a novel of talk and telling. Perhaps an emblem of its oral method lies in Quentin's overhearing several young boys discuss what they would do with twenty-five dollars: "They all talked at once, their voices insistent and contradictory and impatient, making of unreality a possibility, then a probability, then an incontrovertible fact, as people will when their desires become words" (145). Generally in the work, voices echo one another, repeating incidents, restating them anew, yet capturing the sound of what went before, each time bolstering by reiteration the reality of the incidents. Faulkner is cognizant of the relationship between his writing and talking, and in section four, he seems absorbed with the possibilities suggested by black oratory.[35]

34 Faulkner, "Introduction to *The Sound and the Fury*," 412.
35 Faulkner is not alone in recognizing the aesthetic power and potential of the black church service. Many southern writers of the nineteenth century, such as George Washington Cable and Joel Chandler Harris, incorporate sketches of the Negro's religion into their works. And after the turn of the century, writers became increasingly more aware of the Negro and his church. James Weldon Johnson, in *Autobiography of an Ex-Coloured Man* (first published in 1912), treats the sermon as one measure of the achievement of blacks and, in *God's Trombones* (1927), creates a collection of folk sermons as a tribute to the poetic skill of black preachers. In the years just prior to the publication of *The Sound and the Fury*, the resurgence of literary interest in the South and the Negro had produced E. C. L. Adams' *Congaree Sketches* (1927), which draws upon the Negro's religious services, and Roark Bradford's *Ol' Man Adam An' His Chillun* (1928), which makes use of the Negro's interpretation of biblical stories. In fact, Bradford, Faulkner's friend from his New Orleans days, consistently experiments with both black dialects and black religion in his fiction; his Negro-centered novel *This Side of Jordan*, published the same year as *The Sound and the Fury*, relies upon the black preacher and religious conversion for its development.

The rhythms and idioms of Negro speech in particular underscore the innovative uses Faulkner makes of voice in the novel. The Easter sermon preached by the Rev. Shegog, a visiting minister from St. Louis, is a culmination of a pattern of communal experience and of colloquial voice. The sermon section concentrates the verbal resonances which carry the first three monologues by showing in miniature the effect of a speaking voice upon an active, receptive audience. In the sermon, Faulkner attempts a doubly difficult feat: the recording of a "spiritual" as opposed to a manuscript preacher and the capturing in writing of the oral folk sermon. His art welds the essential sound of Negro oratory into a written text. Shegog's sermon gives a figurative representation of Faulkner's own oral art and a literary confirmation of his acceptance of uniquely "American" materials for his fictional matter. He carefully delineates Shegog's rhetorical ability, his expert control of language, and his understanding of the power of gesture and imagery. Shegog's transformation from a white to a black voice and his ability to involve his audience in the waves of his voice suggest the concretizing of sound and sense, voice and meaning in the novel.

The Rev. Shegog, "undersized, in a shabby alpaca coat," has "a wizened black face like a small, aged monkey" (365). In comparison, the local minister, dressed "in a frock coat and white tie," has physical presence: "his head magisterial and profound, his neck rolled above his collar in rich folds" (365). The visitor is "insignificant," "dwarfed," and "countrified" (366) beside the "imposing bulk" of the other minister. Dilsey, in her charity, defends his appearance by saying, "'I've knowed de Lawd to use cuiser tools dan dat'" (366); her statement, a reminder that appearance is not a measure of human worth, foreshadows Shegog's importance as an instrument of Faulkner the artist manipulating the black world for an oblique comment on his white world.

When Faulkner moderates Dilsey's symbolic significance by describing her realistically, he succeeds in preventing her from becoming an inaccessible abstraction; however, when he presents Shegog in terms of animal imagery ("a monkey talking," "his monkey body," 366; "his monkey face," 368), he severely diminishes the minister's stature. The analogy between Shegog and the monkey, frequently associated with mischief and tricks, implies a comic stereotype of the Negro as a primitive not far removed from a jungle.[36] Faulkner's intention may well be to have the minister rise symbolically above his physical self, but his repetitions of "wizened monkey" as a descriptive motif preclude a satisfying corrective to Shegog's reduction.

Although tiny and insignificant in appearance, Shegog has a commanding presence in his voice, which he uses to gain the attention of his audience and control their emotions: "When the visitor rose to speak he sounded like a white man. His voice was level and cold. It sounded too big to have come from him" (366). But from the time Shegog starts to use his voice, he becomes extraordinary. He awakens the congregation to a new consideration of him which places him between the white world ("he sounded like a white man") and the black world:

> They began to watch him as they would a man on a tight rope. They even forgot his insignificant appearance in the virtuosity with which he ran and posed and swooped upon the cold inflectionless wire of his voice, so that at last, when with a sort of swooping glide he came to rest again beside the reading desk with one arm resting upon it at shoulder height and his monkey body as reft of all motion as a mummy or an emptied vessel, the congregation sighed as if it waked from a collective dream and moved a little in its seats. (366)

Faulkner treats Shegog's voice as an aesthetic object which draws response from his listeners and, in the process, connects folk artist and audience in the creation of an emotionally satisfying, aesthetic experience.[37]

36 Faulkner's portrait of Shegog is conventional; often, as James Weldon Johnson points out, "the old time Negro preacher has not been given the niche in which he properly belongs. He has been portrayed only as a semi-comic figure. He had . . . his comic aspects, but on the whole he was an important figure, and at bottom a vital one." Preface to *God's Trombones: Seven Negro Sermons in Verse* (New York: Viking, 1927), 2.
37 Helen Swink has pointed to Faulkner's creation of the "illusion of 'voice'"; she notices that: "In any oral form the encounter between speaker and listener is the essential one. There is active participation by the speaker who depends upon the medium of voice to reach the audience, but there is also the necessary participation on the part of the listener who responds audibly to the cues and suggestions offered by the speaker. The interaction is spontaneous, and from this mutual encounter the speech

However, it is the familiar sound of a distinctly black voice that has the power to sustain a dynamic sense of community. In order to communicate effectively, the black preacher must adjust his language to a variety of contexts within the two cultures, black and white. He understands that the language most comforting to the average churchgoer, who desires messages of strength in racial identity and cultural roots, is the familiar language of blacks. Therefore, at a crucial moment, Shegog sheds his cold, level "white-man's" voice: "They did not mark just when his intonation, his pronunciation, became negroid, they just sat swaying a little in their seats as the voice took them into itself" (368). He drops his associations with outsiders (symbolized by his white man's voice), and identifies himself as one with them, the ordinary, uneducated blacks of the congregation, by changing his pronunciation and rhythmic patterns.

The congregation loses itself in the experience of the minister's voice. Shegog, too, becomes enmeshed in his own voice and the message which it transmits, so that free of self-consciousness he communicates in his own unique style: "the voice died in sonorous echoes between the walls. It was as different as day and dark from his former tone, with a sad, timbrous quality like an alto horn,[38] sinking into their hearts and speaking there again when it had ceased in fading and cumulate echoes" (367). Shegog's conscious descent from the "cold" sound of the white world to what is presented as the rich, moving dialect of the Negro is a movement from a distant, rationalized individuality to an intimate communal existence. It is a way of understanding the preceding sections as isolated narratives of dispersed selves unable to coalesce private experiences into a meaningful whole.

Shegog's shift from white to black voice also repeats and emphasizes the linguistic transformations that the black characters un-

---

grows organically. Perhaps no better example of this oral encounter can be found than the Negro sermon in the South." "William Faulkner: The Novelist as Oral Narrator," *Georgia Review*, XXVI (Summer, 1972), 183–209.
38 The comparison of Shegog's voice to an alto horn is an intrusion which, though poetic, is secular and impious (especially for 1928, when the alto or jazz horn was popular in night life and not in the black church); consequently, the appeal of Shegog's voice to primitive emotions or to the lower instincts seems to be the point, rather than the musicality of his voice.

dergo in this section. In Benjy's monologue, all of the Gibson family members speak nearly standard English, though it is English with a noticeably southern accent. However, in the final section, the surviving Gibsons, Dilsey, Frony, and Luster, speak in a heavily accented dialect. Luster, for example, in Benjy's section says, "'Hush up. . . . You old loony. . . . You want me to whip you'" (19). But in section four, he expresses a similar idea in quite a different voice: "'Hush, now . . . I fixin to whup you'" (393). In Benjy's section he uses fairly straightforward colloquial speech: "'Aint you something, thirty-three years old, going on that way. After I done went all that way to town to buy you that cake. Hush up that moaning. Aint you going to help me find that quarter so I can go to the show tonight'" (1–2). Yet in the final section, Luster's speech pattern and sound change, so that phonetic spelling emphasizes his pronunciation as a black Mississippian. Final *g*'s disappear from the endings of words, and *th*'s become *d*'s: "'He been gwine on dat way ev'y since you sont us outen de house. I dont know whut got in to him dis mawnin'" (359).

Dilsey's idiom also changes in section four. For example, in the first section she states, "' 'Clare I don't see how come Jason wont get a new surrey. . . . This thing going to fall to pieces under you all some day. Look at them wheels'" (9). Dilsey talks about the surrey again in the final pages of the book, but her voice bears little resemblance to the earlier one: "'Luster, honey . . . Will you think about yo ole mammy en drive dat surrey right?'" (396); "'Hush, now. Luster gone to git de surrey en take you to de graveyard. We aint gwine risk gittin you cap'" (396).

It is also apparent that there is little difference between the colloquial speech of the blacks and that of the whites in the first section. Versh, for example, tells Benjy: "'You better keep them hands in your pockets. . . . You get them froze onto that gate'" (4). Similarly, Caddy Compson says to Benjy, "*Keep your hands in your pockets. . . . Or they'll get frozen. You don't want your hands froze on Christmas, do you*"(3). And both Versh and Caddy answer Mrs. Compson with, "yessum" (6, 8). These two characters in particular, but all the others in the first section as well, show that a peculiarly "Negro" dialect is not one of Faulkner's major intentions here.

Faulkner deliberately sought this leveling effect because, according to Emily K. Izsak, "Negro speech in the first section of the novel was revised so as to reduce somewhat its colloquial character." Izsak suggests that the changes were made "probably in the interests of consistency in Benjamin's characterization," in that his mind reshapes "the speech he hears according to a comparatively impersonal pattern of diction."[39] However, it seems more likely that, as an idiot, Benjy would simply mimic the voices he hears. Faulkner's use of a highly differentiated "Negro" idiom, in the last section especially, is his way of reinforcing his depiction of a Negro-centered world, and also of utilizing the resources of black speech in experimental fiction.

In the Easter Sunday section, the Negro's voice is clearly symbol and metaphor. Dilsey speaks in cryptic tones that echo and extend thematically the metaphorical language of Shegog's sermon. At the same time, the speech patterns, inflections, and pronunciation of Dilsey, Frony, and Luster, as well as of Shegog himself, are decidedly those representing illiterate southern blacks. The degeneration of their language from a white standard follows the pattern of the sermon as it moves away from associations with the white world. It appears that the use of a conventional literary conception of Negro dialect in the last section reflects the characters' independence from the white world (possible only in the context of the religious service) and that, although their lives are intertwined with the Compsons, they are not subject to similar limitations because their orientation to life is different.

Rev. Shegog has been called "a conscious artist."[40] He is precisely that because he understands the human voice as an artistic instrument, which carries personal messages outward to a public audience. Though he may be an educated clergyman, Shegog knows that the black minister "must be linguistically flexible in order to communicate with all of his congregation" because "in times of crisis . . . no man hears well the words of a stranger spoken in a

---

39 Izsak, "The Manuscript of *The Sound and the Fury*: The Revisions in the First Section," 199. See Izsak's table of specific word revisions in the diction of blacks (200).
40 Brent Harold, "The Value and Limitations of Faulkner's Fictional Method," *American Literature*, XLVII (May, 1975), 212–29.

strange tongue."[41] Shegog is flexible, as is the black congregation he addresses; they stand in contrast to the Compsons, who are rigid in their approach to life and inflexible in the demands they make on one another. Shegog's changing intonation and pronunciation reveal what Gene Bluestein calls Faulkner's "perceptive insight into the pluralistic pattern of American Negro life."[42] But more importantly, it displays Faulkner's technical dexterity, his ability in this section of the novel to fuse structure and idea, action and theme.

Faulkner dwells upon the congregation's surrender of itself first to Rev. Shegog's voice and then to his subject. Similarly, in the three monologues, Faulkner encourages the reader's giving himself over first to the sound of the voice speaking and then to its meaning or significance. But the difference is that, in Shegog's sermon, voice persuades the audience to abandon individuality for the unifying emotion generated by the voice, while in the interior monologues voice isolates and establishes the individuality of the speaker.

Each participant in the church service is touched partly by the words of the sermon, but primarily by the sound and the feeling of the minister, who by the power of his own transcendency inspires his listeners to move out of their individual troubled selves and to trust in the power of emotion. Benjy and Dilsey are both moved according to their capacity: "In the midst of the voices and the hands Ben sat, rapt in his blue gaze. Dilsey sat bolt upright beside, crying rigidly and quietly into the annealment and the blood of the remembered lamb" (370–71). Benjy is pacified, while Dilsey is strengthened by the memory of the sacrificed Lamb, Christ, whose Crucifixion has made spiritual and moral salvation possible.

Rev. Shegog becomes fused with the idea, subject, and content of his sermon. He is personally the object as well as the subject of "de ricklickshun en de blood of de Lamb." His sermon places him in the central position in the biblical narrative. He says, " 'I sees de light en I sees de word, po sinner'" (368). He has the ability to participate imaginatively in the life of Christ and in the text of the Bible. His vision is analogous to Dilsey's " 'I've seed de first en de last. . . . I

41 Henry Mitchell, *Black Preaching* (Philadelphia: J. B. Lippincott, 1970), 161.
42 Gene Bluestein, *The Voice of the Folk: Folklore and American Literary Theory* (Amherst: University of Massachusetts Press, 1972), 124.

seed de beginnin, en now I sees de endin'" (371). Thematically, Shegog's transfiguration underlines the meaning of Easter: Christ transformed into more God than ordinary man, and his divinity finally proven by his resurrection from the dead. In his Easter resurrection, Christ affirms his power over death and life. And in the novel, the Negro—Shegog, the Gibsons, and the other blacks—ultimately affirm the power of living in the face of death.

The stylized sermon reconstructs the novel's central tensions between past and present. Shegog takes his present-day congregation actively into a time in the historical and mythic past. His action restates the fluidity of past and present and the encroachment of the past upon the present that together define the narrative method in the stream-of-consciousness and narrated monologues comprising the first three sections. The freedom and mobility of his style of preaching recapitulate similar aspects in the larger structure. Shegog's method involves the audience in ideas that are alive, in a morality that is also made to live and provide hope for the future. The sermon creates a sense of oneness, a sense of the congregation's collective involvement with life, and with the temporal struggle against overwhelming odds to live and to achieve future happiness. The text is "de ricklickshun en de Blood of de Lamb," that is, the recollection of Christ's crucifixion and resurrection, his bloody sacrifice of himself as the innocent offering to atone for man's sin and to give him life.

Shegog preaches, "'I sees de resurrection en de light; sees de meek Jesus saying Dey kilt Me dat ye shall live again; I died dat dem whut sees en believes shall never die'" (370). The subject of his sermon is seeing, perception, and knowledge. It is a sermon about participation, and avowing belief, in a living faith, so that the individual possesses "'de milk en de dew of de old salvation when de long, cold years rolls away!'" (369). The sermon is about acting out faith with the anticipation that when "'de generations passed away'" (368), existence will still be meaningful. The climax of the sermon makes this point clear:

> "I can see de widowed God shet His do'; I sees de whelmin flood roll between; I sees de darkness en de death everlasting upon de generations. Den, lo! Breddren! Yes, breddren! Whut I see? Whut I

see, O sinner? I sees de resurrection en de light; sees de meek Jesus saying Dey kilt Me dat ye shall live again; I died dat dem whut sees en believes shall never die. Breddren, O breddren! I sees de doom crack en hears de golden horns shoutin down de glory, en de arisen dead whut got de blood en de ricklickshun of de Lamb!" (370)

Faulkner does not present the entire development of the sermon; instead he attempts to create the impression of a complete text. Just as when the details of a story are not the main consideration, in this sermon Faulkner concentrates on form, assuming that both Shegog's congregation and his novel's audience know the story of Christ's passion and resurrection from memory. But it is a folk poetry in dialect, and that very form makes it largely unintelligible in parts. Faulkner seems so overly concerned with capturing some essentially "Negro" quality in Rev. Shegog's sermon that it is difficult to follow the words of the sermon. Logic is not the issue; the emotional content is the more important aspect of the sermon apparently for Faulkner.[43]

For example, one long sequence of the sermon attempts to heighten the audience's empathy with Mary and Jesus:

"Breddren! Look at dem little chillen settin dar. Jesus wus like dat once. He mammy suffered de glory en de pangs. Sometime maybe she helt him at de nightfall, whilst de angels singin him to sleep; maybe she look out de do' en see de Roman po-lice passin." He tramped back and forth, mopping his face. "Listen, breddren! I sees de day. Ma'y settin in de do' wid Jesus on her lap, de little Jesus. Like dem chillen dar, de little Jesus. I hears de angels singin de peaceful songs en de glory; I sees de closin eyes; sees Mary jump up, sees de sojer face: We gwine to kill! We gwine to kill! We gwine to kill yo little Jesus! I hears de weepin en de lamentation of de po mammy widout de salvation en de word of God!" (369)

The intention is to make the story of Christ immediate by intensifying the very human picture of the concerned mother and her child, who is likened to the children in the congregation. But the section

43 Richard P. Adams demonstrates that "What we are given . . . is a poetically rhetorical development of the emotional pattern of the Passion story, a sequence of feelings associated with the life, death, and resurrection of Christ." *Faulkner: Myth and Motion*, 228.

ends with ideas that move away from the feeling of Mary (or Ma'y, since Faulkner uses both spellings in the section) and the child Jesus to "de weepin en de lamentation of de po mammy widout de salvation en de word of God." Though both Mary and "de po mammy" suffer, the final idea does not establish an empathetic relationship between the two.

Faulkner uses a crude literary representation of Negro dialect which succeeds in creating the Negro-centered reality needed to dramatize his vision of survival in a changing world, but he confuses the reader, who may consequently believe that the Compsons' alienation from the represented black world of faith is justified. His rendition of the sermon lacks the biblical grandeur of language associated not only with Faulkner's own writing, but also with black preaching;[44] moreover, it does not create the illusion of strong emotion as effectively as his descriptive passages surrounding the sermon.

Shegog's sermon is not, as André Bleikasten concludes, "a triumph of Faulkner's verbal virtuosity."[45] Faulkner narrates more about the process and the effects than he renders of the sermon itself. The most memorable passages are not those contained in the actual sermon, but those embedded in the descriptions of it. For instance, his depiction of Shegog preparing for his text sets up a pattern of similes and repetitions: "The preacher removed his arm and

44 Conveying the emotional dynamics and thematic content of a black spiritual preacher is a difficult literary task. While Faulkner's sermon is not completely successful, it is an admirable attempt. The main weakness is his particular construction of dialect and linguistic patterns. In explaining why he did not write his folk sermons in dialect, James Weldon Johnson makes a pertinent observation: "The old-time Negro preachers, though they actually used dialect in their ordinary intercourse, stepped out from its narrow confines when they were all saturated with the sublime phraseology of the Hebrew prophets and steeped in the idioms of the King James English, so when they preached . . . they spoke . . . a language far removed from traditional Negro dialect. . . . To place in the mouths of the talented old-time Negro preachers a language that is a literary imitation of Mississippi cotton-field dialect is sheer burlesque." Johnson, Preface to God's Trombones, 9. See also Bruce A. Rosenberg's helpful discussion in "The Aesthetics of the Folk Sermon," Georgia Review, XXV (Winter, 1971), 424–38.

45 Bleikasten, The Most Splendid Failure, 200. Bleikasten may not mean the sermon itself, because when he claims that "Faulkner's greatest success is that he has . . . managed to capture the musical quality of the sermon" (200), he quotes Faulkner's description of that quality ("sad timorous quality like an alto horn, sinking into their hearts and speaking there again"), and not words actually from Shegog's sermon.

he began to walk back and forth before the desk, his hands clasped behind him, a meagre figure, hunched over upon itself like that of one long immured in striving with the implacable earth" (367). Faulkner's poetic language culminates as Shegog announces his text: "He tramped steadily back and forth beneath the twisted paper and the Christmas bell, hunched, his hands clasped behind him. He was like a worn small rock whelmed by the successive waves of his voice. With his body he seemed to feed the voice that, succubus like, had fleshed its teeth in him" (367). Faulkner's provocative description is rich with sight and motion imagery that is only tangentially connected to sound (Shegog's voice and sermon).

The effects on the congregation also capture Faulkner's imagination:

> And the congregation seemed to watch with its own eyes while the voice consumed him, until he was nothing and they were nothing and there was not even a voice but instead their hearts were speaking to one another in chanting measures beyond the need for words, so that when he came to rest against the reading desk, his monkey face lifted and his whole attitude that of a serene, tortured crucifix that transcended its shabbiness and insignificance and made it of no moment, a long moaning expulsion of breath rose from them, and a woman's single soprano: "Yes, Jesus!" (367–68)

Here Faulkner continues his poetical evocation of emotion primarily through images of motion and sight. While the passage symbolizes the operation of voice, it depends mainly upon reporting the experience of voice. Even the voice of the woman is a result of a description of its movement.

In the sermon section, Faulkner's success lies in his descriptive power—his ability to show vividly the impact of words—before Shegog preaches the body of the sermon. For example, he presents one of his moving descriptions of Dilsey prior to Shegog's delivery of his text: "Dilsey sat bolt upright, her hand on Ben's knee. Two tears slid down her fallen cheeks, in and out of the myriad coruscations of immolation and abnegation and time" (368). This brief picture demonstrates the force of the cumulative religious experience swaying the congregation, but it returns the narrative focus to Dilsey, and the larger fiction of the novel, by reiterating her relevance to the Compsons' story.

Once Faulkner has effectively evoked emotion from his descriptions of Shegog's method and the congregation's response, he uses an abbreviated sermon to connect that emotion directly to his major ideas about the functional religion of blacks and inversely to his primary concerns with the destruction of the Compsons. He intersperses responses from the church members to sustain the feeling of the power of words: " 'Yes, Jesus!' . . . A low concerted sound rose from the congregation: 'Mmmmmmmmmmmmmm!' The woman's voice said, 'Yes, Jesus! Jesus!' " (369). These unifying refrains convey an impression of an entire congregation caught up in religious fervor:

> "Mmmmmmmmmmmmmmmmm! Jesus! Little Jesus!" and another voice, rising:
> "I sees, O Jesus! Oh I sees!" and still another, without words, like bubbles rising in water.
> . . . .
> "Mmmmmmmmmmmmmmm. Jesus! I sees, O Jesus!" (370)

These responses function as verbal reassurances that the sermon is dramatically effective in moving the group to an emotional solidarity. Within these refrains, Faulkner effects a surfeit of feeling which carries over to his dénouement of Dilsey and the blacks as thematic and structural contrasts to a lost white world.

Though more fully developed, Faulkner's central vision of the black church service in *The Sound and the Fury* does not differ in any significant way from his conclusion in *Soldiers' Pay*. In both works, he depicts the traditional black church, specifically the power of voice and feeling, as an expression of stability, love, and communion, of moral consciousness and spiritual faith, which for him augurs endurance and transcendence in a troubled modern world. What does change in *The Sound and the Fury* is his conception of how the church service might be brought to bear on the meaning and cohesion missing from the lives of whites, because in his first novel, reflective white characters see and hear—though from the outside— blacks performing their religious rituals.

While the sermon section in *The Sound and the Fury* is a significant part of a movement toward spiritual resolution, it poses ideas that are not transferred to the central condition of Faulkner's white pro-

THE SOUND AND THE FURY 125

tagonists. Whites have no access to the rituals. As a result, the progress within the sermon section toward vision, especially Rev. Shegog's ability to see his subject clearly, cannot affect the Compsons.
The transformations, engendered by vision through voice and emotion, are restricted to blacks and therefore are not sufficient to
change fractured selves into wholes. In fact, Faulkner does not
probe deeply into the meaning of the transformation of Shegog's
voice; he allows it to stand without substantial transference to the
Compsons' condition. Although Faulkner fuses Shegog with his sermon, he does not transfigure the preacher into Christ, which might
forward a suggestive connection to the white world; instead, the
closest he comes is to an image relating Shegog's shape to the cross
on which Christ dies. (Perhaps he starts with too low a picture of
Shegog the monkey to fuse him with the Christ Himself.)[46] Faulkner
contains the experience of the sermon in the black environment,
and in effect, he relegates it to a position of minimal influence in his
narrative. Faulkner uses the black church as an affirmation only of
the values and faith that give meaning to the Gibsons' world, and
thereby he resolves his attention to the black world, but the service
is not a resolution to the problems and tensions he develops for his
white characters.

The final section of the novel is an ironic analogue to the sermon.
Luster, in an attempt to show off, turns the surrey carrying Benjy to
the left of the Jefferson monument. Benjy's voice mounts in bellows,
"with more than astonishment in it, it was horror; shock; agony eye-
less, tongueless; just sound" (400). Jason rushes up, hurls Luster
aside with a backhand blow, and strikes him over the head with his
fist. He strikes Luster not just to restore order for Benjy, but also to
release his own tension and frustration. Jason has not been able to
seize his own destiny as he has led himself to believe he could;
therefore, his violent act is a reassertion of his notion of self-deter-

46 The pattern of fusing the preacher with the central figure from his biblical text is
the usual one in literary and authentic folk sermons. See, for example, Waldo Frank's
striking depiction of a black minister's becoming Paul on the road to Damascus in *Holiday* (New York: Boni and Liveright, 1923), 52. Frank also uses the idea of the southern black congregation's becoming "Voice" (55) in his fictional version of an emotional
church service, which is contrapuntal to his development of a sterile white community and its unemotional religion.

mination and power. In a sense, he does stop sound and the emotion generating it. He directs Queenie homeward, and Benjy stops screaming: "His eyes were empty and blue and serene again as cornice and façade flowed smoothly once more from left to right; post and tree, window and doorway, and signboard, each in its ordered place" (401).

Just as Rev. Shegog and the black congregation receive physical release from their pain and suffering by means of "little Jesus," who brings with his crucifixion and death a peace and promise of life, so the violence done to Luster ironically brings about some measure of peace—to Jason directly, but only indirectly to Benjy. This resolution, technically the second of the "April Eighth 1928" section, ultimately points out that there can be no reconciliation of Dilsey's faith and Jason's fantasy, and no reconciliation of the vision that Benjy inherits and the one Luster embodies. Black life remains a foil to emptiness, the loss of value and meaning, in white southern life. The novel concludes with two distinct resolutions; neither is satisfactory to the life and orientation of the other.[47]

Faulkner's dual resolution suspends *The Sound and the Fury* between the two worlds of blacks and whites. The Compsons and the Gibsons are held in their separate places without either a sense of ending or a statement of essential conflict in their division. Faulkner has successfully utilized the structural condition of his southern heritage for creating his first major novel. Moreover, he has claimed the lives of black servants, their folk religion and language, as vital to his experiment in literary modernism, which is one culmination of his thinking about innovative techniques and valid materials begun during his days in New Orleans.[48] These are remarkable feats for a white southern writer who only a few years earlier had shown little literary interest in his culture.

However, as an artist attempting to capture a substantive reality whole, Faulkner evidences dissatisfaction with the suspension at

47 In this dual resolution relying in one part upon the religious experience of southern blacks, *The Sound and the Fury* anticipates another major southern novel, *Lie Down in Darkness* (1951), by William Styron, who, in the tradition Faulkner made meaningful, writes about a black revival and baptismal meeting.

48 Another culmination is *As I Lay Dying* (1930), which also uses the voices and lives of distinctly southern folk as significant subject and method.

the end of *The Sound and the Fury*. He returns, in fact, to the Compsons and Gibsons in his 1946 appendix.[49] Perhaps he goes back out of a recognition that the basic social and historical conflicts separating their worlds and destroying individuals had not been developed, because a large portion of this "fifth section" provides the familial and cultural background shaping the novel's characters. He tries, it seems, to make more explicit the conflicts keeping the divided worlds apart and, in spite of their tensions, to bring them closer together. But the novel could not be rewritten by appending his new perspective.

In *Light in August, Absalom, Absalom!* and *Go Down, Moses*, Faulkner resumes within the fictions themselves his struggle with form in an art shaped out of the ethical and intellectual duality of his South. These later works reflect his finding a more focused direction for the conflicts—emotional, psychological, and physical—within the racially divided worlds. In these novels, Faulkner overtly sustains their intensity and pursues their implications, neither of which his former dependence upon conventional portraits allowed. With this finer recognition of the artistic possibility fundamental to the special circumstances of his South, he frees his fiction from the suspension between worlds—a suspension dictated by the partial acknowledgment of conflicts between blacks and whites in *The Sound and the Fury*. His apprehension of conflict within southern life transforms his work into powerful expressions of the human condition. Although this later fiction may be no greater literary achievement than *The Sound and the Fury*, it is the product of an artist who, whether able or not to transcend the polarity of races, is secure in his personal vision of a polarized world and confident of his ability to express that vision in his art.

---

49 In a February 4, 1946, letter to Robert N. Linscott, Faulkner discusses his "new section" for *The Sound and the Fury*, the Appendix: "I should have written this new section when I wrote the book itself. . . . When you read it, you will see how it is the key to the whole book, and after reading it, the 4 sections as they stand now fall into clarity and place. . . . When you issue the book print the sections in this order, print this appendix first, and title it APPENDIX." Blotner (ed.), *Selected Letters of William Faulkner*, 220–21.

CHAPTER IV

Light in August

It is possible that the white race and the Negro race can never really like and trust each other; this for the reason that the white man can never really know the Negro, because the white man has forced the Negro to be always a Negro rather than another human being in their dealings, and therefore the Negro cannot afford, does not dare, to be open with the white man and let the white man know what he, the Negro, thinks.

> "Address to the Raven, Jefferson, and O D K Societies of the University of Virginia," Charlottesville, February 20, 1958, *Essays, Speeches and Public Letters*, p. 157.

The suspension between the Gibsons' black world and the Compsons' white one which concludes *The Sound and the Fury* becomes a major premise for the development of *Light in August*. White and black worlds as separate realities (with all of their cumulative connotations) shape both place and person in this work, which Faulkner first called "Dark House" in manuscript form. Faulkner starts with the assumption that race not only separates whites and blacks, but dictates social convention and personal conduct as well. He creates a controlling situation in which one person, Joe Christmas, becomes aware of the psychological, emotional, and physical conflicts caused by racial distinctions, but attempts to exist suspended between two worlds. Out of this controlling situation,

Faulkner shapes his primary narrative focus: the development of character in both public and private spheres of southern life. His narrative progresses then with the central action taking place in the dominant white world, but with the central issues examining the meanings of "Negro" in the lives of individual characters and in their collective society.

Light in August is the first of Faulkner's novels to treat the Negro as an abstraction rather than merely a physical presence in the southern world. The strength of this treatment lies in Faulkner's ability to infuse the abstraction into the lives of his major characters without delineating individual black characters. Joe Christmas, Lena Grove, and Gail Hightower all search for abstractions: Joe quests inward to uncover the self; Lena journies into the world to discover a wider context for her life; Hightower searches into a mythical past to lose himself. By means of these three characters separately and the tensions among their stories, Faulkner reveals the special meaning of abstraction in the lives of his people, and he suggests that the greatest abstraction within their culture is the Negro.

The novel extends Faulkner's use of counterpoint[1] as a means of probing shades of meaning. While he does not ignore the family, which helped to shape his subject in The Sound and the Fury, he shifts his emphasis to the larger possibility of the individual's relationship to community or society. Faulkner places Joe Christmas' quest and Lena Grove's journey in a contrapuntal design so that they become two different perspectives from which the nature of the individual's relationship to self and society may be viewed. He compounds the complexity of "seeing" self and society by adding a third perspective, that of Gail Hightower. His use of multiple perspectives demonstrates that absolute meanings are impossible.

Joe Christmas' story, combined with those of Lena Grove and Gail

---

1 One of Francois Pitavy's major assumptions in his carefully developed work on Light in August is that the novel "does mark the beginning of a search for a new form—a contrapuntal structure—which reaches an extreme development . . . in The Wild Palms." Faulkner's "Light in August" (Bloomington: Indiana University Press, 1973), 7. Pitavy's observation regarding the development of contrapuntal form through The Wild Palms in 1939 is accurate if deemed to refer to one work made up of separate and distinct narratives which do not depend upon the same set of characters or even upon parallel action. However, Light in August is an extension of the contrapuntal structuring Faulkner began in Soldiers' Pay (1926).

Hightower, establishes the novel's dual movement: outward toward connection with the larger world, and inward toward understanding of self-motivation (whether or not the individual has a chance to act upon his discovery). The outward movement involves society. The movement inward is less readily apparent as a major formal principle of the novel, yet its operation is clear. The three characters following this pattern, Joe, Gail, and Lena,[2] turn their center of concentration inward and begin the often painful process of ordering their perceptions of themselves. It is only after this ordering process takes place that they can realign their conceptions of society.

At the center of the alternate ways of "seeing" is the Negro. Faulkner's concern lies with the meanings of "Negro" which shape the lives of various characters, primarily Joe Christmas—a man who lives in a region demanding strict racial allegiance, but whose racial origins are unknown. In revealing Joe's history and destiny, Faulkner presents "Negro" as a behavioral pattern (especially from the point of view of other characters, such as the dietitian, the sheriff, Halliday, and Percy Grimm); as a social construct (according to the views of Gavin Stevens, Joanna Burden, and Gail Hightower); and as a subjective projection (particularly in the case of Doc Hines and Joe himself). From the perspective of the white South, Faulkner presents what it means to be "Negro" and what "Negro" means to the general society. He accomplishes this feat without allowing the lives of Negro characters to represent that meaning; that is, individual black characters are not depicted as either symbolic or realistic representations of "Negro." His method reiterates what Hugh Kenner terms "Faulkner's root need": "to expand, expand: to commence with the merest glimpse and by way of wringing out its significance arrange voices and viewpoints, interpolate past chronicles, account for just this passion in just this ancillary passion, and tie the persons together, for the sake of intimacy, intensity, plausibility, with ties of blood and community and heritage."[3]

2 I include Lena here because the final vision shows her in touch with her motivations in continuing on the road. The furniture dealer reveals that Lena seems to be aware that she is just traveling and no longer pursuing Lucas Burch (Joe Brown). He also suggests that Lena wants Byron Bunch to continue his efforts to claim her and that she intends that he do so.
3 Kenner, A Homemade World, 205–206.

An expanding rather than condensing approach to fiction-making clarifies the meaning of Negro in *Light in August*. Within the story of Joe Christmas, Faulkner dramatizes his conception that a social, not a biological, definition of Negro underpins southern thought. The Negro is the African, heathen and primitive, but at the same time, the Negro is a form of actual or imagined behavior: the slave, brutish and ignorant; the "nigger," menacing and surly. From these various perceptions, Faulkner presents the social and psychological implications of the Negro as a concept in a closed society. He treats perceptual changes in group attitudes toward the Negro. For example, the anxious crowd outside the burning Burden house shifts from considering that the crime has been committed by "a negro" or even "the Negro" to believing that it has been committed by "Negro," an ominous abstraction. Somehow the crowd "believed aloud that it was an anonymous negro crime committed not by a negro but by Negro."[4] The ways of viewing "Negro" dissolve reality into varied reflections of individual perceptions. The entire group, made up of "casual Yankees," "poor whites," and "southerners who had lived for a while in the north," also "knew, believed, and hoped that she had been ravished too: at least once before her throat was cut and at least once afterward" (271—72). They are linked by their stereotyped conception of the "brute Negro," who maniacally rapes his white victim whether or not she is alive.

Through Joe's ironic predicament—his not knowing whether he is black or white—the problem of assigning absolute meanings to abstractions becomes clearer. Joe Christmas has the racial freedom feared most by the conservative South. Orphaned in infancy and abandoned without any clear family connections, he can be either Negro or not-Negro by choice. If Joe is *not* "Negro," but is made "Negro" by the projections of white consciousness (the combined forces, for example, of Doc Hines, Joanna Burden, and the mob), and by his own acceptance of their projections, then "Negro" becomes a superficial delineation which is not a matter of blood but a matter of life style, adherence to preconceived behavioral norms. A social code defines "Negro" as a prescribed pattern of acting, not as

4 William Faulkner, *Light in August* (New York: Harrison Smith and Robert Haas, 1932; rpt. Random House, 1963), 271.

a state of being (or blood). If, on the other hand, Joe is "Negro," by virtue of blood, then the fact that he could have been in a position to choose his racial affiliation denies that southern racial codes and concepts (particularly "blood tells") have any validity in "fact."

A passage introducing Joe addresses the issue of labels, including names, that function to limit human possibilities:

> "His name is what?" one said.
> "Christmas."
> "Did you ever hear of a white man named Christmas?"
> "I never heard of nobody a-tall named it," the other said.
> And that was the first time Byron remembered that he had ever thought how a man's name, which is supposed to be just the sound for who he is, can be somewhat of an augur of what he will do if other men can only read the meaning in time. (29)

Given the nature of southern beliefs, Joe's name must be either white or black, and as one or the other, the name carries and sets the limits of what the bearer can do.

The label "nigger" with all of its negative and defeating connotations operates from the time of Joe's childhood in an orphanage to constrict his development and self-expectations. When he is called "nigger" by other children, Joe does not understand that the word is intended to communicate the experience of "the Negro" in the South. The word itself is a personal experience for Joe, so that much of his later life may be interpreted as analysis of his initial experience of the word.

Faulkner uses "Negro" as a socially defined term: "None of them knew then where Christmas lived and what he was actually doing behind the veil, the screen, of his negro's job at the mill" (31). This reference links work to prescribed notions of the Negro and his capacities, but throughout the novel, social configurations create and reinforce the meaning of Negro. In a discussion of "Negro" as a social creation, Robert Penn Warren points out that: "Insofar as he [Joe] is a Negro, he is such by social definition and not by blood; . . . Faulkner here undercuts the official history and mythology of a whole society by indicating that 'nigger' is a creation of the white man."[5] The "official history and mythology" are undermined as well

5 Warren, *Faulkner: A Collection of Critical Essays*, 259.

by the lives of other characters, especially Hightower, whose story ultimately presents the past minus its glorious trappings. What Faulkner seems to offer is a view of the individual and collective beliefs of southerners as based upon inventive but ultimately unhealthy conceptions of their past and their destiny.

One of the most revealing passages related to the "nigger" as a social category occurs during the Mottstown sequence just before Joe's capture. An observant townsman, Halliday, spots Joe on the street and a colloquial narrative voice reports the event: "'He never acted like either a nigger or a white man. That was it. That was what made folks so mad. For him to be a murderer and all dressed up and walking the town like he dared them to touch him, when he ought to have been skulking and hiding in the woods, muddy and dirty and running. It was like he never even knew he was a murderer, let alone a nigger too'" (331). Ironically, at this point Joe has, in fact, accepted his place as a "nigger," but again his external appearance (a white man and non-murderer) does not coincide with the interior reality. Immediately after Halliday recognizes Joe and Joe admits his identity, Halliday begins to hit him in the face. He "'had already hit the nigger a couple of times in the face, and the nigger acting like a nigger for the first time and taking it, not saying anything: just bleeding sullen and quiet'" (331–32). Faulkner seems to say that social identity may well be a perversion, since it is not at all synonymous with wholeness or even with health in this society.

When Joe tells Joanna Burden that he believes he is "Negro," he also states the irony of that belief: "'If I'm not, damned if I haven't wasted a lot of time'" (241). The point is that he has wasted a lot of time, that southerners, both white and black, have wasted a lot of time. Perhaps Joe suspects as much because, although he tells Joanna that one of his parents was "part nigger," he also admits that he has no proof ("'I dont know it,'" 240).

Joe Christmas refuses to accept the terms for his existence dictated by southern society. Those terms—to be either white or black, to live as one or the other—are in themselves limiting and dehumanizing. Joe's refusal, though effectively defeated, is a positive, progressive impulse, but one doomed to failure because it cuts so sharply against the grain of traditional southern life and thought. Joe's naysaying in the broadest sense is a revolt against sterile community conformity and against acceptance of a racist code which perpetuates division and isolation. It is a revolt against the pressures and forces of history. Ironically, Joe's revolt, when viewed from the perspective of his culture, is a death wish, because in this case to choose the human principle above the social obligation is to reject "life" (here the tenets of a specified southern life) and to accept death. Curiously, critics tend to speak of the "life" in *Light in August* as all life.[6] But Joe rejects the terms for living laid down by southern law and custom, even though he has not the strength of moral character to understand the implications of his rejection.

Whether or not Joe Christmas is taken to be "Negro," his life encompasses a struggle for survival that is magnified by the accepted myth and the social reality of the black experience. Joe's odyssey is concerned with the social definition of Negro. He suffers aloneness and a crisis of identity as well as the trials of northern migration and life as an industrial laborer—all new experiences to the white southerner during the Depression, but after the Civil War a familiar pattern in black life. Joe is initially described as a man on the road:

> He looked like a tramp, yet not like a tramp either. His shoes were dusty and his trousers were soiled too. But they were decent serge, sharply creased, and his shirt was soiled but it was a white shirt, and he wore a tie and a stiff brim straw hat that was quite new, cocked at an angle arrogant and baleful above his still face. He did not look like a professional hobo in his professional rags, but there was something definitely rootless about him, as though no town nor city was his, no street, no walls, no square of earth his home. And that he carried his knowledge with him always as though it were a banner with a quality ruthless, lonely, and almost proud. (27)

In addition to the emphasis of rootlessness, the ambiguity of Joe's physical appearance forms an important part of this description. He

6 Sally R. Page, for instance, states that "Joe's inability to accept life on its own terms is the most admirable refusal of life Faulkner has created." *Faulkner's Women*, 146. However, it is not so much a refusal of life as it is a refusal to submit to a certain kind of wrong, one prescribing a limited way of life. Page reduces the central conflict of Joe's life to a "struggle between the forces of life and death." This reduction is too simplistic as it leads to misreadings such as ". . . the tension between black and white is actually symbolic of the more basic conflict between the instinct for life and the drive toward death."

looks like a tramp, yet not like one. His clothing is soiled, yet neither worn out nor of poor quality; it is proper dress, yet out of joint with the wearer. Joe is and is not what he appears to be. His costume is contrived for his first appearance on the Jefferson stage.

Faulkner casts Joe's appearance and personality so that his singularity stands out. He signals Joe's alienation from the worlds of blacks and whites, yet he also makes Joe's clothing symbolize the two worlds. One result for the reader is an ambivalence toward Joe—a dissatisfaction with his lack of a precise place. However, a desire for Joe's acceptance of either world implicitly condones the racial segregation of Faulkner's South. There is no comfortable emotional response to Joe's position. To envision his escape without punishment is to encourage the social outlaw. To applaud his final "peaceful" return to Jefferson wearing "nigger" shoes is a tacit admission that the survival of order and morality in southern life depends upon the existence of the "nigger." Even though Faulkner permits the reader to react safely with moral indignation or outrage at Percy Grimm's superficially rational act, he incorporates a moral ambivalence, because the reader may also feel relief at Joe's death, almost as Joe himself approaches his death with relief after a lifetime of not belonging.

Faulkner maintains that Joe Christmas is *both* black and white, rather than, as some critics conclude,[7] that he is neither black nor white. Joe lives both existences, contrary to the accepted standards of the South. During his wandering, he exists as a black man with other blacks and also as a white man with other whites. He can and does occupy both spaces, sometimes even simultaneously as when he cohabits with Joanna Burden.

While Faulkner may claim that Joe Christmas never knows conclusively whether he is white or black, he does provide details which link Joe to the black side of Jefferson life, though the smells and sights of the black community obviously repel him. Joe lives in "a tumbled down negro cabin on Miss Burden's place" (32). He does a "negro's job at the mill" (31). He enters Joanna's house like a nigger invading in the night, and he eats coarse food set out in her kitchen

7 See Nilon, *Faulkner and the Negro*, 74, for example.

for the nigger (224). Even before he tells Joanna that he believes he is a Negro, Joe apparently sees himself as the "nigger" in her bed.

At the same time, Faulkner also establishes Joe's white ties. Regarding those same excursions into Joanna's house, Faulkner states, "Sometimes the notes would tell him not to come until a certain hour, to that house which no white person save himself had entered in years" (245). And when Joe lived with a black woman who resembled an ebony carving, he would lie awake "watching his white chest arch deeper and deeper within his ribcage, trying to breathe into himself the dark odor, the dark and inscrutable thinking and being of negroes . . . trying to expel from himself the white blood and the white thinking and being" (212).

Joe is an allegory of the South in a particular sense. He portrays the South's fragmentation, but also the pathetic nature of its attempts at wholeness and unity. Those attempts, Faulkner seems to say, are doomed to failure. Joe's rare chance is not to live as either white or black, but to live as both and to mingle the two modes of existence. The merging of the two worlds would unleash the unknown and signal the loss of the ability to retreat into rigid patterns of caste, class, or custom in times of stress, uncertainty, or difficulty. Therefore, even in theory such merging is a serious, clearly dangerous threat to the society. That Joe fails and drops all racial designations is a helpless admission of the impossibility of uniting the two worlds.

Joe asks, in terms of blood, the rhetorical question, " 'Just when do men that have different blood in them stop hating one another?' " (236). The answer, in this novel, is never, not even in death. Although posed in relation to North and South, the question has to do with blood, and so symbolizes as well the state toward which Joe moves—a state in which individuals of black blood and white blood do not hate one another.

John Longley identifies a central issue regarding Joe's racial status by discriminating between the attitudes of the community and those of the individual. Joe, according to Longley, "ultimately . . . chooses to be neither—he will simply be himself. Until the very end, the community cannot decide what he is; their deep distrust grows from his refusal to declare himself one or the other in a social pattern in which this is the most important distinction of all. He will insist on his right simply to be; he has defined himself and has fought hard for the definition."[8] One basis, however, for Joe's self-definition has to do with his existence as both a black and a white individual. Living at once as a black man and as a white man brings Joe Christmas close to the symbolic possibility of racial amalgamation expressed in Faulkner's later novels. That he fails is both the result of his own personality and of social and environmental pressures. Joe is free to choose his race, but he *must* in fact *choose*—choose or face destruction. Only by making a choice can he continue to exist in Jefferson and, by extension, in the South.

Joe's interlude with Joanna Burden breaks down precisely because society, Joanna in particular, cannot allow Joe or any other southerner, whether white or black, to fuse the two worlds in his own existence. Joanna attempts to destroy Joe's freedom to be both black and white when she demands that he become a "Negro." She desires a definite racial identity for him because race is the central area of alliance in her South, and more important in terms of her self-awareness, it is the issue which brought her family south and took the lives of her grandfather and brother; it is also the social pattern which gives her meaning even as it restricts her existence.

Joanna Burden's name, interpreted as symbolic of her view—one frequently held by whites—that the Negro is the white man's burden, has both moral and religious overtones.[9] Yet the name also suggests two other applications. One has to do with Joanna's own childhood and family background which has placed on her the "burden" of being not only a southerner with all of the pressures of race and history, but also a northerner with the added pressures of politics and religion. Like others living in the divided world of the South, Joanna, in a confessional speech about her personal history, portrays

8 Longley, *The Tragic Mask,* 196.
9 Hyatt Waggoner, for instance, considers the "clue" offered by Joanna's name and her symbolic role: "She accepts the burden of working for human betterment and the other, often painful, burden it entails. Her isolation in a hostile community has been the price *she* has had to pay . . . for working for the cause of Negroes. For her, the white man's burden is her own burden." *William Faulkner: From Jefferson to the World* (Lexington: University of Kentucky Press, 1959), 112.

her own childhood as a weight which she can manage neither to forget nor to accept comfortably. A second application of the name "burden" has to do with Joanna herself. She literally becomes a "burden" to Joe Christmas. She bears down upon his consciousness to the extent that he finds he cannot abandon *her*. She inevitably becomes a burden to whatever possibility Joe has of existing in freedom from a declaration of race and of resolving the conflicting demands of self and society.

Joe actually begins to fear Joanna; she begins to corrupt him, in spite of his own years of "anonymous promiscuity" which in comparison to Joanna's corruption have been a conventional life of "healthy and normal sin" (246). Joe watches himself "being sucked down into a bottomless morass" (246). He finds himself speaking aloud, " 'I better move. I better get away from here' " (246). Yet he remains, as though held by something. He likens his position to that of one who has fallen into a sewer (242). The "imperious and overriding fury of those nights" (246) submerges him more and more. The narrator theorizes that Joe as a "fatalist" is held "by curiosity, by pessimism, by sheer inertia" (246), and that "perhaps he realized that he could not escape" (246).

Joe describes his relationship with Joanna in three phases: "During the first phase it had been as though he were outside a house where snow was on the ground, trying to get into the house; during the second phase he was at the bottom of a pit in the hot wild darkness; now he was in the middle of a plain where there was no house, not even snow, not even wind" (254–55). His description suggests that customs, mores, and conventions have no meaning for him throughout his affair with Joanna. For the first phase, he uses the color white and the sensation of cold; the image symbolizes Joe's physical isolation from the rest of the world, from both domestic and natural environments. The second phase associates blackness with both spiritual damnation and sexual primitivism, and represents the most threatening exterior condition. The third phase creates a twilight zone of physical and psychological dislocation in which neither the laws of humans (no house) nor the laws of nature (no snow or wind) apply. It is on the level of this "plain" that Joe and Joanna conclude their relationship and their lives.

Joe's fears regarding Joanna, and the imagery symbolic of their relationship, suggest another aspect of their liaison. Joe, if he were black, would traditionally be considered the corrupter, the one to approach the affair with sexual abandon. He would then be considered the hot, dark primitive whose place is in the night. However, it is Joanna who is described as "something growing in a swamp" (248), and who seems "to exist somewhere in physical darkness" (248). Joanna is associated with night, with Dionysian irrationality and sexual abandon. Joe, though acquiescent, does not initiate the sexual games. In presenting Joe, the man who may have Negro blood, as approaching the affair with some degree of rationality and without being completely caught in the throes of physical pleasure, Faulkner operates against one set of beliefs regarding blacks and sexuality (particularly beliefs about black men and white women).

Faulkner explores other myths about black-white sexual relations. When Joe realizes during the early stages of his affair with Joanna that " 'it was like I was the woman and she was the man'" (222), he implies the relationship that has existed between the Negro and the white South.[10] The Negro has been castrated by his subservient role in southern life. Unable to express his manhood, he has assumed external behavioral patterns which the dominant culture associates with the female. Joe reveals that "at first sight" of Joanna "there had opened before him instantaneous . . . a horizon of physical security and pleasure" (221). Joe's revelation places him in one of the traditional conceptions of the psychology of women: that their search for security and comfort is to be provided by the male. Included, too, is a scene symbolic of the reversal of traditional male and female roles; Joe lies on his cot in an old slave shack provided by Joanna, while Joanna sits at her desk attending to business.

In a general sense, black life in the novel is closely associated with the female. The "hot wet primogenitive Female" describes Joe's sense of "the Negro" (107). When he stands in Freedman Town, Joe

10 Though Joe quickly denies his statement ("But that was not right, either," 222), he uses an analogy which suggests that his lifelong resistance of women may stem at least partially from a fear of being womanlike himself in a society adhering to a strict distinction between male and female and having fixed roles for each in the scheme of things.

hears "the bodiless fecundmellow voices of negro women" and feels trapped: "It was as though he and all other manshaped life about him had been returned to the lightless wet primogenitive Female" (107). The primary images connecting the Negro and the female are primitive, having to do with fertility and birth, and they recur throughout the novel.

Hightower, for example, looks at the charred ruins of the Burden house and thinks: "'Poor, barren woman. To have not lived only a week longer, until luck returned to this place. Until luck and life returned to these barren and ruined acres.' It seems to him that he can see, feel, about him the ghosts of rich fields, and of the rich fecund black life of the quarters, the mellow shouts, the presence of fecund women, the prolific naked children in the dust before the doors; and the big house again, noisy, loud with the treble shouts of the generations" (385). Hightower envisions fecund black life in a romantic time past. His notion of the Negro incorporates a picture of the antebellum, slave-holding South as rich and fertile. His conception is a stereotyped one of the happy and contented slave—the primitive native living an idyllic "fecund rich black life," filled with "mellow shouts," "fecund women," and "prolific naked children"; essentially, the emphasis on women, fertility, and birth duplicates Joe's reaction to Freedman Town.

The equation of the Negro and the female principle suggests the powerful depths of racial stereotyping. Such a conception of the male leads to a denial of his masculinity. The male Negro, then, is emasculated by a cultural consciousness which submerges the male's personality in a hazy, but useful, conception of the woman, the mammy. Joe, though his personality is warped by a variety of experiences, rebels against the conception of the Negro as female; he attacks the woman of either race and gropes for the masculine in all things.

Neither the woman nor the Negro is attractive in the novel. And it is not immediately apparent that either represents the fertility of life. The early portraits of white women, for instance, juxtapose Lena Grove, an almost grotesque figure, and Martha Armstid, who foreshadows Joanna Burden in her "manhardness." Martha is "the gray woman not plump and not thin, manhard, manwork, in a serviceable gray garment worn savage and brusque, her hands on her hips, her face like those of generals who have defeated men in battle" (14). Although Martha is a sympathetic character because she gives her egg money to Lena so that the younger woman may have some funds to continue her journey, Martha seems more masculine than feminine. Despite her description as "the gray woman with the cold, harsh, irascible face, who bore five children in six years and raised them to man- and womanhood" (13), Martha does not seem maternal. Far from being an image of the fertility of life, she appears symbolic of stoic endurance, particularly her appearance: "with a savage screw of gray hair at the base of her skull and a face that might have been carved in sandstone" (15). It is as though Martha Armstid is a portrait of man in the generic sense.

Joanna, like Martha, has "mantrained muscles and [a] mantrained habit of thinking" (221–22). She is at once drab and masculine: "a figure . . . in a severe garment . . . that looked as if it had been made for a careless man. Above it . . . a head with hair just beginning to gray drawn gauntly back to a knot as savage and ugly as a wart on a diseased bough" (260). A virginal spinster ("calm, cold-faced, almost manlike, almost middleaged woman who had lived for twenty years alone, without any feminine fears at all," 244), Joanna is far removed from the fertility of life; she does not even know how to live fully, and consequently her existence is barren both in the sexual sense and in the sense of the rich experiences normal life offers. Faulkner's narrator observes that when Joe first takes Joanna sexually, "It was as if he struggled physically with another man for an object of no actual value to either, and for which they struggled on principle alone" (222). Joanna's code, like Martha Armstid's, is forthright and direct; she possesses the "strength and fortitude of a man" (221). Neither of these women, as Faulkner describes them, is attractive in appearance or mannerisms.

Similarly, the Negro in the novel is not an attractive conception. Joe's introduction to race is through taunts of "nigger" made by children in the orphanage where he lives for a time as a small boy. Joe also has the epithet "You little nigger bastard!" hurled at him by a dietitian whom he observes in an illicit sexual encounter (114). The word "nigger" acts as object in confounding Joe's normal growth and development. "Nigger" comes to mean inferiority and something womanlike (mysterious and unpredictable), so that by the time Joe is fourteen, he has a violent reaction to a black girl who sexually accommodates five white youths:

> He could not move at once, standing there, smelling the woman, smelling the negro all at once; enclosed by the womanshenegro and the haste, driven, having to wait until she spoke: a guiding sound that was no particular word and completely unaware. Then it seemed to him that he could see her—something, prone, abject; her eyes perhaps. Leaning, he seemed to look down into a black well and at the bottom saw two glints like reflection of dead stars. He was moving, because his foot kicked her. He kicked her hard, kicking into and through a choked wall of surprise and fear. She began to scream, he jerking her up, clutching her by the arm, hitting at her with wide, wild blows, striking at the voice perhaps, feeling her flesh anyway enclosed by the womanshenegro and the haste. (146–47)

The smell of woman and Negro is so unpleasant that Joe reacts like a madman. At this point in the narrative, it seems apparent that even at fourteen Joe already is unable to free himself of the traditional, puritanical, and provincial conception of the Negro. The pressures and stereotypes of blackness shape his self-conception, thwart his emotional growth, and warp his development as a whole person. Somewhat like Lena, Joe functions on the animal level, riding what Hightower terms the "sheer tremendous tidal wave of desperate living" (458).

In *Light in August* Faulkner makes no attempt to make "Negro" palatable or attractive. Joe's own conduct and life style as a black man seem calculated to repel rather than attract. Hyatt Waggoner contends that Faulkner "attempts to make us pity, identify ourselves with and even, in the religious sense of the word, love, a man who would be rejected not only by Southern mores with their racial bias but by any human standard."[11] Waggoner's assessment and Joe's

---

11 Waggoner, *William Faulkner*, 102. Waggoner has a realistic view of Joe as "a man of whom we might say that it is surprising not that he commits one murder but that he has not committed more, a man apparently capable of any violent and repulsive deed, a man who hates not *even* those who love him but *especially* those who love him" (103).

own comment, "God loves me too" (98), stress the irony of the situation: Joe is not a lovable person. In Joe Christmas' case, Faulkner asks the reader to suspend usual notions of morality and to love in spite of the character's faults.

The union between the female and the Negro in the novel implies that the fear and fantasy of the white male is precisely that these two crucial elements of his world will form an alliance which will operate to defeat him. For example, before Percy Grimm races for the kitchen where Joe awaits capture, he shouts in disgust and outrage: "'Has every preacher and old maid in Jefferson taken their pants down to the yellowbellied son of a bitch?'" (439). The allusion is sexual, but the suggestion is that the weak links in southern society will accommodate the Negro and undermine the larger group.

Grimm's comment reiterates, too, that all the major characters are inextricably linked in a masochistic union of racial fantasy and religious hysteria. Joanna Burden, in particular, exemplifies this process. Joanna's racial and religious beliefs appear in two ways. One is in her calling Joe Christmas, "'Negro! Negro! Negro!'" (245), during their sexual encounters. She uses the term to debase not Joe, but herself. Her libertine actions are a part of her attempt at self-damnation. Joanna abandons herself to Joe as "Negro," not simply to the "wild throes of nymphomania" (245). Not the sexual act alone, but sexual mating with the Negro will condemn her to hell. Miscegenation merits hell because the Negro is cursed by God and doomed to Satan according to her Calvinistic beliefs.

The second way in which Joanna's beliefs about race and religion are revealed also suggests the basic tenets of white supremacy. In a lengthy section, Joanna recounts her family's history and her father's views of the Negro. Her father, Nathaniel, in showing her the secret family graves of her grandfather and brother, two Calvins by name, had said, "'Your grandfather and brother are lying there, murdered not by one white man but by the curse which God put on a whole race. . . . A race doomed and cursed to be forever and ever a part of the white-race's doom and curse for its sins. . . . His doom and his curse'" (239). Joanna's father sees the black race as the doom and curse of the white race and emphasizes that neither Joanna nor any other white child ever born can escape this curse. She responds to

her father's notions in her relationship with Joe Christmas, who becomes "Negro" in her mind.

In translating Nathaniel Burden's words into a personal code,
Joanna formulates her own "vision":

> "I thought of all the children coming forever and ever into the
> world, white, with the black shadow already falling upon them be-
> fore they drew breath. And I seemed to see the black shadow in
> the shape of the cross. And it seemed like the white babies were
> struggling, even before they drew breath, to escape from the
> shadow that was not only upon them but beneath them too, flung
> out like their arms were flung out, as if they were nailed to the
> cross. I saw all the little babies that would ever be in the world, the
> ones not yet even born—a long line of them with their arms
> spread, on the black crosses." (239)

Joanna's vision is guilt- and fear-ridden. Her father's advice regarding the vision is, "'You must struggle, rise. But in order to rise, you
must raise the shadow with you. But you can never lift it to your
level'" (240). Blacks, then, remain inferior to whites, yet they are the
means by which whites may work out their own expiation.

Joanna remembers exactly the final words of her father's treatise
on race: "'The curse of the black race is God's curse. But the curse of
the white race is the black man who will be forever God's chosen
own because He once cursed Him!'" (240). The logic here is obscure
and irrational, yet Joanna not only accepts it as a child, but also lives
by it as an adult. Her father's racial views sustain Joanna, and they
lead to her death. The vengeful God of her father receives His due.

Joanna's final insistence that Joe kneel and pray with her because
"God" asks it is the demand of a fanatical woman.[12] Her object is not
to get Joe to become a "nigger"; she believes that God—not herself—demands it. Religious faith upholds the Burdens' views on
race. In Joanna's attempt to get Joe to pray, she recalls the persistence
of the South in believing that it performed God's will in upholding
slavery and maintaining Jim Crow. While her exterior may not be
hysterical, Joanna still is suicidal and driven. She has no authority to

---

12 Cleanth Brooks, however, makes the point that "Joanna's final gesture is not the
spiteful reaction of a jilted woman. There is something almost impersonal about it."
William Faulkner, 58.

force Joe into prayer, yet she attributes her own desires to the will of God. Her protestantism and race justify her vengeance. However, the description of Joanna's face during her confrontation with Joe over his attending a school for Negroes attests to her irrational state of mind: "Their faces were not a foot apart: the one cold, dead white, fanatical, mad; the other parchment-colored, the lip lifted into the shape of a soundless and rigid snarl" (262). Joanna is both mad and a fanatic.

Joanna Burden is not so different from the other more obvious fanatic, Doc Hines, who preaches white supremacy under the guise of Christian asceticism and a sense of mission in converting blacks. Hines is the character who is totally obsessed with race. He believes that God has spoken directly to him and said: " 'You can go now. You have done My work. There is no more evil here now but womanevil, not worthy for My chosen instrument to watch' " (365). These words of his God free the old man to leave the orphanage after Joe's adoption by the McEacherns. Doc Hines suggests the allegory of a southerner who expends all of life's positive values by hating the Negro and by tormenting himself about the place and activities of the Negro. Even after Doc Hines no longer observes Joe's growth and development firsthand, he keeps in touch through his God: "one night he wrestled and he strove and he cried aloud, 'That bastard, Lord! I feel! I feel the teeth and the fangs of evil!' and God said, 'It's that bastard. Your work is not done yet. He's a pollution and a abomination on My earth' " (365). Doc Hines's God is a reflection of Hines himself. A crazed parasite, Hines feeds his hatred by preaching to black congregations who never know that he preaches hatred and damnation of the Negro. His view mixes racial and religious fanaticism: it links Doc Hines to Calvin Burden and his biological and ideological heir, Joanna.

Like Doc Hines, Joanna Burden actually believes that she is an instrument of her God, one shaped by a distorted personal vision and zeal. In her final days, she prays aloud in a voice "monotonous, calm, and despairing" (264). She talks to God "as if He were a man in the room" (265). By her actions, Joanna establishes her basic emotional instability; she is, like Hines and possibly Hightower, mad. It is difficult to dismiss her previous conduct with Joe and accept her final moments as those of a rational individual. Joe even considers her, "there in the house, patient, waiting, inescapable, crazy" (254). Joanna becomes a mirror image of Joe, who sees himself as the "volitionless servant of the fatality in which he believed that he did not believe" (264). Both struggle against, but ultimately succumb to, a power which they attribute to forces outside of themselves, yet which seems also to emanate from within. Faulkner suggests that though ideological pressures exist externally they may be creations of the human psyche at work individually and collectively over a period of time.

In the relationship between Joe and Joanna, Faulkner explores the private sphere of southern life that develops character and racial conceptions. However, because his concern is also with the public, social sphere, he examines as well the role of the larger external southern world which he presents as a land both blessed and cursed, both fecund and sterile. He balances his characters as self-willed individuals with imagery indicative of their being controlled by external forces. Those forces include the region's social patterns and beliefs, which Joanna Burden acknowledges when she tells Joe, "'A man would have to act as the land where he was born had trained him to act'" (241). Social conditioning has its effects on all of the characters, and Faulkner makes its most detrimental effects visible in juxtaposing the stories of Joe, Lena Grove, and Gail Hightower.

In setting up the major triad of the novel, Faulkner seems preoccupied with a connection between the theater and his fictional characters. A submerged metaphor—life as a play, culture as a stage—holds characters and actions together. Jefferson and its environs are like a cardboard stage. His characters are both types and abstractions who are not fully developed human beings, at least partly because their roles do not demand that they be. The character-actors are at once operating under their own volitions and at the same time controlled by the stage world with its script and directions. Not only their words but their actions as well are manipulated by external forces. Yet they appear to the audience to be free and willful in their movements. The player-actor metaphor reminds the reader that the

actor is simultaneously himself and the character and every other actor who has played the part.

Faulkner suggests that there is some value in knowing how to
play out assigned roles, how to improvise in the face of uncertainty,
how to endure patiently in light of nonacceptance. And at the same
time, he criticizes the debilitating effects of prescribed roles and suggests that they contribute to the decadence of Jefferson and the de-
humanization of its residents.

Giving shape to the play-drama is the Negro, the pervasive abstraction behind the scenes, prompting actions, ideas, and responses. Blacks in Faulkner's world understand better than anyone
else the significance of acting out assigned roles, especially those of
"Negro" and "nigger," because often their very life depends upon
the ability to stay within the confines of their role. Survival in a hostile environment has depended upon the degree to which blacks
could play "Negro," though ironically their adeptness at the role
leads to entrapment in it. This circular existence continues tragically,
unaltered in spite of any accurate perceptions of self.

Hightower, for instance, recounts his black nurse's vision of the
war knowing that it has shaped his youth and adulthood: " 'Now
this is what Cinthy told me. And I believe. I know. It's too fine to
doubt. It's too fine, too simple, ever to have been invented by white
thinking. A negro might have invented it. And if Cinthy did, I still
believe. Because even fact cannot stand with it' " (458). Even in this
tribute of sorts to Cinthy, Hightower acknowledges the finely drawn
lines between black and white life in his society; moreover, he reveals the Negro as the creator of southern myth and legend, and not
simply a component of those stemming from the white psyche. Significantly in *Light in August,* the player-actors take their cues from
preconceived definitions, descriptions of the Negro and his place in
their lives and society. That they all misjudge and misconstrue the
meaning of the Negro because of the collective regional fantasy at
work ultimately becomes the actual tragedy enacted in the novel.

Clear perception of self and others becomes a key to the health
and stamina of the characters whether in roles created for them
by the divisive forces constricting southern life or roles they create
for themselves out of personal responses to their society, such as

rebellion (Joe Christmas), frustration (Hightower), and boredom (Lena Grove).

Joe, in particular, makes himself. Once he opens his bedroom window at the McEacherns, his adoptive parents, Joe escapes into a makeshift life of his own creation. Other forces may have conspired against him and attempted to mold him, but he wills himself into the personality and being that he is. For example, he resists Joanna Burden's desire for a child and marriage with the thought, "'No. If I give in now, I will deny all the thirty years that I have lived to make me what I chose to be'" (250–51).

Joanna, too, invents scenes and situations, especially for her interaction with Joe: "She could have had no such experience at all, and there was neither reason for the scene nor any possible protagonist. . . . It was as if she had invented the whole thing deliberately, for the purpose of playing it out like a play" (244–45). Joanna acts out her own fantasies ("the faultlessly played scenes of secret and monstrous delight and jealousy," 249), but she involves Joe in them. In this sense she is unlike Hightower, whose fantasies remain private inside his own mind. Not only does Joanna involve Joe in her fantasies, but she also involves the entire community. In death she becomes a modern link in the region's collective fantasy of the white woman and "the Negro"—precisely the roles she invents for herself and Joe.

When the sheriff and his deputy accompany an anonymous "Negro" into the cabin for interrogation, they leave outside a crowd merging into a frightening oneness: "with avid eyes upon which the sheer prolongation of empty flames had begun to pall, with faces identical one with another. It was as if all their individual five senses had become one organ of looking, like an apotheosis, the words that flew among them wind- or air-engendered *Is that him? Is that the one that did it?*" (Faulkner's italics, 275). The crowd begins at once to respond to the old code: "Behind them . . . the dying fire roared, filling the air though not louder than the voices and much more unsourceless *By God, if that's him, what are we doing, standing around here? Murdering a white woman the black son of a . . .* (Faulkner's italics, 275). They become characters in a play defending the honor and virtue of the white woman. In death Joanna Burden becomes what she was not in life: "None of them had ever entered the house. While she was alive they would not have allowed their wives to call on her. When they were children (some of their fathers had done it too) they had called after her on the street, 'Nigger lover! Nigger lover!'" (275). In death Joanna is recognized as a white woman deserving the loyalty and protection of the white community, which is interested in protecting its self-image and the distinctive roles it has inherited.

Similarly, Lena Grove's characterization as a poor-white woman establishes her as a particular character type, operating within fixed, predictable social and environmental limits. Lena may appear fluid and mobile, yet the mode of her character development precludes the possibility of change in her life. Not only is she an actress who plays a self-created role, but she is also, despite her seeming freedom, fulfilling another function which Faulkner adapts from the conventions of the poor-white in southern life. In many respects, Lena is placed puppet-like upon the road and drawn animal-like away from the past. Her depiction prepares the way for Joe Christmas as an individual whose self-image has been unduly determined by social distinctions and cultural perceptions. Lena plays out her role, while Joe refuses to act out the part assigned to him.

Lena Grove sets up a social type which is a parody of Christmas as a socially defined "nigger" in southern life. Lena and Joe are related to a system of values that emanates from rigid social and cultural mandates. Adherence to types and to the system assures Lena of acceptance, or at least charitable tolerance. Even as a recognized poor-white, Lena can find a place in Jefferson.

On the other hand, Joe (whether as Mexican, exotic foreigner, or as native black) wavers between acceptance of and rebellion against the values of his culture, and therefore cannot find a place in Jefferson. He must exist on the fringes and in the background as all "niggers" must—the only exception being house niggers like Dilsey Gibson. In all his endeavors, Joe is an actor who plays to the audience of his choosing. He seeks the greatest possible reaction from that audience; for a white audience he uses the shock value of blackness appearing surreptitiously in their midst; for a black audience, he asserts the superiority of his whiteness. If he fails with either tactic, he can blame the script, the racial situation in the South and his own non-family background. If he succeeds, he can praise his own ingenuity, all the while cursing his having to execute roles.

During the course of the novel the reader comes to know Joe Christmas as a man in the process of creating an identity, shaping a personality, and evolving a "self" concept, though the reader has to measure Joe's success and its meaning in relation to Lena Grove's search. When in the end their separate existences take on opposite meanings, even those opposites must be viewed together somehow, perhaps not quite comfortably but certainly in a tangential relationship whose resonances meet in Hightower's awakening to life and himself.

Hightower, the other character of the major triad, is similar to Joe in that he does not have a place within the community. He, too, is an outsider because he has refused to leave once his traditional position in the community has dissolved (that is, after he can no longer function as minister, and has no prescribed role in Jefferson). Hightower's lot is as much his own making as it is the town's. If Joe can never know the biological details of the past and his origins, Hightower can never face the reality of his. He escapes his past, and consequently himself, by romanticizing it and merging with the romance. Hightower is an actor who ignores the audience almost completely in favor of his own script. He interprets his role solely in light of the imagined conduct of his ancestors, earlier actors. In the final analysis, he sees himself clearly: "He seems to see reflected . . . a *figure antic* as a *showman*, a little wild: a *charlatan* preaching worse than heresy, in utter disregard of *that whose very stage he preempted*" (my italics, 462).

Essentially Hightower yields to the pressure of the community following the embarrassing death of his wife and resigns his pastorate, only after a prolonged attempt to ignore everything. His succumbing to the collective will of the congregation and the town (despite the obscurity of the moral issues) foreshadows Joe's giving in to the social forces at work making him a nigger. A narrative comment regarding the reaction of the town to Hightower's yielding suggests a relationship to Joe's own yielding: "Then the town was sorry with being glad, as people sometimes are sorry for those they have at last forced to do as they wanted them to" (64). The specific details of

Hightower's treatment by the town link Hightower to Joe and undermine the moral values and integrity of the community.

Once the town recognizes that Hightower "would be a part of its
life until he died," it left him alone: "As though . . . the entire affair
had been a lot of people performing a play and that now and at last
they had all played out the parts which had been allotted them and
now they could live quietly with one another" (67). The cohesive-
ness of the South depends upon role playing, on the acceptance of
the roles, and on agreement on their meanings. Hightower has not
been exact in fulfilling the role of the minister; he has changed the
part without community consent. Though he reenacts the great
drama of the Civil War, Hightower does not recognize that it is not
his private domain. He fails to understand that the legacy of the war
is a collective fantasy in which all participate.

It is no wonder that when the townsmen move against Hightower, they move in fixed roles that stem from a time that is past but
which lingers in their minds. When Hightower involves "the Negro"
in his situation, he gives the community its justification and motivation for purging him. The townsmen accuse Hightower of having
been an unnatural husband because of a Negro woman who cooked
for him. Masked men frightened the woman away from her job, but
Hightower remains. (Faulkner reveals in an ironical aside that the
woman was a high brown, that is a bright-skinned Negro considered unusually attractive, and that there were two or three men in
the town who had personal stakes in keeping her away from Hightower.) Regarding the actions of the townsmen against Hightower,
Byron observes: "in a small town, where evil is harder to accom-
plish, where opportunities for privacy are scarcer, . . . people can
invent more of it in other people's names" (65–66). The community
invents Hightower's sins, then doles out the age-old prescribed punishment. After he ignores an ultimatum from the KKK, Hightower is
taken into the woods, tied to a tree, and beaten unconscious.

Jefferson acts out the part of the avenger, though as Byron points
out, "the town had a habit of saying things about the disgraced minister which they did not believe themselves for too long a time to
break themselves of it" (69). In part they act out their fantasies even
when they recognize them as fantasies. " 'Because always,' " Byron

reflects, "'when anything gets to be a habit, it also manages to get a right good distance away from truth and fact'" (69). Byron voices an awareness of Jefferson's common assumptions which persist apart from truth or fact. What results when the townsmen react to habit is a highly stylized play duplicating what they perceive as life.

Similar to Hightower, Lena Grove is a character given to private fantasies which ultimately involve the larger community. She creates romance and adventure out of her rather ordinary life and predicament. Despite her apparent rootlessness or her enjoyment of her mobility, Lena is on the road not simply because Lucas Burch is on it ahead of her; she is on it because her life and the life of her family have been confined to the area surrounding Doane's Mill. It would appear that place, the southern physical setting, is not always wholesome and healthy. In her simple way, Lena wishes to escape the past and all ties to the drab existence of her kind. As a child going into town with her father, she would get out of the wagon at the edge of town and walk the rest of the way because (and this she would not tell her father) "she believed that the people who saw her and whom she passed on foot would believe that she lived in the town too" (1–2). Lena's action suggests both an exaggerated sense of pride and a romantic self-image—two major aspects of her personality as an adult.

When she does move into town, it is as an orphan in her brother's house, where she "did all the housework and took care of the other children" for her brother's "labor- and childridden wife" (3). Her simple observation on her own pregnancy addresses her own motivations perhaps more than she is fully aware. Summing up her lot in her brother's house, she states, "'I reckon that's why I got one so quick myself'" (3). The notion of escape from her drab life is plainly the reason why Lena chooses to leave on her journey into the world at night and through the window when she could well have gone out the door during the day.

Along the way Lena labors to be "proper" and a "lady." In a display of pride, she refuses food because the refusal makes her appear ladylike. When she eats breakfast with Armstid, Lena causes him to notice that she eats with "the tranquil and hearty decorum of last night's supper, though there was now corrupting it a quality of polite and almost finicking restraint" (19–20). Absorbed with the appearance of eating "proper," Lena contemplates buying sardines and crackers because they present her as quality, a lady:

> She is remembering breakfast, thinking how she can enter the store this moment and buy cheese and crackers and even sardines. . . . At Armstid's she had had but a cup of coffee and a piece of cornbread: nothing more, though Armstid pressed her. "I et polite," she thinks, her hands lying upon the bundle, knowing the hidden coins, remembering the single cup of coffee, the decorous morsel of strange bread; thinking with a sort of serene pride: "Like a lady I et. Like a lady traveling. But now I can buy sardines if I should wish." (23)

Lena conducts herself on the road according to her own dreamlike sense of propriety and decorum. She creates an image of herself, and then she sets out to live that image. Lena Grove is a natural actress. Lucas may have initially sparked her decision to set out on the road, but Lena is where she is in Mississippi by an act of will and determination, an outgrowth of how she perceives herself in the world. Her acceptance of Byron stems, at least in part, from his unabashed devotion: he feeds and confirms her romantic notion of herself.

Ironically, it is Hightower who, although he sees through Lena's pretenses with Byron, voices what may be Lena's own idealized conception of herself: "*She will have to have others, more* remembering the young strong body from out whose travail even there shone something tranquil and unafraid. *More of them. Many more. That will be her life, her destiny. The good stock peopling in tranquil obedience to it the good earth; from these hearty loins without hurry or haste descending mother and daughter. But by Byron engendered next*" (Faulkner's italics, 384). Hightower's vision ignores at least a part of the reality of Lena's life. His faulty perception here is akin to his romanticizing of his grandfather's heroism during the Civil War.

Hightower builds romantic notions about the heroics of the war into his way of seeing himself. Because he grows up "among phantoms, and side by side with a ghost" (449), Hightower himself becomes a phantom attempting to re-create his illusions in the actual world. His parents and his mammy, the three phantoms in his world, reinforce his fantasies about the war by turning his grandfather, the ghost in Hightower's life, into a valiant Civil War officer-hero. The truth is, however, that Hightower's grandfather was shot probably by a Confederate soldier's wife during a raid on a chicken house—in other words, shot by a woman as he tried to steal chickens (459).

Hightower's self-image has been molded by an old black woman who told stories of his grandfather. Cinthy, the storyteller, is the third phantom in Hightower's world; she was "a huge woman, with a face both irascible and calm: the mask of black tragedy between scenes" (450). Faulkner describes Cinthy's face both in terms he frequently uses for blacks, "irascible and calm," and in symbolic terms that suggest the role of the Negro in the total drama of *Light in August:* "the mask of black tragedy between scenes." Cinthy is the phantom who fed Hightower's childhood visions of the heroic past and caused him to see life in tragic terms. Because of Cinthy and the historical forces acting upon him, Hightower apprehends the world and himself through distorted images of the past and the Civil War.

Hightower, then, is too much the dreamer to have his simple, ennobling opinion of Lena taken literally. Because he has little direct experience of life, Hightower cannot be accepted as an authority on living. He lives in the past, an antebellum past as far removed from the reality of Lena's situation as is her conception of herself as a "lady." Both are guilty of falsely perceiving themselves and their world. The sad reality is that Hightower's vision is a romanticizing of the fate which Lena's own sister-in-law and other poor women have suffered: "labor- and childridden," "for almost half of every year . . . either lying in or recovering" (3).[13]

Faulkner insinuates that Lena is aware that once her traveling stops she will never be able to resume it again; he does not intimate the reasons why. He presents Lena in all her earthy, primitive simplicity as admirable for her capacity to trust, love, hope, but also as

13 In spite of its brief delineation, the condition of Lena's sister-in-law is similar to other naturalistic portraits of regular childbearing among poor white women. Judy Pippinger in Edith Kelley's *Weeds* (1923) is one example; another is Ellen Chesser of Elizabeth Madox Roberts' *The Time of Man* (1926). Both women are essentially broodmares who are painfully aware of themselves becoming less human with the birth of each child.

offensive because of her mindlessness, animal-like sensibilities, and self-deception. The portrait suggests the role of the "nigger" in southern life. She is a homeless wanderer, unwed mother, and outlander drifting through the South in brogans. She is the "noble savage," the white primitive, who drops her baby and then continues on, practically uninterrupted by its birth.

Lena's journey from Alabama through Jefferson and on into Tennessee offers one perspective from which the nature of the individual's relationship to self and society may be viewed. Lena is alone, without family connections in a society that is historically conscious of ancestors and family ties. She is not accepted so much as she is pitied, but the fact is, Lena does not *see*, cannot see how other people see her. She remains oblivious to her actual condition and excludes all external views of herself until Hightower confronts her about Byron Bunch; then she allows to the external world a meaning other than the one she has assigned in her role playing: "she begins to cry. She sits upright, the child at her breast, crying, not loud and not hard, but with a patient and hopeless abjectness, not hiding her face. 'And you worry me about if I said No or not and I already said No and you worry me and worry me and now he is already gone. I will never see him again'" (390). At that moment, Hightower realizes her simplicity. He knows that he has penetrated her shell; he "rises and stands over her with his hand on her bowed head thinking *Thank God, God help me*" (Faulkner's italics, 391).

All of these characters are outsiders; none properly belongs to the town of Jefferson. All attempt to ignore the immensity of the "Negro" question in the daily life of the South. Only Lena and Byron manage to slip away unscathed by the complex moral issues involved. That they do so, but escape onto Lena's road which is not unlike Joe's street, seems fitting because the road is dissociated from the reality of southern life. Its unreality is perhaps best emphasized by first Lena and later Joe as they ride along on wagons which seem to separate living occupants from a backdrop of unchanging cardboard scenery.

The image of a wagon drawing slowly toward Lena Grove as she waits for a ride into Jefferson suggests the advance of the three plots: "And no one could have known that he had ever looked at her as, without any semblance of progress in either of them, they draw slowly together as the wagon crawls terrifically toward her in its slow palpable aura of somnolence and red dust in which the steady feet of the mules move dreamlike and punctuate by the sparse jingle of harness and the limber bobbing of jackrabbit ears, the mules still neither asleep nor awake as he halts them" (8). A key clause in this passage ("without any semblance of progress in either of them, they draw slowly together") describes the method used in moving the three central storylines (if not the figures) toward one another. The description of the mules in a dreamlike state ("neither asleep nor awake") points to Joe Christmas because Faulkner closely associates mules and the Negro in creating his South.[14] The conjunction of the two (mules and Negroes) suggests something about the unreality of the region, and about the lethargic state in which Joe finds himself during his flight from Jefferson.

The wagon and driver taking Lena into Jefferson foreshadow Lena's relationship to the Joe Christmas story. "The wagon moves slowly, steadily, as if here within the sunny loveliness of the enormous land it were outside of, beyond all time and all haste" (24). Like the individuals in the novel, the wagon depicts the solitude possible even when nature is not a hostile environment but simply a huge canvaslike backdrop accommodating a linear passage. The wagon's slow forward momentum creates expectancy: "The wagon goes on, slow, timeless. The red and unhurried miles unroll beneath the steady feet of mules, beneath the creaking and clanking wheels" (25). Lena herself is, like the motion of the wagon, unhurried, slow, yet she moves deliberately toward Jefferson and the events enveloping Joe Christmas. Following the pattern of her actions, the reader moves directly to the town's search for Joe as an accused murderer and into Joe's own search for self-actualization.

The driver's attitude toward Lena anticipates the failure of Joe and Lena to meet: "Apparently he has never looked at her, not even

14 Faulkner uses *niggers* and *mules* in the impressionistic town scenes in *Soldiers' Pay* and in Quentin Compson's vision of Jefferson and home in *The Sound and the Fury.* Quentin also points out that only niggers know whether mules are asleep or awake, and thus suggests both some vague natural relationship between them and, more important here, a keener perception or ability to discern reality in a marginal situation that blacks possess.

when she got into the wagon. Apparently she has never looked at him, either" (24). The two, Lena and the driver, share the same physical space but do not communicate by word or glance. Each is isolated in a private reaction to self and to the monotonous scene. The two plots, Lena's and Joe's, are analogous to this situation; they share the same fictional space but do not technically respond to each other. Their autonomous situations suggest the rigid caste and class lines drawn by the South's social structure, and the difficulty of communication within that structure.

The wagon is a motif linking Joe and Lena, and its forward motion is a metaphor for the movement of the two stories: "backrolling now behind her a long monotonous succession of peaceful and undeviating changes from day to dark and dark to day again, through which she advanced in identical and anonymous and deliberate wagons or through a succession of creakwheeled anad limpeared avatars, like something moving forever and without progress across an urn" (5). The movement, timeless and perpetual yet without noticeable progress (the urn image), recurs in the passage describing Joe Christmas' final wagon ride to Mottstown:

> [Joe] thinks that perhaps, sitting with the wagon's motion to lull him, he will sleep. But he does not sleep. He is not sleepy or hungry or even tired. He is somewhere between and among them, suspended, swaying to the motion of the wagon without thought, without feeling. He has lost account of time and distance; perhaps it is an hour later, perhaps three. The youth [the driver] says:
> "Mottstown. Dar tis."
> Looking, he can see the smoke low on the sky, beyond an imperceptible corner; he is entering it again, the street which ran for thirty years. It had been a paved street, where going should be fast. It had made a circle and he is still inside of it. (321)

The wagon ride into Mottstown recalls Lena's ride into Jefferson. In each case, the passenger appears to move by some force other than will and to be caught in an interminable process, symbolized by the circle (for Joe) and the urn or the spool (for Lena). Just as the "smoke low in the sky" signals the approach to Mottstown and portends Joe's doom, so the image of smoke on the horizon announces Jefferson and is an ominous suggestion of fortune for Lena: "she sees two columns of smoke: the one the heavy density of burning coal above a tall stack, the other a tall yellow column standing apparently from a clump of trees some distance beyond the town. 'That's a house burning,' the driver says. 'See?'" (26). Lena, however, is not concerned with the twin columns of smoke; she is lost in her own reflections, unaware that the planing mill and the Burden estate are to be her principal contacts with Jefferson.

As Joe reflects on his position inside the circle, he thinks: "'And yet I have been further in these seven days than in all the thirty years. . . . But I have never got outside of the ring of what I have already done and cannot ever undo'" (321). He essentially repeats one of Lena's first observations as she approaches Jefferson: "*although I have not been quite a month on the road I am already in Mississippi, further from home than I have ever been before. I am now further from Doane's Mill than I have been since I was twelve years old*" (Faulkner's italics, 1). In these corresponding passages, Faulkner connects two isolated characters and the journey-search motifs defining them.

Faulkner's description of scenery viewed from the wagon suggests that the southern landscape as a reality recedes into the background, despite its psychological significance to both Lena in her travels and Joe in his flight: "Fields and woods seem to hang in some inescapable middle distance, at once static and fluid, quick, like mirages. Yet the wagon passes them" (24). It is not the natural environment, but rather the social environment that is most prominent in the novel. The statement of place as fluid and static echoes an earlier statement by Varner, who owns the store where Lena awaits a ride into Jefferson, and it prefigures Joe's dreamlike experience of the land. Varner thinks, "'I reckon that even a fool gal don't have to come as far as Mississippi to find out that whatever place she run from ain't going to be a whole lot different or worse than the place she is at'" (23). Varner's statement applies equally to Lena and Joe, as well as to the fact that they do indeed "come as far as Mississippi" in order to make their discoveries.

The duality of place as fluid and static appears in Joe's flight sequence; for example, when he awakens from a sleep,

Time, the space of light and dark had long since lost orderliness. It would be either one now, seemingly at an instant, between two moments of the eyelids, without warning. He could never know when he would pass from one to the other, when he would find that he had been asleep without remembering having lain down, or find himself walking without remembering having waked. Sometimes it would seem to him that a night of sleep, in hay, in a ditch, beneath an abandoned roof, would be followed immediately by another night without interval of day, without light between to see to flee by; that a day would be followed by another day filled with fleeing and urgency, without any night between or any interval for rest, as if the sun had not set but instead had turned in the sky before reaching the horizon and retraced its way. (291)

Though primarily a description of the temporal confusion that Joe experiences during his flight, this passage also takes the initial drowsy, dreamlike sequence to its nightmarish extensions. The arbitrary conditions of light and dark are at the opposite pole from the "monotonous changes between darkness and day" that Lena experiences (6). In fact, a long passage describing Lena's journey presents the sense-dulling effect of the wagon rolling by and caught in the landscape:

The sharp and brittle crack and clatter of its weathered and un-greased wood and metal is slow and terrific: a series of dry sluggish reports carrying for a half mile across the hot still pinewiney silence of the August afternoon. Though the mules plod in a steady and unflagging hypnosis, the vehicle does not seem to progress. It seems to hang suspended in the middle distance forever and forever, so infinitesimal is its progress, like a shabby bead upon the mild red string of road. So much is this so that in the watching of it the eye loses it as sight and sense drowsily merge and blend, like the road itself . . . like already measured thread being rewound onto a spool. So that at last, as though out of some trivial and unimportant region beyond even distance, the sound of it seems to come slow and terrific and without meaning as though it were a ghost travelling a half mile ahead of its own shape. (5–6)

Both the wagon, which emerges "without meaning" from some "region beyond even distance," and the ghost, "travelling a half mile ahead of its own shape," prefigure Joe Christmas riding into Mottstown and his death: "with planted on the dashboard before him the shoes, the black shoes smelling of negro: that mark on his ankles the gauge definite and ineradicable of the black tide creeping up his legs, moving from his feet upward as death moves" (321).

The movement of the wheel, its paradoxical negligible progress, the suspension of time, its confusion and monotony, all merge in Hightower's final vision, in which Faulkner employs the metaphor of a vehicle with its wheel of thinking to identify the workings of Hightower's mind. In that scene Hightower acknowledges, "'I have bought my ghost, even though I did pay for it with my life'" (464). After Joe's death, Hightower sits at his window, and his thinking "slows like a wheel beginning to run in sand, the axle, the vehicle, the power which propels it is not yet aware" (464). This retardation allows him to focus on the previously ignored aspects of his life. When he becomes aware of "the sand," the slowed movement, he thinks: "Progress now is still progress, yet it is now indistinguishable from the recent past like the already traversed inches of sand which cling to the turning wheel, raining back with a dry hiss" (464).

Sitting motionless in his window, which frames him like an actor on stage, Hightower reviews the facts of his own guilt; his "wheel of thinking turns on with the slow implacability of a mediaeval torture instrument" (464–65). He slowly reconstructs his life (this time with understanding and responsibility). He envisions a halo which he recognizes as filled with faces, "peaceful, as though escaped into apotheosis" (465). He sees the faces, his own included, "in the lambent suspension of August into which night is about to fully come" (465). The suspended August light and the peaceful faces recall Lena Grove and also Joe Christmas. When he sees the confused, yet peaceful, composite face of Joe and Percy Grimm, Hightower has his climactic vision, and "the wheel turns on. It spins now, fading, without progress, as though turned by that final flood which had rushed out of him, leaving his body empty and lighter than a forgotten leaf and even more trivial than flotsam lying spent and still upon the window ledge which has no solidity beneath hands that have no weight" (466).

Hightower's "wheel" and "window" link him to Lena and Joe. For all three characters, a window is an entry into the social world. Joe escapes from the confines of his adoptive parents by going out a window. Lena leaves her brother's house through the same window she uses for her rendezvous with Lucas Burch. Lena and Joe open windows for experience and enter into a knowledge of life. Lena especially, for all her passive exterior, is actively involved in living. Gail Hightower, however, sits passively before his window and is content to observe life; the window forms a barrier which prevents him from confronting experience directly. Nonetheless, his vision makes explicit Faulkner's use of life as a play enacted before an audience and of culture itself as a stage world dictating the movements of all the character-actors.

Jefferson, Mississippi, provides the backdrop for the action in *Light in August*. Its residents are both audience to and participants in the drama of Joe Christmas. An understanding of Jefferson forwards an understanding of the individual's responsibility to self and to community in the novel.

Although the most insightful revelations about Jefferson occur after Joanna's murder, there are several that appear in connection with Lena Grove. Lena travels along in a society-involving journey; she is out to experience the world and to complete her family circle. Within Jefferson, Lena serves as a catalyst by which the community draws back the isolated or alienated figures, Byron Bunch and Gail Hightower, into its fold. However, because Hightower's return to the community, precipitated partly by his delivery of Lena's baby, amounts to nothing more than a vision of death in life that perhaps culminates in his own death, Lena's impact on Byron is the more revealing.

Although Byron Bunch moves away from his social isolation by following Lena, he becomes, in effect, an obedient boy-figure, whose actual involvement in the community is minimal. Byron's portrait as the surviving, redeemed white male is by no means flattering, because he follows the implicit dictates and whims of the simple-minded Lena. Moreover, Lena and Byron neither settle in Jefferson nor accept active participation in the Jefferson community. They return to the road, which, like Joe's street, remains on the perimeter of the community. Their continued movement belies the assumption that the community is morally sound and upright, as well as that there is one large community in the novel.

The Faulknerian world as it reflects and takes impetus from the southern world is basically a dual culture, a divided world. There is not in fact one larger sense of community capable of containing all the people of a given town. While the reader may assume the existence of a traditional community in *Light in August* (largely oriented toward rural, agrarian, familial values), the reader perhaps should not automatically assume that its morality is an ideal norm. In the world of Jefferson as much fanaticism and misperception lie within the white community as without. Its citizens may have common purposes shared by some others; nevertheless, because of the basic acceptance of a fractured, divided society, individuals learn to relate to distortions, and their personal values become a warped reflection of the social isolation of their racial community. Faulkner does not uncritically celebrate the community or uphold its standards of religion, race, sex, or ethics. In fact, a major cause of ambiguity in Faulkner may well stem from his own inability to determine exactly how to remain a part of a flawed community while exposing its flaws and questioning the validity of its fundamental assumptions.

Faulkner shows a deep affection for his native land. He has provided numerous descriptions of the virginal beauty of that land, while maintaining a graphic fidelity to actual settings. Yet his land is Mississippi, a land of violence, brutality, and oppression. In fact, one source for Joe's murder of Joanna, as well as for his death and castration by Percy Grimm, comes from the history of Oxford, Mississippi.[15]

In 1908 Nelse Patton, a black man, was accused of murdering a white woman, Mrs. Mattie McMillan, by almost severing her head from her body with his razor. Patton was captured, lynched, and

15 Joseph Blotner provides an additional source at least for the death of Joe Christmas. According to Blotner, who uses the Oxford *Eagle* as the basis of his account, Leonard Burt, a black man, disemboweled his wife in September, 1919, and set the bed on fire to hide his crime. He was captured four months later. On Wednesday, March 12, while being taken from the jail to the courthouse, Burt broke away from his escorts and ran up the alley between the jail and a row of stores. He was shot four times as he ran by an officer, T. G. Mertz, who did not castrate him. Burt died the following day. Blotner, *Faulkner: A Biography*, I, 762–63.

castrated by a mob of Oxford's average citizens who had been incited
by a prominent politician, Senator W. V. Sullivan in particular. John
B. Cullen, in *Old Times in the Faulkner Country*, recounts the details of
the event. Although only fourteen at the time, Cullen himself captured Patton, and his own account is a graphic one:

> I yelled for him to halt and when he kept on running, I shot at him
> with both barrels of my shotgun. This stopped him. . . . my squir-
> rel shot were far to small to do much damage at that distance.
>
> I reloaded and ran up close to him and told him to put up his
> hands. He said to my brother, "Mr. Jenks, you knows I'se a good
> nigger."
>
> "I know you're a good nigger," my brother said, "but get your
> hands up." But Nelse never did put his hands up.
>
> He was still standing up, and I believe he was trying to get a
> chance to grab my gun. If he had tried this, I was ready to shoot
> him between the eyes.[16]

Starkly honest, the man recalls that he was ready to shoot Patton
between the eyes, though he was "a good nigger." Cullen's account
of the capture and lynching is important here, not solely because of
the factual parallels between Patton and Joe Christmas, but because
of the conception and treatment of blacks by whites in Faulkner's
Mississippi.

The mob that lynched Patton included the Cullen brothers and
other boys in the community. These boys played a primary role in
taking the jail and subduing the guards ("After Senator Sullivan's
speech, the mob began pitching us boys through the jail windows,
and no guard in that jail would have dared shoot us. Soon a mob
was inside. My brother and I held my father, and the sons of the
other guards held theirs").[17] The adult members of the community
had so wholly accepted violence as a necessity that they allowed the
involvement of their youth. Even the fourteen-year-olds like Cullen
demonstrate a matter-of-fact acceptance of violence as a way of life.
Cullen concludes his account of the actual lynching in a few sparse
sentences: "When the mob finally got through and broke the lock off
the murderer's cell, Nelse had armed himself with a heavy iron coal-

16 John B. Cullen and Floyd C. Watkins, *Old Times in the Faulkner Country* (Chapel
Hill: University of North Carolina Press, 1961), 90.
17 *Ibid.*, 91.

shovel handle. From a corner near the door, he fought like a tiger, seriously wounding three men. He was then shot to death and thrown out of the jail. Someone (I don't know who) cut his ears off, scalped him, cut his testicles out, tied a rope around his neck, tied him to a car, and dragged his body around the streets. Then they hanged him to a walnut-tree limb just outside the south entrance to the courthouse."[18] Over fifty years later, Cullen can still provide the specific details of the lynching; there is no indication in his account to suggest remorse for his own part or even suppression of the bloodier details of the gruesome incident.

The Nelse Patton case suggests the coexistence of innocence and evil in the Oxford community; the use Faulkner makes of this case in *Light in August* suggests that there are no sharp divisions between good and evil, within and without the Jefferson community. Further, accepting the complexity of Jefferson resulting from this fusion of good and evil corrects the assumption that "Faulkner's criticism of Jefferson is relatively mild" in that "after the arrest of Christmas it is the peace and quiet of the town that is insisted upon."[19]

Neither the peaceful exterior nor the momentary lull in activity can negate the presence of destruction or evil. The situation in Jefferson is comparable to the peace and quiet within the eye of a hurricane; the danger is still present and carried by the total organism. Though the windless and rainless eye follows in the wake of the initial devastation and precedes the final torrents, it is an integral part which cannot be separated from the whole. Within the eye the threat of violence is all pervasive. When Faulkner tells us that Percy Grimm "recrossed, the empty square, the quiet square empty of people peacefully at suppertables about that peaceful town" (430), he makes a pointed, ironical statement. That peace is not a facade; it does exist. However, the presence of evil exists alongside it and is accepted in Jefferson during the most ordinary, mundane activities, so that even while the external texture involves dinner the internal reality is that the forces of evil are accumulating for a climactic assault.

18 *Ibid.*, 93.
19 Millgate, *The Achievement of William Faulkner*, 128.

Acceptance of the community means acquiescence in the rigid racial codes of the South; to join the community, Joe must accept either blackness or whiteness. Because he has been pushed so far outside the set limits and standards of white society, he must accept being a "nigger" if he is to join any community at all. Yet Faulkner's message is not as clear-cut as it appears. Race, and its meaning to the community, comes to the forefront as a major social issue with the discovery of Joanna Burden's death, which is aptly termed "an emotional barbecue" (273). The sheriff, anxious to discover who lived in the cabin behind the Burden house, calls out, "'Get me a nigger'" (274). Any "nigger" will do; any one is the same as any other. At the root of the sheriff's request is the white South's failure to see blacks as individuals. Ironically that failure is Joanna's as well, because even if Joe were to accept her offer to become publicly "Negro," he would still not have been free to be an individual "Negro," but would have had to conform to her image of "the Negro."

The southern community insists upon maintaining its "nigger," its simple, uncomplicated scapegoat as a category of human life. One of the deputies suggests as much when he assumes the murderer to be "a nigger": "'She might have had niggers living in the house with her, from what I have heard. What I am surprised at is that it was this long before one of them done for her'" (274). And from the time of the murder on, Joe becomes more and more white Jefferson's "nigger" and scapegoat, just as in the eyes of first Doc Hines and later the dietitian he has become "nigger" and scapegoat.

The murder of Joanna Burden is ultimately an affirmation of Joe's "Negroness." The nigger's lust for the white woman and the white man's heroism in thwarting that satanic sexual drive are enduring myths that surface as soon as Joe Brown (Lucas Burch) informs the sheriff that Christmas is black. Once Joe kills Joanna, he gives in to the social pressures at work. His only freedom has been that of ignoring his race and living as both black and white. He maintains freedom from entrapping circumstances throughout most of his life, but the cost is suspension between worlds, a static state of nondevelopment. With the violence and the murder, Joe makes a choice; ironically he becomes precisely "the nigger" Joanna has tried to force him to become. His return to Jefferson, and the awaiting community, is synonymous with death.

Regarding Joe's death, Melvin Backman asks, "Although Christmas' death seems a crucifixion, is it not also a form of suicide? His submission to pain and death reflects a lifelong pattern of masochism."[20] Acceptance of "nigger" status is indeed masochistic, because pain and suffering are a foregone conclusion. The crucial single test for Faulkner's Negro is the test of endurance. Joe does not have the capacity to endure. Joe's death becomes inevitable because, though he seems to accept emotionally the role of the Negro in society, he is not capable of accepting that role logically or intellectually. For instance, when he wanders into Freedman Town, he feels suffocated by the nigger smells and sounds: "As from the bottom of a thick black pit he saw himself enclosed by cabinshapes, vague, kerosene-lit, so that the street lamps themselves seemed to be further spaced, as if the black life, the black breathing had compounded the substance of breath so that not only voices but moving bodies and light itself must become fluid and accrete slowly from particle to particle, of and with the now ponderable night inseparable and one" (107). The voices and buildings of Freedman Town cause Joe to panic, to breathe hard and run. His image of himself at the bottom of a black pit illustrates the claustrophobia he experiences among blacks. The curious mixing of black (including the humans and the night) with light (kerosene light, street lamps) emphasizes his severe confusion. His reaction to Freedman Town is not an isolated occurrence; it is similar, for example, to his lying in bed at night beside "a woman who resembled an ebony carving" in a condition of panic, "sleepless, beginning to breathe deep and hard" (212).

In *Light in August* Faulkner poses a resolution to Joe's dilemma that feels right because of the manner in which he has manipulated emotions. Joe must die and he must die as a "nigger" to reinforce his acceptance of "nigger" space in a racially divided community. Joe's place is settled as it is because maintaining everything in its proper, assigned place is the end of the southern code of order. However, social order is in this case equated with emotional disorder. Individ-

20 Melvin Backman, *Faulkner: The Major Years, a Critical Study,* (Bloomington: Indiana University Press, 1966), 86.

uals as diverse as Joanna and Percy Grimm move against Joe to protect the social order; Hightower attempts to remain aloof from that order, but in the end he recognizes that he, too, must either accept or reject it.

Thus, though Joe's actual blood heritage remains unresolved, he dies the death traditionally accepted for the "nigger." His ultimate racial classification, then, is as a black person whether or not he feels comfortable with the label. Because Joe is accused of the rape-murder of Joanna Burden and because he is labeled "nigger" by Joe Brown and consequently hunted as a "nigger," Joe dies a nigger's death. While Joe's death at the hands of Percy Grimm should not be technically termed a "lynching," the withholding of the term does not negate the fact that Grimm's method, the sexual mutilation and castration of a Negro, was an accepted punishment meted out to those blacks accused of any license with a white woman. Grimm's actions fall almost predictably within the accepted mold, and it matters little that his subconscious and conscious motivations do not mesh.

Gavin Stevens, Faulkner's Harvard-educated district attorney, attempts to explicate the confusion of Joe's final hours. He presents the case plainly in terms of the dichotomy between Joe's black blood and his white blood. Stevens rationalizes the situation into language and conceptions that the townsmen could easily understand. His superficial yet elaborate explanation makes use of the simple stereo-typed hybrid, the doomed, ill-fated mulatto:

"All those successions of thirty years . . . which had put the strain either on his white blood or his black blood . . . which killed him. . . . But his blood would not be quiet, let him save it. It would not be either one or the other and let his body save itself. Because black blood drove him first to the Negro cabin. And the white blood drove him out of there, as it was the black blood which snatched up the pistol and the white blood which would not let him fire it. And it was the white blood which sent him to the minister, which rising in him for the last and final time, sent him against all reason and all reality, into the embrace of a chimera, a blind faith in something read in a printed Book. Then I believe that the white blood deserted him for a moment. Just a second, a flicker, allowing the black to rise in its final moment and make him turn upon that on which he has postulated his hope of salvation. It was the black blood which swept him up into that ecstasy out of a black jungle where life has already ceased before the heart stops and death is desire and fulfillment. And then the black blood failed him again, as it must have in crises all his life. He did not kill the minister. He merely struck him with the pistol and ran on and crouched behind that table and defied the black blood for the last time, as he had been defying it for thirty years. He crouched behind that over-turned table and let them shoot him to death, with that loaded and unfired pistol in his hand." (424–25)

Stevens' theorizing is purely fantasy and a whimsical, romantic fantasy at that. Yet his theory has been assumed to be Faulkner's own. It is a tight theatrical presentation not of facts but of material which plays well to an audience long familiar with the general out-line and which adheres to the thematic ideas of this particular Faulkner novel.[21] The lines of blood distinctions are clearly drawn. Cowardice and criminal tendencies are the by-products of black blood. White blood accounts for the rational and humane side. Black blood is equivalent to primitive lust, instinct, and irrationality; white blood is the civilizing and moral influence.

Gavin Stevens presents an allegory not of Joe Christmas' blood but of tensions in the South. The ease with which he spins off the balanced, point-counterpoint theory, and its facile acceptance by his Harvard-trained, professor friend, affirms the basic divisiveness of the society and the widespread racism among all segments of the community. Both men, well-educated and not immediately vulnera-ble to mob hysteria, clearly subscribe to the notion of racial blood itself creating behavioral patterns. Gavin Stevens' description of Joe's final hours reveals Stevens' own creation of the myth of "the Negro." It is a tall tale spun off in a leisurely way for his guest and himself. It is as fraught with stereotyped racial assumptions as those provided by the covert fanatic Joanna Burden and by the overt fa-natic Doc Hines, albeit rhetorically more palatable. Stevens certainly

21 My reading of Faulkner's typescript for *Light in August* supports this conclusion. Faulkner revised a portion of Steven's theory for consistency with the general notions of black and white blood in this novel. For instance, "And then the white blood drove him out of there, as it was the black [*black*, the original word in the typed sentence is crossed out and *white* inserted, but subsequently deleted for *black*] blood which snatched up the pistol and the white ["*white* is inserted after *black* is crossed out] blood which would not let him fire it." See 467, *Light in August* typescript, Faulkner Collec-tion, Alderman Library, University of Virginia.

appears linked to the major white characters in the perpetuation of race propaganda, as well as in a need to articulate personal conceptions of "Negro."

By the inclusion of Gavin Stevens, Faulkner reiterates a dominant motif and at the same time dispels the notion that his racial views in this novel are simplistic. Faulkner depicts an unwholesome Jefferson in presenting Stevens. In establishing Stevens as a part of the old aristocracy, Faulkner relates something of the convictions of Stevens' ancestors as well: "His family is old in Jefferson; his ancestors owned slaves there and his grandfather knew (and also hated, and publicly congratulated Colonel Sartoris when they died) Miss Burden's grandfather and brother" (419–20). The reference is to the shooting of Joanna Burden's grandfather and brother by Colonel Sartoris "over a question of negro voting" (235). In a subtle aside about Stevens' family, Faulkner suggests the longevity of Jefferson's perversity.

Gavin Stevens' theorizing also shows Faulkner's understanding of the popular misconceptions held by his culture: that blood conflict or warfare takes place inside the mulatto. During the 1920s and 1930s, the mistaken notion of blood conflict was frequently used as motivation for characters.[22] Joe Christmas, however, is not the "tragic Mulatto," a set character type. He does not neatly fit the mold. Faulkner carefully establishes Joe as a man who does not know his biological background. Joe as an orphan is unable to determine his race according to the usual procedure of blood lineage. The words of a black man working in the yard of the orphanage reflect that neither racial designation alone nor the odyssey of the tragic mulatto is at issue in Faulkner's treatment of Joe. When Joe approaches the man with a question about his race, he receives the re-

22 For example, Jean Toomer, himself a man who chose his race, relies on it in *Cane*, especially for his primitive females of mixed blood, Fern and Esther. A person of mixed blood could never be at peace or happy in life. The mulatto's fate was always to be driven by the turmoil in his or her blood through a turbulent life to a tragic death. Even when ostensibly successful (as in the case of Johnson's nameless protagonist in *The Autobiography of an Ex-Coloured Man*), the mulatto suffered internally from the contradictory impulses of black and white blood which permanently trap the individual in an unsatisfactory life. See Sterling Brown's presentation of the mulatto in "A Century of Negro Portraiture in American Literature," *Massachusetts Review*, VII (Winter, 1966), 73–96.

tort: "'Who told you I am a nigger, you little white trash bastard? I aint a nigger. You are worse than that. You dont know what you are. And more than that you wont ever know. You'll live and you'll die and you wont ever know'" (363). Joe's problem is one of personal identity, not anonymous assimilation into a racial group. Faulkner attempts to make Joe's tragedy his not knowing, and not, as Gavin Stevens claims, a blood conflict.

The ironical placement of Stevens' exegesis just prior to the narrative of Percy Grimm stresses by means of structure the general racist views of the townsfolk. Grimm has: "a sublime and implicit faith in physical courage and blind obedience, and a belief that the white race is superior to any and all other races and that the American uniform is superior to all men, and that all that would ever be required of him in payment for this belief, this privilege, would be his own life" (426–27). He is a supreme example of the blind acceptance of unfounded generalities as cultural imperatives. Though more bluntly emotional than Gavin Stevens', Grimm's conception is the cultural mandate of white supremacy. The literal juxtaposition of Grimm's notions on race with those of Stevens demonstrates that the two, though different in character type, psychology, and class, are not so far apart in race ideology.

Importantly, however, Faulkner continues the idea of manipulation by external forces beyond the characters' control. He has Gavin Stevens reveal that Mrs. Hines wanted Joe Christmas to die "decent": "'Decently hung by a Force, a principle; not burned or hacked or dragged dead by a Thing'" (421). The distinction Stevens makes between a "Force" and a "Thing" has little significance because both represent an inflexible domination over a victimized human being. The theme of a dominated human being moved about like a chess piece reaches a climax in the section leading up to Joe's death at the hands of Percy Grimm.

With the introduction of the special Grand Jury (431), Faulkner moves into the very center of the drama to be played out in the capture and death of "the Negro," Joe Christmas: "somehow the very sound of the two words [Grand Jury] with their evocation secret and irrevocable and something of a hidden and unsleeping and omnipotent eye watching the doings of men, began to reassure Grimm's

men in their own makebelieve" (432). The makebelieve is both
watched and controlled by external forces: "So quickly is man unwit-
tingly and unpredictably moved that without knowing that they
were thinking it, the town had accepted Grimm with respect and
perhaps a little awe and a deal of actual faith and confidence, as
though somehow his vision and patriotism and pride in the town,
the occasion, had been quicker and truer than theirs" (432). Grimm's
vision creates the occasion for the drama. He seems at first to direct
the spectacle, which quickly becomes a costumed production:

> After the sleepless night, the tenseness, the holiday, the suttee of
> volition's surrender, they were almost at the pitch where they
> might die for him, if occasion arose. They now moved in a grave
> and slightly aweinspiring reflected light which was almost as pal-
> pable as the khaki would have been which Grimm wished them to
> wear, wished that they wore, as though each time they returned to
> the orderly room they dressed themselves anew in suave and aus-
> terely splendid scraps of his dream. (432)

The townsmen become volitionless actors in prepared roles which
Grimm seems to control. Out of his dream of himself as defender of
his race and his culture, Percy Grimm creates an image of himself
and urges it upon the rest of his society who, morally weakened by
generations of race prejudice and stringent racial codes, acquiesce in
Grimm's mania for heroism and a starring role in the collective
make-believe. It is his will to which others bow. Eventually Grimm
supersedes the sheriff, and his men do wear the uniforms so that
the costumed drama is set.

However, just as he has the chance to perform what he wills (re-
capturing the escaped "nigger," Christmas), Percy Grimm becomes
himself a victim: "He was moving again almost before he had ever
stopped, with that lean, swift, blind obedience to whatever Player
moved him on the Board" (437). Grimm is himself manipulated: "He
seemed indefatigable, not flesh and blood, as if the Player who
moved him for pawn likewise found him breath" (437). Grimm is a
pawn moved by the Player, who like Doc Hines's "God" is a projection of the combined racial fantasy and hysteria long ingrained in
southern society. Grimm's external reality is make-believe that confirms his inner scenario. At the same time, that external reality is not

unique to Grimm; it is a set stage prepared by each generation of southerners who enact a drama whose precise author no one remembers (or needs to remember, so mindless has the rote participation become). Percy Grimm is controlled by a fatality and a fanaticism as extreme and extensive as those controlling Doc Hines, Joanna Burden, or Joe Christmas himself.

Percy Grimm, Gavin Stevens, Eupheus Hines, Joanna Burden, and Gail Hightower (and even Joe Christmas himself) all work out a "truth" about "the Negro" which they attempt to live by. Their individually perceived truths actually distort their perceptions of other areas of life and of themselves as human beings. Grimm's truth demands that the Negro know his place. After he castrates the dying Christmas with a butcher knife, Grimm gloats: "'Now you'll let white women alone, even in hell'" (439). His brutal act implicates all of those present and indicts all of Jefferson. Because aspects of his particular "truth" about the Negro coincide with the collective "truth" created by the community, Percy Grimm acts with community approval, or at least the force of the community behind him.

Faulkner builds the involvement of the community right from the discovery of the murder when members of the white Jefferson community not only begin "to canvass about for someone to crucify" (272) while the Burden house is still burning, but also labor "for that end whose ultimate attainment would leave them with nothing whatever to do" (273). From the beginning the crowd, women included, want a victim. Even before the chase, the men appear caught up in "something terrible and eager and impotent" (280); "It was as if the very initial outrage of the murder carried in its wake and made of all subsequent actions something monstrous and paradoxical and wrong, in themselves against both reason and nature" (280). Yet they persist; they do so because the excitement of the "emotional barbecue," the "Roman holiday" (273) of Joanna Burden's death at the hands of a nigger is more than enough to sustain them.

After Joe's capture and jailing, Hightower watches from his window and observes the atmosphere of the supposedly Christian town: "the doomed man in the barred cell within hearing of them and of the two other churches, and in whose crucifixion they too will raise a cross. 'And they will do it gladly. . . . Since to pity him would be to admit selfdoubt and to hope for and need pity them-selves. They will do it gladly, gladly. That's why it is so terrible, terri-ble, terrible'" (348). Though he is not necessarily anticipating a lynching per se, Gail Hightower is expecting a crucifixion. Joe Christmas will die—a victim—in order to preserve Jefferson as it is. Hightower knows from his personal experience that the town is ca-pable of "insult and violence upon those who like them were created by the same God and were driven by them to do that which they now turn and rend them for having done it" (345). By means of the accretion of such details, Faulkner prepares for the community's par-ticipation in Joe's death.

Moreover, Faulkner focuses on the other men accompanying Grimm on the final chase. As these men follow Grimm into the "stale and cloistral dimness" of Hightower's house, they bring with them "something of the savage summer sunlight which they had just left" (438). Grimm's companions reflect the savagery which en-gulfs them all, not Grimm alone. Faulkner adds more detail to the image: "It was upon them, of them: its shameless savageness. Out of it their faces seemed to glare with bodiless suspension as though from haloes" (438). In the image the mixture of good and evil, the confusion of heavenly and satanic references connect all the men to the grotesque act that follows.[23] The potential for evil within each of the men, Grimm included, becomes a probability as they enter the house, and a fact once Grimm actually commits the deed.

Like the men themselves, readers can become confused in follow-ing the ideology behind the action. Faulkner plays upon that confu-sion; he causes them to dread and expect the outcome. In the final moment when Grimm has carried out the horrible southern punish-ment, castration, readers may recoil from the act itself and from their own part in the mass excitement of the preceding events. The pat-tern may be much like that of the lone man who "stumbled back into the wall and began to vomit" (439).

And yet the fatal scene in Hightower's kitchen does not end there.

---

23 W. M. Frohock discusses Percy Grimm's relation to the rest of the mob in the con-texts of the literature of the Renascence and Faulkner's different emphasis. *The Novel of Violence in America* (2nd ed.; Boston: Beacon Press, 1957), 157–58.

It concludes with an image of Joe's rising (despite Grimm's reference to hell) and being transformed into legend:

> He just lay there, with his eyes open and empty of everything save consciousness, and with something, a shadow, about his mouth. For a long moment he looked up at them with peaceful and unfathomable and unbearable eyes. Then his face, body, all, seemed to collapse, to fall in upon itself, and from out the slashed garments about his hips and loins the pent black blood seemed to rush like released breath. It seemed to rush out of his pale body like the rush of sparks from a rising rocket; upon that black blast the man seemed to rise soaring into their memories forever and ever. They are not to lose it, in whatever peaceful valleys, beside whatever placid and reassuring streams of old age, in mirroring faces of whatever children they will contemplate old disasters and newer hopes. It will be there, musing, quiet, steadfast, not fading and not particularly threatful, but of itself almost serene, of itself alone triumphant. Again from the town, deadened a little by the walls, the scream of the siren mounted toward its unbelievable crescendo, passing out of the realm of hearing. (439–40)

Joe's face, triumphant and serene, rises and soars into the memories of all those present as a reminder not of his crime but of theirs. Waggoner calls his death "a kind of metaphoric ascension," which "constitutes a rebuke of the community, a measure of its sin of racial arrogance and of its corruption of Christianity from a religion of love and life to one of hatred and death."[24] In death the complex duality of Joe Christmas continues. The "truth" of Joe's death as "Negro" which Faulkner seems to advance is that it means both redemption and depravity.

None of the men will escape the memory of Joe's face, connected symbolically to the scream of the siren, which signals the end of the community pageant just as it had signaled the beginning or the lifting of the curtain when it was heard screaming out at the old Burden place after the discovery of Joanna's body. The siren at its crescendo moves beyond the range of hearing but not out of the realm of knowing or consciousness of its continuing existence, so that its sound suggests Joe's apotheosis after death. What the men will experience along with the image of Joe's face is guilt. Hence the Christmas-Grimm story is transformed into an explanatory myth of the or-

24 Waggoner, *William Faulkner,* 107, 108.

igin of modern guilt in Jefferson. Grimm may be the racist extremist among them, but he acts out their collective fear and fantasy: to brutalize the nigger for his deception of the community and his attack upon the white woman by making him recognize his inferiority.

When Hightower confronts the self that he has created in the wake of the fine storytelling by the Negro woman, Cinthy, he makes an observation about heroes which addresses Joe's final transformation, and Percy Grimm's dilemma (essentially the dilemma of all the major figures). Hightower surmises that the "'fine shape of eternal youth and virginal desire . . . makes heroes'" and that "'the doings of heroes border so close upon the unbelievable that it is no wonder that their doings must emerge now and then like gunflashes in the smoke, and that their very physical passing becomes rumor with a thousand faces before breath is out of them, lest paradoxical truth outrage itself'" (458).

A problem not confronted by Faulkner in asking the reader to accept Joe's meteoric rise to canonization as "hero" and "Negro," who endures life and death in the South and the modern world, is the underdevelopment of the black side of the divided world. For example, Joe's death asserts the efficacy of love and piety in defeating the forces of degradation. One feels free to assume, therefore, that Joe obtains these virtues along with his acceptance of "blackness," since he has not shown any prior inclination toward them. Yet if these virtues are, in fact, characteristic of black life in Jefferson, then they are not revealed as such in the course of the novel. If love and piety are simply *human* virtues, then their assumption alone without the acceptance of "Negro" should be sufficient to affirm Joe's spiritual ascendancy. But because of Faulkner's presentation, these virtues seem insufficient in themselves, and are inexplicably linked to the black world. Seemingly he assumes that the reader understands the nature of the black South, yet his primary agent for revealing that side of the South, Joe Christmas, never shows any understanding of it. Faulkner does not portray, what are apparently for him, the salient features of the black portion of the divided world to which Joe finally gravitates. He provides but a few glimpses of that world, and those primarily during Joe's tense encounters with blacks after the murder.

The problematic area for Joe is identity, not race. Faulkner, after all, has insisted that the novel's ultimate tragedy is Joe's not knowing who or what he is. In *Light in August* race is the vehicle for exploring the modern problem of identity,[25] but Faulkner specifically presents Negro as an abstraction. If the novel stems from Faulkner's increasing awareness of the dilemmas and ambiguities of complex modern relationships (emotional, economic, political, or social) and a corresponding need to simplify them to comprehensible terms, then *Light in August* does not seem convincing in its presentation of Joe's acceptance of blackness because Faulkner reveals so little of Joe's interior responses and feelings. This criticism is not to suggest that the novel lacks power; rather, it is intended to suggest that Faulkner does not penetrate Joe's psyche, be it white or black.

Light in August does not delve into "Negro" consciousness of self as "Negro"; nor does it present Joe Christmas as a black man.[26] Joe's characterization encompasses a level of abstraction and generalization which undermines his humanity, no matter whether he is black or white. Joe is almost purely a symbolic persona in what appears at least on the surface to be a realistic novel. Arguing that Joe's very lack of individualization is a part of Faulkner's thematic message evades the issue. Sympathetic involvement with Joe as a person, a human being in trouble, is virtually impossible for most of the plot, so that certainly there is none with him as "Negro" toward the conclusion. Consequently, the immensity of his private dilemma and his agony does not come through to the reader. And because Faulkner does not penetrate the black world, his presentation of Joe's turmoil seems false. Joe's choice between the races (though symbolic in terms of the larger identity issue) is not much of a choice at all. His death as "nigger" does not lead to transcendence, despite the symbolic language Faulkner uses to describe it.

In the final analysis, it seems that one way of approaching Faulkner's emphasis on the unreality of Joe's life and death is to consider the whole as a fantasy with only the veneer of a realistic novel. By

25 Gwynn and Blotner (eds.), *Faulkner in the University*, 118.
26 There seems to be little justification for Howe's contention, "If in the earlier work the focus of attention is on the white man's feelings toward the Negro, now there is a shock of discovery—a discovery of the Negro *as Negro*, blackness stripped to pariah." "William Faulkner and the Negroes," 362–63.

fantasy I mean something closer in kind to the early morality plays rather than to modern absurdist dramas. Faulkner suggests the comparison himself in his Virginia conferences when he pointed out that the naming of characters in *Light in August* is "out of the tradition of the pre-Elizabethans, who named their characters according to what they looked like or what they did"; Faulkner concludes his observation by saying, "it came from the—my memory of the old miracle plays, the morality plays in early English literature."[27]

My suggestion is that in *Light in August* there is the creation of symbol and significance which does not duplicate the ordinary aspects of life but which celebrates the extraordinary in a manner reminiscent of the miraculous scenes from the Old or New Testament and of the allegorical dramas of abstract concerns making up the miracles and moralities. To be sure, Joe is first of all a fictional creation of Faulkner's. But further, within the context of Yoknapatawpha, he is purely a creature of fantasy. He himself creates part of the personal fantasy of his life, while a nexus of sociohistorical, cultural, and religious forces creates the remainder of the fantasy for him. Joe's transcendence into legend immediately upon his death is a myth by which Faulkner attributes meaning to the death of a self-created and socially created "nigger." Like the expected allegorical aspects of the morality play, each part of the final action is imbued with meaning. What meaning Faulkner assigns is not as important as his affirmation of meaning inherent in the actions themselves not simply as an appendage to the process.

In this novel Faulkner seems much more interested in the process by which the individual is made, almost forced, to become "Negro" in order to "save," in a secular and religious sense, himself and the society creating the "Negro," than he is in *the Negro as Negro*. Although the idea is more fully developed than in *The Sound and the Fury*, it remains basically the same one informing the portrayal of the Gibsons in that novel. While *Light in August* does appear to be a

---

27 Gwynn and Blotner (eds.), *Faulkner in the University,* 97. In pointing to this statement, I am not suggesting a detailed structural comparison between extant miracle cycles or medieval moralities. If Faulkner worked at all with either in mind, he would have done so only in that very general way in which accumulated or absorbed knowledge finds expression in "new" independent creations.

result of Faulkner's preoccupation with "Negro," it seems to be especially an outgrowth of his interest in problems of consciousness of self and society generated by the dual southern world and by the black presence in the white South. "Negro," then, functions as a conception which impinges upon the internal and external realities of whites, just as it does in an embryonic form in *Soldiers' Pay;* however, a major difference between *Light in August* and Faulkner's earlier novels is his underlying assumption that both the complex factors shaping conceptions of self and the variable ways of perceiving experience are complicated further by racial tensions within a dual culture. Reality becomes even more subjective and fragmented in his imaginative world, even though there may be no attendant development in his overall stylistic complexity. But in *Absalom, Absalom!* Faulkner fuses subjective realities in an intricate aesthetic design which depends upon "the Negro" as a forceful abstraction in southern life.

CHAPTER V

Absalom, Absalom!

And those of us who were born in Mississippi . . . who have continued to live in it . . . simply because we love Mississippi and its
ways and customs and soil and people; who because of that love
have been ready and willing at all times to defend our ways and
habits and customs from attack by the outlanders who we believed
did not understand them, we had better be afraid . . . that we
have been wrong; that what we had loved and defended not only
didn't want the defense and the love, but was not worthy of the
one and indefensible to the other.
Letter to the Memphis *Commercial Appeal,* March 26, 1950,
Essays, Speeches and Public Letters, p. 204.

Implicit in Joe Christmas' apotheosis into a myth of the Negro that
bears meaning for the white South is Faulkner's reliance on an aesthetic fusion of realism and symbolism related to the black and
white worlds of his South. Dilsey Gibson in *The Sound and the Fury* is
the forerunner of this fusion, but the meaning of her existence remains inaccessible to the whites in that novel. With his focus on the
white world in *Light in August,* Faulkner explores, on literal and
symbolic levels, what the Negro means to whites publicly and pri-
vately. He emphasizes that racial tension distorts and damages the
lives of modern southerners, who inherit their conceptions of the
Negro from both cultural and familial pasts. In *Absalom, Absalom!*
(1936), Faulkner resumes the theme of the necessary apotheosis of

society's "nigger" into myth, and he achieves an artistic plateau in transforming the raw materials of his familiar world into fiction.

The Negro in this novel is not one myth, but a series of myths by which Faulkner shows how the Negro fits into the white world, either figuratively or imaginatively, and suggests the missed possibilities of his belonging in that larger world. A white world is created in broad historical outline and sufficient psychological depth to subsume the myths of the Negro, but that world fails, and the vision creating it is reduced to an emotional paralysis. Henry, son of Thomas Sutpen, and Quentin Compson, one of the narrators, are both catatonic figures at the conclusion of the novel; their condition is one result of their joint creation of Charles Bon as "nigger."

While abstraction in *Absalom* is similar to the pattern of abstraction in *Light in August*, it lacks any one representative figure as inclusive as Joe Christmas. The novel does not actively incorporate from the early sections any major black characters or characters thought to be black; neither does it initially appear to be concerned with race. Nevertheless, Faulkner explores the meanings of "Negro" from multiple historical and narrative perspectives by means of a unique interaction between past and present, between participants and tellers. He presents, against a backdrop of slavery, the Civil War, and their dual legacies, the chronicle of Thomas Sutpen as he is imaginatively understood by four narrators alive during the early days of the South's modernity. Faulkner's narrative strategy (accretion of materials filtered through layers of time and individual perceptions), combined with the absence of a black narrator among the four rendering the story, retards any immediate recognition of the Negro's significance. Because of a complex interplay between the Sutpen legend and the four narrators, the novel relies in general upon an oblique apprehension of "fact" and "truth," and upon the discernment that neither is absolute. The treatment of the Negro follows this pattern.

The narrative design recalls the fragmented monologues of *The Sound and the Fury* that work together although occurring in ostensible isolation; however, *Absalom* lacks a central vision of black life comparable to that provided by Dilsey Gibson and the Easter sermon, and its Negro is not antithetical to a deteriorating white world. In fact, though the resolution of the novel depends upon the existence, and firm acceptance, of two southern worlds that must never be joined by interracial marriage, *Absalom, Absalom!* paradoxically plays down the polarities of black and white life. As a result of both narrative strategy and thematic ideas, the conception of Negro is more fragmented and illusive than the social definitions in *Light in August*, yet more intense than the myths of custom and manners in *The Sound and the Fury*. Accordingly, the Negro in *Absalom, Absalom!* seems analogous to Hugh Kenner's assessment of an ideal Faulkner novel: "dense with specificity but difficult to specify."[1]

Yet a black presence dominates this work as it does perhaps no other Faulkner novel. Nowhere else is it so apparent that the Negro is an abstract force confounding southern life both past and present even while, paradoxically, stimulating much of that life and art. A symbolic statement of this idea is suggested by the action of Miss Rosa Coldfield, one of the participants and narrators, who attempts to lift the weight of a coffin bearing the body of Charles Bon (whom she has never seen either alive or dead) in order to ascertain whether Bon's body is inside. In essence, she desires to validate Bon's existence from sense evidence; she is determined to know whether he is flesh or an imaginative construct. However, Miss Rosa is forced to apply not the most expedient sense mechanism (that is, sight), but the only one available to her, and that one is insufficient for such a determination. She recalls:

> I tried to take the full weight of the coffin to prove to myself that he was really in it. And I could not tell. . . . Because I never saw him. . . . There are some things which happen to us which the intelligence and the senses refuse . . . occurrences which stop us dead as though by some impalpable intervention, like a sheet of glass through which we watch all subsequent events transpire as though in a soundless vacuum, and fade, vanish; are gone, leaving us immobile, impotent, helpless; fixed, until we can die.[2]

Her metaphorical language suggests the white South confronted with the Negro—its morally paralyzing abstraction. No one sense test is capable of validating the existence of the Negro; even sight

1 Kenner, *A Homemade World*, 205.
2 William Faulkner, *Absalom, Absalom!* (1936; New York: Modern Library, 1964), 151–52.

has traditionally been insufficient, not only because blacks who are visibly white in color exist, but also because the white southerner has persistently refused to see the Negro, despite living and dying with the effects of his presence. In Rosa Coldfield's mind Charles Bon becomes "the abstraction which we nailed into a box" (153), but like the Negro in the South, the abstraction in this novel refuses to remain in a box. Bon is always flesh *and* imaginative construct, both of which excite the rational and creative faculties of the narrators. His presence, whether seen or felt, is an inescapable reality. He becomes, like the Negro in general, the metaphorical embodiment of all that is invisible in southern life.

The Negro supplies the central focus—albeit the most illusive— and the major tensions in the pre- and postwar South of Thomas Sutpen, a man born into the poor white mountain culture of western Virginia. Sutpen formulates a grand design for living, labors to execute his design, and comes extremely close to completing it. A synopsis of the Sutpen legend without the inclusion of the Negro is a story without motivation or significant meaning. In June of 1833, Sutpen mysteriously arrives in Jefferson and resolutely establishes a plantation, wealth, and respectability. He marries Ellen Coldfield, whose sister Rosa is one of the principal narrators, and he begets two children, Henry and Judith. Prior to the outbreak of the Civil War, Sutpen's son renounces his birthright and departs from Sutpen's Hundred, his father's plantation, with a University of Mississippi classmate, Charles Bon, a New Orleans creole and Judith Sutpen's intended husband. The two youths do not reappear until the end of the war when Henry shoots Bon at Sutpen's Hundred and then disappears. Sutpen himself returns from the war a decorated colonel but poverty-ridden (having lost both his only son and most of his plantation). He salvages a mile of land, consorts with a poor white, Wash Jones, and opens a small store with Jones as partner; he is eventually killed by Jones.[3]

3 A possible source for Wash Jones is a character by the same name, Washington Jones, which is shortened to Wash Jones, in "Ananias," a short story by Joel Chandler Harris. I do not wish to emphasize the coincidence of the name; however, the situation is suggestive. Wash Jones, a lower class white, is the one-time overseer of Col. Benjamin Flewellen's plantation who becomes rich after the war and is the colonel's chief creditor. Jones is a commission merchant who forecloses the mortgage on the Flewellen plantation and thereby becomes the owner. See Joel Chandler Harris, "Ananias," in *Balaam and His Master* (Cambridge: Riverside Press, 1891), 113–48.

The addition of the Negro lifts the Sutpen legend from a flat canvas and transforms it into a powerful vehicle of individual will, of complex human motives and emotions, of personal, social, historical interaction. For example, the Negro shapes, motivates, and determines Sutpen's design from the beginning. As a boy of thirteen or fourteen, Sutpen approached the big house on a Tidewater Virginia plantation with a message from his father to the owner Pettibone. He is thwarted in his attempt to deliver the message (and see the inside of the house) by a black house slave who turns Sutpen away from the front entrance and directs him to the back door. The black man becomes the "monkey nigger" in Sutpen's accounts, and the boy Sutpen becomes "the boy-symbol."

According to Sutpen's own version which he gave to General Compson, Quentin's grandfather and Sutpen's sole confidant if not friend: "He had never thought about his own hair or clothes or anybody else's hair or clothes until he saw that monkey nigger, who through no doing of his own happened to have had the felicity of being housebred in Richmond maybe, looking at them and he never even remembered what the nigger said, how it was the nigger told him, even before he had had time to say what he came for, never to come to that front door again but to go around to the back" (232). Sutpen regards the incident as a denial of his individual value by the "monkey-dressed nigger butler" and the plantation owner and the system he represents. This recognition forces Sutpen to evaluate personal and societal estimations of human worth. He has an epiphany regarding himself and his society:

> (Not the monkey nigger. It was not the nigger anymore than it had been the nigger that his father had helped to whip that night. The nigger was just another balloon face slick and distended with that mellow loud and terrible laughing so that he did not dare to burst it, looking down at him from within the half-closed door during that instant in which, before he knew it, something in him had escaped and—he unable to close the eyes of it—was looking out from within the balloon face just as the man who did not even have to wear the shoes he owned, whom the laughter which the balloon held barricaded and protected from such as he, looked out from whatever invisible place he (the man) happened to be at the moment, at the boy outside the barred door in his patched garments and splayed bare feet, looking through and beyond the boy, he

himself seeing his own father and sisters and brothers as the owner, the rich man (not the nigger) must have been seeing them all the time—as cattle, creatures heavy and without grace, brutely evacuated into a world without hope or purpose for them, who would in turn spawn with brutish and vicious prolixity, populate, double treble and compound, fill space and earth with a race whose future would be a succession of cut-down and patched and made-over garments bought on exorbitant credit because they were white people, from stores where niggers were given the garments free, with for sole heritage that expression on a balloon face bursting with laughter which had looked out at some unremembered and nameless progenitor who had knocked at a door when he was a little boy and had been told by a nigger to go around to the back.) (234–35)

Compressed into Sutpen's epiphany are all the tensions of caste and class struggles in the South, the brutalization of human beings, black and white, inherent in the slave system, and the moral ambiguities engendered by social problems. In closing the door, the "monkey nigger" opened the boy Sutpen to a painful awareness of the inner dynamics of southern life. Because of his action, the "monkey nigger" balloons up larger than life; he becomes at once a visible metaphor for social reality and an allusive, invisible presence in the boy's life. The incident precipitates Sutpen's rejection of his family's simple way of life in favor of all that the "monkey nigger" held the door against. As a result, Sutpen desires not simply wealth, but slaves and a plantation, all the trappings designating the value of a human being in the antebellum world. He realizes, " 'You got to have land and niggers and a fine house to combat them with' " (238). He works for the indisputable, visible and material, right to assert his superiority over the "monkey nigger" and his kind, whom he further abstracts by means of the "balloon" metaphor. The intent, then, of Sutpen's design is to elevate himself into the landed gentry against whom no "nigger" can close doors.[4] Sutpen feels compelled

---

4 Ilse Dusoir Lind calls Sutpen's motivation "the negative impetus upon which his entire design was constituted." "The Design and Meaning of *Absalom, Absalom!*," *PMLA*, LXX (December, 1955), 887–912; rpt. in Wagner (ed.), *Faulkner: Four Decades of Criticism*, 291. Or as Vickery puts it, "At the core of Sutpen's design and of the social structure of the South is the concept of the 'Negro' as an inferior being or social pariah." *The Novels of William Faulkner*, 97–98. And Melvin Seiden terms the Negro both "the silent unseen antagonist in the savage familial and social struggles that are

to prove that he is better than the "monkey nigger," and of course better than his owner. His self-image, personality, and life goals are shaped by the "monkey nigger," who is ultimately the personification of an entire society.

Some critics see Sutpen's eventual downfall as inevitable because he substitutes his personal design in place of an existing moral and social order.[5] However, Sutpen's encounter with the "monkey nigger," as well as the resulting self-debate, leads to a recognition of his design as one complying with the existing social order and the prevalent moral order. In fact, because Sutpen's way of life is so in tune with the dominant southern way, his personal history can become one, in Quentin and Shreve's construction, with the progress of southern history. The South's retreat and surrender, in particular, are imagined as occurring simultaneously with the failure of Sutpen's design (347–50). What Sutpen violates in accepting the principles of the "monkey nigger" and Tidewater Virginia is precisely a personal code of honor and moral behavior derived from the social and ethical order of his own mountain society. Albeit more primitive, the mountain society has values that are more in keeping with the purer dictates of the human heart to which Faulkner frequently refers.

Sutpen's "design" is preeminently a drive toward completion of self. The irony is that he strives to complete an image of self constructed from models alien to his "natural" state. His failure is ordained from the moment he loses touch with that inner self which

waged in the book" and "that fearful abstraction of the Southern mind . . . of immense importance in determining the fate of the Sutpen family." "Faulkner's Ambiguous Negro," *Massachusetts Review*, IV (Summer, 1963), 675–90. Lind, Vickery, and Seiden all point to the significance of the Negro to Sutpen's design.

Cleanth Brooks, in clarifying Sutpen's relationship to the southern planter class, labels Sutpen one "possessed by an almost malignant demon of abstraction," because "the irony of Sutpen's life is . . . that he was fixated on his image of the plantation which for him was an abstract idea—since he had had scant participation in it as lived experience—and that . . . Sutpen pursued an ideal of gracious ease and leisure with a breathless ferocity." "Thomas Sutpen: A Representative Planter?" in *William Faulkner: Toward Yoknapatawpha and Beyond* (New Haven: Yale University Press, 1978), 300, 296. Although Brooks does not make this point, the "abstract idea" (Sutpen's image of the plantation) is intricately connected with the Negro.

5 See, for example, Elisabeth S. Muhlenfeld, "Shadows with Substance and Ghosts Exhumed: The Women in *Absalom, Absalom!*," *Mississippi Quarterly*, XXV (Summer, 1972), 289–304.

demands of the aware individual a completing of self. That initial loss of harmony is irreparable. Sutpen strives vaingloriously to complete Pettibone and his kind. Like those slave owners who upon seeing the African's black skin deemed him animal rather than human, Sutpen settles for appearance rather than substance as an estimate of human worth. Thus, he is essentially always about the business of duplication instead of true self-completion. Because an imitation is, by its very nature in the usual order of things, less than the original, his process of duplication, despite its unfinished state, can never attain the status, albeit morally questionable, of the model.

Moreover, because Sutpen's understanding of completion is literally a body fitted to the prescribed mold of Pettibone's kind, his design has as its ultimate goal the heir, the male figure, a replica of the model, which is again Pettibone's kind, not Sutpen himself but the Sutpen who is an imitation of Pettibone. Therefore, Charles Bon appears as a threat to Sutpen's design, not simply because Bon himself by virtue of his blood from the slave class cannot duplicate Pettibone's model, but primarily because Bon exercises such a powerful hold over Henry Sutpen, the heir apparent to Sutpen's design, that Bon possesses the potential of becoming himself a Pettibone, a model for Henry instead of that one laid out for Henry by his father.

Because he bases his design mimetically upon a negative, unwholesome model, Sutpen lacks the stature of a man who has failed in the attempt to achieve something magnificent or laudable. He, finally, can be reduced to a pathetic old man literally killing himself by trying to place his seed in an available and remotely acceptable (that is, "white") female in order to produce a male child. His ultimate failure is not a tragedy; he has denied his "central I-Am" (139). Yet because Faulkner presents that poignant boy-symbol and with it the possibility of harmonious self-completion, he shows in that moment of faulty, but private, individual choice, Sutpen's lost potential. Though haunted by the boy-symbol and the "monkey nigger," Sutpen understands neither the proportions nor the implications of his choice. Consequently, he never knows that his choice of Pettibone as a model for self-completion corrupts the boy-symbol and signals waste and loss, which ultimately justify the laughter of the balloon-face "monkey nigger."

The Negro provides the modern survivors of Sutpen's South (specifically three of the four narrators: Jason Compson, his son Quentin, and Rosa Coldfield) with one means of approaching, understanding, and living with their past, the collective southern past, if they prove capable of reading the meaning of Sutpen's story. The opportunity that the story represents for them is reminiscent of an observation on race relations made by Joel Chandler Harris: "The problems of one generation are the paradoxes of a succeeding one, particularly if war, or some such incident intervenes to clarify the atmosphere and strengthen the understanding."[6]

The four narrators help to clarify the novel's intricate design and to determine the Negro's relationship to the verbal design, because narrating or "telling" in this novel is a way of establishing the concrete reality of narrator-characters, both those participating in the legend and those attending its re-creation. At the same time, the lack of "telling" by the blacks who inhabit the world of *Absalom, Absalom!* reduces them to an involved dependency upon the actual narrators, and their lack of "telling" functions, inversely, to establish the abstract quality of their existences.

In the narrative development, counterpoint reappears, an extension of Faulkner's way of seeing and rendering anticipated by *Soldiers' Pay.* However, in *Absalom, Absalom!* it is not a matter of thematic counterpoint; the Negro neither presents a different perspective of the function and meaning of life, nor voices, by either word or deed, opposition to the decay of moral and spiritual values. Counterpoint occurs in its most sophisticated and artistic form in that the method entails a multiplicity of narrators at work creating themselves in a concentric design and creating out of themselves experience from a common stockpile of "facts." It is only by means of their individual perceptions that specific portraits of blacks occur.

6 Joel Chandler Harris, "Free Joe and the Rest of the World," in *Free Joe and Other Georgian Sketches* (New York: Charles Scribner's Sons, 1887), 1.

In discussing *Absalom*, Faulkner has pointed out, "every time any character gets into the book, no matter how minor, he's actually telling his biography—that's all anyone ever does, he tells his own biography, talking about himself, in a thousand different terms, but himself."[7] Faulkner's notion of character is especially relevant to the narrators in the novel, because each one is a character telling about himself in the process of telling about the Sutpens.

Mr. Compson suggests the narrative method in his attempt to grasp the reality of the legend from "a few old mouth-to-mouth tales" and "letters without salutation or signature" exhumed "from old trunks and boxes and drawers" (100–101). He recognizes that fragments from the past are "almost indecipherable, yet meaningful" (101) and that the "living blood and seed" of people "in this shadowy attenuation of time" (101) create him and generate his absorption in their lives. He tells and sees both as himself, a sardonic and disillusioned southerner (an image which results from narrative voice rather than his actions), and as his father, General Compson, who had been Sutpen's lone intimate among the Jefferson townspeople, and whom the reader gets to know from his reported voice as much as from his interactions with the Sutpens. Although Mr. Compson understands the magnetic nature of the past and its inhabitants, he cannot explain the legend, not even in his own version, because "something is missing" (101). He has "the words, the symbols, the shapes themselves," but they remain "shadowy inscrutable and serene" (101). When, for example, he spins the tale of Charles Bon and his octoroon, Mr. Compson withdraws his final approval of it because his rational vision that "something is missing" is at odds with his creative impulse. He emphasizes Faulkner's main point: there is no true design for the telling, only the most expedient, practical, or communicative in a given situation.

Mr. Compson's acknowledgment that "something is missing" reminds the reader that *Absalom* is not about Sutpen, Charles, Henry, Judith, but about Rosa, Mr. Compson, Quentin, and Shreve—about those inhabitants of a modern world (which is growing increasingly more complex) as they reveal and react, by force of habit, inclina-

7 Gwynn and Blotner (eds.), *Faulkner in the University*, 275.

tion, curiosity, or need, to aspects of themselves which appeared long ago, were illuminated, and faded only to be dusted off and held up to the light at the time of an impending personal crisis. At the same time, "something is missing" also suggests the absence of the Negro from the narrators' initial formulations of the past. The Negro's place in the whole pattern is revealed gradually.

The device of gradual revelation is a significant aspect of *Absalom*. It is a device having cultural origins in the method of the oral story-teller who gradually reveals more not necessarily about his story—though that in itself may be refined again and refracted anew as each thread unfolds—but about the narrator himself as storyteller.[8] This process is the lesson in craftsmanship at the heart of Sherwood Anderson's turning back Faulkner's first-written tall tale. It perhaps explains as well why the gradual revelation of details in the Sutpen legend does not lead closer to understanding the meaning of the legend, or of the Negro in it. The intellectual construction of the Sutpen story leads to an emotional experience. The method leads closer to the narrators, and to the personal beliefs and obsessions which cause them to create and solve the Sutpen legend in a manner suitable to their individual characters.

The methods of the four narrators suggest that the work is more about process than end result. An integral part of that process has to do with the old abstraction, "Negro," almost as a matter of course, because the experience created is "southern" first of all in its specifics. "Negro" is the one major element that operates with some degree of consistency both in the legend and in the narrative reconstructions. Even more intriguing than a pattern, identified by Vickery, in which the "narrators see each of the characters in the legend as confronted by a human being who is also a Negro,"[9] is one in which the narrators themselves create the Negro. Each of the narrators invents his own "Negro" in defining himself and in expressing the limits of his imagination, personality, and humanity. Miss Rosa creates Clytie, Sutpen's slave daughter, and the "wild niggers" who

---

8 For a useful discussion of this process, though in the context of humorous tales, see John Donald Wade, "Southern Humor," in W. T. Couch (ed.), *Culture in the South* (Chapel Hill: University of North Carolina Press, 1935), 616–28.
9 Vickery, *The Novels of William Faulkner*, 92.

build Sutpen's Hundred. Mr. Compson draws the New Orleans octoroon and her son Charles Etienne St. Valery Bon. Quentin and Shreve imagine Charles Bon and his mother Eulalia. They have the most complete authorial control over the Negro because his actual physical presence is the least documented by "facts" from the past. All of their projections operate to enrich the significance of "Negro" as both abstraction and metaphorical reality in *Absalom, Absalom!*

The most readily apparent example of this process is Rosa's construction of the "wild niggers," Sutpen's original band of slaves. She sees them as "his band of wild niggers like beasts half tamed to walk upright like men, in attitudes wild and reposed" (8). This recurring image of the slaves grounds her telling in a recognizable, if distorted, reality which attempts to wrench a personal moral order out of confusion. Because Sutpen is her private demon, she makes the "wild niggers" an extension of Sutpen himself and synonymous with Sutpen's Hundred. The "wild niggers" are her stage props and stage crew, just as they are the actual work horses who clear the virgin land and build Sutpen's plantation.

Beginning with the early segments of Rosa's narrative, the "wild niggers" become an obsessive presence in her mind. She calls them "a herd of wild beasts that he [Sutpen] has hunted down single-handed because he was stronger in fear than even they were in whatever heathen place he had fled from" (16). She imagines their origins "in the mud" of a "dark swamp" (24) in order to complete her construction of their bestiality. The slaves, according to Rosa, are from a nameless "heathen place," which is a "much older country than Virginia or Carolina but it wasn't a quiet one" (17); her statements link Sutpen to the same place reference. She perceives Sutpen's "wild niggers" as his mirror reflection (somewhat similar to Quentin Compson's view in *The Sound and the Fury* of blacks as an "obverse reflection of the white people" they live among). The appearance of the blacks becomes the irrevocable proof of Sutpen's nature ("anyone could look at those negroes of his and tell," 17). They are imaginative projections of Rosa's feelings about Sutpen, about blacks, and about Sutpen's Hundred.

The "wild" slaves as an imagined reality in the novel serve to create psychological atmosphere and mood similar to the function of natural landscape or setting in some nineteenth-century novels (such as the moors in *Wuthering Heights*). For instance, every appearance of Sutpen in Jefferson is colored by Rosa's association of him with his "wild" slaves and land. Her version of the arrival of the Sutpen family for Sunday church services is typical of her perception of Sutpen's union with his slaves: "this is my vision of my first sight of them which I shall carry to my grave: a glimpse like the forefront of a tornado, of the carriage . . . and on the front seat the face and teeth of the wild negro who was driving, and he [Sutpen], his face exactly like the negro's save for the teeth (this because of the beard doubtless)—all in a thunder and a fury of wildeyed horses and of galloping and of dust" (23).

Rosa's words, "my vision of my first sight," are aptly chosen, because it is apparent that she is shading a real incident with her own peculiar way of seeing Sutpen. Not only does the driver look exactly like Sutpen, but he is also "the wild negro," Sutpen's surrogate who emerges from "the mud of that swamp" (24) to drive the horses too fast and to beat them for running away. He is, like his owner, more devil than man.[10] The mere sight of him "in a thunder and a fury" extends the demonic atmosphere and adds density to Rosa's dramatic rendition of the legend.

Rosa's conception of Sutpen's slaves as an extension of their owner seems related to a picture of Sutpen's house as assuming his personality and character. Mr. Compson draws the comparison while reporting that Sutpen's slaves deserted the plantation to follow the Union troops:

> [It was] as though his [Sutpen's] presence alone compelled that house to accept and retain human life; as though houses actually possess a sentience, a personality and character acquired, not so

10 Moreover, because the driver is dressed "like a performing tiger in a linen duster and top hat" (24), he repeats the pattern of imagery used for Sutpen's "monkey-dressed nigger butler"; both of these black servants are reduced to animal level by the perceptions of whites. In a discussion of the animal as a metaphorical vehicle, Joseph Reed observes that the "bestial reductions of the slaves . . . also works in the opposite direction, to comment upon the masters' degraded view of human chattel and their own bestiality." *Faulkner's Narrative*, 154. However, Miss Rosa makes Sutpen a beast out of a different awareness of his role in relation to the slaves. They do not dehumanize him (by his ownership of them); they serve as an extension of Sutpen's self, a concrete representation of Sutpen's demon nature.

much from the people who breathe or have breathed in them inherent in the wood and brick or begotten upon the wood and brick by the man or men who conceived and built them—in this house an incontrovertible affirmation for emptiness, desertion; an insurmountable resistance to occupancy save when sanctioned and protected by the ruthless and the strong. (85).

Mr. Compson's analogy is clear; Sutpen created his living space and it responded to him by reflecting his personality.[11]

Mr. Compson's narrative, gathered primarily from his father, General Compson, but also from other members of the community, serves as a corrective to Rosa's presentation of Sutpen and his niggers. The townspeople and Mr. Compson are by no means egalitarian when it comes to the slaves, yet they do not evidence Miss Rosa's fanatical view of the blacks. Mr. Compson admits that there is a legend of the wild blacks, and that there is some element of "truth" contained in the legend:

So the legend of the wild men came gradually back to town, brought by the men who would ride out to watch what was going on, who began to tell how Sutpen would take stand beside a game trail with the pistols and send the negroes in to drive the swamp like a pack of hounds; it was they who told how during that first summer and fall the negroes did not even have (or did not use) blankets to sleep in, even before the coon-hunter Akers claimed to have walked one of them out of the absolute mud like a sleeping alligator and screamed just in time. The negroes could speak no English yet and doubtless there were more than Akers who did not know that the language in which they and Sutpen communicated was a sort of French and not some dark and fatal tongue of their own. (36)

The view of blacks in this less emotional account is still that of primitive men close to instinctual communication with animals and nature. Mr. Compson suggests, however, that the "wild men" were the mental projections of Sutpen created by the town, as well as

11. Mr. Compson's equating of Sutpen with his house and Rosa's creation of the "wild beasts" recall a convention of the gothic novel which depicts the haunted castle and its environs as representative of the owner's psychological state. That Sutpen's house assumes his personality seems directly related to the tradition, whereas the portrait of his slaves as "wild beasts" seems to be an inversion of the convention because the mind they best reflect is Rosa's rather than Sutpen's.

Miss Rosa, in its ignorance. Sutpen's slaves, for instance, are not using a heathen tongue, but are West Indians (either from Haiti, as is Sutpen's first wife, or from Martinique, like the architect) speaking a French dialect. Akers and the other townspeople, Rosa included, fill in the shadowy outlines of the real Sutpen slaves with information that appeals to their imaginations.

Other versions balance Miss Rosa's misplaced emphasis, although they, too, maintain that Sutpen's relationship with his slaves is different from that traditionally depicted between master and slave. For example, General Compson told his son that "while the negroes were working Sutpen never raised his voice at them, that instead he led them, caught them at the psychological instant by example, by some ascendancy of forbearance rather than brute fear" (37). Sutpen, in other versions besides Miss Rosa's, worked intimately with his twenty slaves, all of them "plastered over with mud against the mosquitoes and . . . distinguishable one from another by his beard and eyes alone" (37). The others, too, stress the primitive nature of Sutpen's slaves and actively mythologize them into an integral part of the community legend. But they do not resort to calling them wild beasts; for example, one quite civil reference is to Sutpen's "crew of imported slaves" (though the added comment is that Sutpen's "adopted fellow citizens still looked upon [his slaves] as being a good deal more deadly than any beast," 38). And another reference terms the slaves "human," even while exalting their animal instincts: "human beings who belonged to him body and soul and of whom it was believed (or said) that they could creep up to a bedded buck and cut its throat before it could move" (40).

These views reflect a matter-of-fact depiction of blacks as slaves and whites as masters; they are glimpses of the minds of individuals thoroughly in tune with the dominant social practices. But these other observations of Sutpen's slaves are secondary; Rosa's vision of the "wild niggers" dominates the narrative. Her image of the "wild" slaves emanates from a mind out of joint with reality; it becomes a metaphor which the reader comes to identify, not with the demon Sutpen, but with the dark mysterious force at the center of southern life that, as portrayed in *Absalom, Absalom!*, the southerner creates out of an unfailing reserve of self-flagellation and mental anguish.

When Rosa takes fragments of the actual and then envisions an extensive, self-satisfying whole, she duplicates in microcosm the process of the novel as a whole. She projects precisely what she has made herself see and what she has come to feel after forty-five years of static rage. Her imaginative process is a more exaggerated version of Quentin's, Shreve's, and Mr. Compson's (as well as of the collective mind of Jefferson, because Rosa's view of Sutpen's slaves is but an exaggeration of the one held less rigidly by the town). In transforming Sutpen's human chattels into an extension of his demon-self and into a synonym for his plantation, Rosa reveals the narrow limits of her personality and her humanity. Her picture of the slaves is the most revealing in what it reflects about Rosa herself, her mental condition and conflicting emotions.

Rosa's creation of the "wild niggers" is related to the larger meaning of the novel. It brings into the open the hysterical image of blacks which undermines the rational appeal of Charles Bon, Sutpen's elegant mulatto son, who seeks paternal acceptance without regard to race. Because of its intensity and obstinacy, Rosa's distorted vision of the slaves pervades the entire novel and operates as a psychological backdrop for Sutpen's rejection of Bon and his black blood. The struggle between father and son can take on colossal proportions with far-reaching historical and cultural consequences in part because Rosa has so effectively created a forceful, larger-than-life, demonic landscape for the action.

Rosa's personal vision lays bare the threat facing Quentin Compson. Her resolute grasping after poetic impressions as valid "fact" has isolated her from meaningful contact with the contemporary world; the process of conjecture for her is grounded in emotion. Her life is a projection of her warped inner reality. She is an old woman, deranged and obsessed, for whom the present is only an access route to the past and the future is nonexistent. Her condition, clarified by the Negro she invents, suggests the fate awaiting to engulf Quentin.

Significantly, then, in "seeing" and "telling" the Sutpen legend, the narrators must attend to their individual perceptions, and they have as well to attend to the Negro. Faulkner uses the Negro in various manifestations, such as Rosa Coldfield's "wild niggers," as a constant by which the narrators' conceptual structuring of the legend can be judged. Societal values and individual attitudes are made clear, even in a diffused state, because the narrators all base their conceptions of the Negro upon factors in their external world. Essentially, they present not only themselves, but also their society as well. Their world becomes known and accessible by means of the Negro that they conjure up.

Absalom, Absalom! is, in a convoluted way, developed at least partially around (and out of) the white man's reaction to socially established images of the Negro, as opposed to contextually determined conditions involving individuals who happen to be black. The Negro is primarily a social rather than a racial concept, just as it is in *Light in August*. Faulkner weaves his design, as ambitious as Sutpen's own, around various perceptions of the Negro's place in the southern world. The images presented of blacks are the creations of whites who are in a position to "see" the Negro—that is, to observe him but not necessarily to know him with insight; however, all of the images are carefully woven into the larger portrait of a society.

The minor representations of blacks fall into three categories which reflect the reality of a divided world, or what Faulkner calls in this novel "a country all divided and fixed and neat with a people living . . . all divided because of what color their skins happened to be and what they happened to own" (221). The first category involves "field niggers," those who planted and worked the land. An example is the Tidewater plantation blacks whom Sutpen saw as "regiments of niggers with white men watching them [who] planted and raised things that he had never heard of" (227).

The second category is made up of body servants who physically maintained the whites and the aristocratic pretensions of plantation society. These are the blacks who drive carriages, serve food, carry packages, hold umbrellas, adjust cushions, shout "Christmas gift," or perform countless other services, "endless repetitive personal offices" (221–22). In a long digression Faulkner presents a picture of the black grooms of white university students who are:

> only in the surface matter of food and clothing and daily occupa-
> tion any different from the negro slaves who supported them—the
> same sweat, the only difference being that on the one hand it went
> for labor in the fields where on the other it went as the price of the

spartan and meager pleasures which were available to them because they did not have to sweat in fields: the hard violent hunting
and riding; the same pleasures: the one, gambling for worn knives
and brass jewelry and twists of tobacco and buttons and garments
because they happened to be easiest and quickest to hand; on the
other for the money and horses, the guns and watches, and for the
same reason; the same parties: the identical music from identical
instruments, crude fiddles and guitars, now in the big house with
candles and silk dresses and champagne, now in dirt-floored cabins with smoking pine knots and calico and water sweetened with
molasses. (97–98)

This juxtaposition of masters and servants provides an example of
blacks who come under the second category.

The third category involves the "ingrates," those well-treated,
seemingly "content" slaves who did not appreciate their "good"
treatment; for example, the Coldfields' two servants who were free
and paid wages "in return for which they had been among the first
Jefferson negroes to desert and follow Yankee troops" (84). However, even the "content" slaves are chattel sustaining the plantation
tradition by means of their labor.

All of these anonymous blacks in the world of *Absalom, Absalom!*
represent the paradox of "a soil manured with black blood from two
hundred years of oppression and exploitation until it sprang with an
incredible paradox of peaceful greenery and crimson flowers" (251).
These blacks appear to specify the paradoxical nature of the southern world constituting the novel, and at the same time their presence insinuates that the Negro's "place" is not simply subordinate to
whites, but that its dimensions are different, smaller by comparison.
Their presence suggests that the Negro is intended, in the proper
order of things, to serve the white man. Generally, it is this provincial view of "Negro" growing out of his social functions in the South
to which Sutpen adheres in formulating his design and to which the
narrators conform in creating the legend.

The more significant configurations of the Negro also stem from a
notion of blacks as servers, but in a more involved way. These include the wild, primitive blacks ("beasts of burden") who helped to
build the South's agrarian tradition (Sutpen's "wild niggers," for example); the "big house" slaves who in their inflated position carried

out the plantation's domestic chores (the "monkey-dressed nigger butler"); and the exotic women of color who became involved in interracial liaisons (both Eulalia Bon, Sutpen's first wife, and Charles Bon's octoroon, for instance). These blacks serve in a dual way: physically as a matter of natural course given the order of the southern world, and psychologically as inspiration for either activity or imagination. The "monkey nigger" serves as the white man's butler, but he is also the means by which the class conflicts and moral complexities inherent in the slave system are made meaningful in the narrative development. As Sutpen's first wife, Eulalia Bon was to serve a purpose in Sutpen's design by helping him to accumulate wealth and offspring, but instead her more meaningful function in the novel is psychological rather than physical. Her shadowy presence inspires Shreve and Quentin to invent a fine tale of revenge and suffering with Eulalia as the avenging angel-victim. Whether it is the "wild niggers" building Sutpen's Hundred, or the New Orleans octoroon bringing feminine grace, beauty, and pleasure, or Clytie serving as companion and keeper of the house, Faulkner depicts the Negro in *Absalom* as making a necessary contribution to the white world. Even the young Charles Etienne Bon provides Judith Sutpen, barren spinster, with the opportunity to become a surrogate mother, and by means of maternal obligations to soften her hardened exterior.

The major black figures emerge out of conceptions of blacks accommodating themselves to the white world. They evolve out of two rather conventional literary images of blacks; significantly both involve mixed-bloods. One is the free mulatto during pre- and postwar years who, envisioned as searcher, occupies the tragic "no-place" in southern life; the second is the slave daughter of the master who remains on the family plantation in an ambiguous maternal role as member and non-member of the family. In fact, all of the blacks in *Absalom* who are given names and delineated in detail are mixed-bloods, or presumed to be by the narrators. Clytie and the Bon men are representative characters. Whereas the Bons are obviously crucial to the resolution of the novel, Clytie reveals the most about Faulkner's art and the Negro in this novel.

Throughout the work, Clytie is the felt black presence that pervades the South. She embodies this presence much more than Charles Bon, the abstraction who is made "nigger" in order to complete the pattern of the legend. She, more than any other character, reveals the ultimately inexplicable nature of human motivation. Both the tension of her existence and the obscurity of her involvement in the lives of others manifest Judith Sutpen's metaphor: " 'You get born and you try this and you dont know why only you keep on trying it and you are born at the same time with a lot of other people, all mixed up with them, like trying to, having to, move your arms and legs with strings only the same strings are hitched to all the other arms and legs and the others all trying and they dont know why either except that the strings are all in one another's way'" (127). The process of life, as Judith describes it, means that Clytie is irrevocably connected to other individuals, so that her very existence, not merely her actions, affects and is affected by others.

Clytie is symbolically and literally a fusion of the two worlds of southern life; yet like the other mixed-bloods in the novel, Clytie does not experience the black world as a black person. Nonetheless, like Charles Bon and his son, Charles Etienne St. Valery, Clytie knows what it is to be treated as "nigger" in the white world. She is, for instance, greeted differently by Sutpen upon his return from the war. Instead of the kiss and touch he gives Judith, Sutpen merely "looked at Clytie and said, 'Ah, Clytie'" (159). And Rosa Coldfield, who recoils from Clytie's "nigger" touch on the day of Charles Bon's death, has from childhood "instinctively" feared her and shunned objects she has touched (140).

Bereft of all that gave meaning to black life, Clytie is denied access to the only two institutions available to blacks—the family and the church. She is deprived of the sustenance of communal identity. Clytie is far from Elnora, the hymn singing cook-housekeeper of *Flags in the Dust* who is also the daughter of the white master. In addition, she is unlike Dilsey, who so staunchly endures with the help of the religion of the black community. Clytie is neither hymn-singing nor church-going; for her there is no refuge in a private life as a black person. Her lack of affiliation with the black world illuminates Faulkner's development of the black housekeeper-servant in his fiction, for in portraying Clytie he moves away from the character type as it appears in the earlier novels.

Clytie is an attempt at a more innovative, and psychologically modern, character, though she is a less successful characterization than Dilsey. Dilsey is conventionally a more imposing and prominent character; however, Faulkner creates her primarily as a character who obviously and symbolically elucidates and embodies theme. Despite the innate nobility with which Faulkner endows her, Dilsey is and remains the Compsons' servant who on Easter Sunday emerges phoenix-like encompassing the extant possibility for human survival with dignity and love. But Clytie is not simply a member of the Sutpen household. She is a member of the family, marked, according to all accounts, with the Sutpen face. She has no connections with individuals who are not Sutpens; her mother, one of Sutpen's original band of slaves, is not even given to her as a memory in the novel. Legally chattel before the war and an institution afterwards, Clytie is a coffee-colored Sutpen. She is defined mainly in terms of her Sutpen heritage and blood. In terms of traditional place and order, then, she is where she belongs. There are no possibilities suggested for her living apart from Sutpen's Hundred; she has no alternative form of existence.

Clytie's singular position may initially suggest a realistic mode of characterizing blacks; however, the fictional method by which she achieves life, primarily through Rosa Coldfield's imaginative construction of her, is a break with conventional portraits. Clytie's presence, unlike Dilsey's, is not intended to provide ethical certainty or emotional comfort. Instead it evokes the duality of human nature. Whereas Dilsey lacks close personal identification with any member of the Compson family, Clytie is closely identified with both her half-sister Judith and her father Sutpen. Described as "at once both more and less Sutpen" (140), she is an extension of the physical selves of Judith and Sutpen, as well as an imaginative projection by the narrators of some dark essence of the Sutpen being. Whatever reality Clytie attains as a character, she attains in the minds of her narrators, but that reality primarily reinforces their central visions. All that readers know of her is filtered through the consciousness of others.

Clytie is preeminently a silent, shadowy presence which, imaginatively delineated, assumes force in the lives of those around her. Her position in the narrative challenges conventional mechanisms contrived for identifying family members and for defining the "central I-Am" of the individual. At the same time, her personal responses to her status as a slave-daughter and to her world go unarticulated by words or gestures. What Clytie herself feels remains a mystery, despite the fact that she is one of the participants in the Sutpen legend who survives into the novel's present.

Clytie is no more enigmatic, however, than the other inhabitants of Sutpen's legendary world. As a pivotal character in the legend and in the reconstruction of it, Clytie reveals Faulkner's innovative handling of experience, characterization, and motivation. Yet she is the character frequently passed over in discussions of the novel.[12]

Although Judith and her brother Henry are described as "that single personality with two bodies" (9–10), the description is even more fitting when applied to Clytie and Judith. Except for physical coloring, the two could be twins. They appear together initially, and from that first appearance, they are twin, silent, and calm figures of strength. Both frequently are called "inscrutable," "impenetrable," and "serene." As they age, they become more alike and gradually assume the status of living legends in the Jefferson community. Clytie is the shadowy complement of her white sister. In a sense, she is Judith's double, functioning to complete Judith's fragmented self. For example, after Bon's death Judith tells the Compsons that she will not commit suicide because "'somebody will have to take care of Clytie'" (128). Yet because a Clytie who needs Judith's care is never visible, the reader may speculate that she is instead another part of Judith's own self which cannot be denied as long as there is some external manifestation of it. Symbolically, Clytie represents both Judith's inner self and the social environment in which Judith functions and exists.

Because Clytie is Judith's complementary part, she follows out to conclusion the pattern of action established by Judith and supported by the two of them while Judith lived. She pays for Judith's and

---

12 See, for example, Backman, *Faulkner: The Major Years*, 109; George E. Kent, "The Black Woman in Faulkner's Works with the Exclusion of Dilsey," *Phylon*, XXXV (December, 1974), 430–41; Elisabeth S. Muhlenfeld, "Shadows with Substance and Ghosts Exhumed: The Women in *Absalom, Absalom!*" *Mississippi Quarterly*, XXV (Summer, 1972), 302.

Charles Etienne's tombstones, raises Jim Bond, and harbors Henry. Her final action, the burning of the Sutpen mansion, is a desperate attempt to preserve the house and the family from violation by outsiders because the Sutpens have earned that right. As she observes, "'Whatever he done, me and Judith and him have paid it out'" (370).

Clytie, as black twin to Judith, becomes a subtle statement of the oneness of humankind. The common bonds of temperament, interests, duty, and affection unite the two women in a sisterhood that transcends race. Their relationship is a more sustained and meaningful version of that between Henry and Charles. Because Clytie and Judith relate to each other as "womenfolk" first, then as "daughter" and "sister," they partly escape the racial burden placed on their brothers. Their personal relationship provides a model of sibling cooperation and harmony in the novel, and by extension it suggests the possibility of a different order of social interaction between races in the South.

The limits of Clytie's existence are set not by her slave status but by her identity as a Sutpen, and in that regard she is also Judith's counterpart. The two are locked into a narrow existence; uncomplaining and stoical, they make the best of their lives. They share the *"indomitable woman-blood"* (153) and are as close to survivors as Faulkner comes in *Absalom, Absalom!* They accept a life without joy or frivolity; they assume the burden of existence and accept each other as human beings. Consequently, Clytie and Judith emerge together as the most admirable characters in the novel. Certainly, Faulkner endows them with dignity and endurance, with pity and love—the virtues he esteemed most and identified with his beloved mammy, Caroline Barr, whom Clytie alone of his black women characters resembles in both physical and personal characteristics.[13]

13 In "Mississippi," Faulkner describes Callie Barr as wearing an "immaculate white cloth-headrag" and sitting with "the five-year-old white child [Faulkner's daughter Jill] in a miniature rocking chair at one side . . . and the aged Negress not a great deal larger, in her chair." Meriwether (ed.), *Essays, Speeches and Public Letters by William Faulkner,* 40. John Faulkner also remembers Callie as "small and black (she weighed only ninety-eight pounds), standing unobtrusively to the side, always with a head rag and some sort of bonnet on, a snuff stick in her mouth, and always in a fresh-starched dress and apron and soft-toed black shoes." *My Brother Bill,* 48. Another brother, Murry, adds to the portrait by recalling Callie as "small, neat, completely unselfconscious, a kerchief wrapped just so about her little gray head and her lower lip

Clytie, then, has no life clearly defined as her own, but the implication is not that she has none because she is "black" and "slave," but rather that she has none because she is, like Judith, "daughter" and "sister." The familial demands extend beyond their individual existences, just as they do for their brother Henry, but the restrictive burden of family is less severe for them.

The relationship between Clytie and Judith is critical to the meaning of the novel because it achieves a level of communication and kinship across social barriers, but also because it precipitates the destructive cycle of Charles Etienne St. Valery Bon, the son of Charles Bon and a New Orleans octoroon. Charles Etienne's story moves the Sutpen legend into the postwar period and enlarges its social significance. Clytie prevents the boy on his first visit to Sutpen's Hundred from playing with a black youth. Even after Charles Etienne arrives to live on the plantation, he is not allowed to have contact with blacks or whites. By watching him with a "brooding fierce unflagging jealous care" (200),[14] Clytie virtually isolates him from members of either race. It seems that as long as she can keep him on Sutpen's Hundred, Clytie believes that she can protect Charles Etienne from the knowledge that barriers exist between races and that those barriers are socially real. She knows that the plantation is a self-contained world sustained only by Judith and herself, for whom racial distinctions no longer have social meanings. Clytie—not Judith—is the boy's guardian and protector. She becomes "the fierce, brooding woman" (197), who in a "curious blend of savageness and pity, of yearning and hatred" (198) cares for Charles Etienne. Clytie's efforts, nevertheless, lead the boy to a much more painful and premature

---

filled with snuff." "The Wonderful Mornings of Our Youth," in James W. Webb and A. Wigfall Green (eds.), *William Faulkner of Oxford* (Baton Rouge: Louisiana State University Press, 1965), 11. Similar to Callie Barr, Clytie Sutpen is a tiny, neatly dressed woman whose "body just grew smaller and smaller" (215). Shreve envisions her when she is over seventy: *"a dried-up woman not much bigger than a monkey and who might have been any age up to ten thousand years, in faded voluminous skirts and an immaculate headrag . . . smoking a clay pipe"* (Faulkner's italics, 214).

14 The drawing of Clytie in these terms suggests Callie Barr, whose sharp tongue and watchful presence have been recorded by the Faulkner brothers. John, for instance, reveals, "I am sure when our time comes, she will demand an explanation even of Him if we are denied admittance Up There, and as sure that her staunch vehemence will bring for each of us at least a resigned 'All right, Let them in.'" *My Brother Bill,* 52.

knowledge: the awareness that the barriers between races and individuals are psychically real. Sutpen's legacy to his rejected black son, Charles Bon, is thus perpetuated in the next generation.

When taken abruptly from the "padded and silken vacuum cell" (199) of his life in New Orleans, Charles Etienne encounters the "gaunt and barren" (197) world in which Clytie and Judith live. Once he crosses the threshhold of Sutpen's Hundred, his "very silken remaining clothes, his delicate shirt and stockings and shoes which still remained to remind him of what he had once been, vanished, fled from arms and body and legs as if they had been woven of chimaeras or of smoke" (197). His silk clothing is symbolic of more than the white world;[15] it represents the hedonistic, cosmopolitan world of New Orleans, "where pigmentation had no more moral value than the silk walls . . . and the rose-colored . . . shades, where the very abstractions which he might have observed—monogamy and fidelity and decorum and gentleness and affection—were as purely rooted in the flesh's offices as the digestive processes" (199). The city with less rigid racial codes and more indulgent mores forms a contrast to the closed world of the plantation and Jefferson. Compared to the delicate, mythical existence Charles Etienne experiences in New Orleans, Sutpen's Hundred (as introduced by Clytie and the denim jumper) is the abrasive, "actual world"; Mr. Compson envisions Charles Etienne as "produced complete . . . in that cloyed and scented maze of shuttered silk as if he were the delicate and perverse spirit symbol, immortal page of the ancient immortal Lilith, entering the actual world not at the age of one second but twelve years, the delicate garments of his pagehood already half concealed beneath that harsh and shapeless denim cut to an iron pattern and sold by the millions—that burlesque of the Sons of Ham" (196).

When Clytie covers Charles Etienne with a coarse denim jumper, she burdens him with a second existence without explanation. She begins the process of alienating the boy and destroying the world he knows to be real. Neither Clytie nor Judith recognizes that Charles

---

15 Nilon limits the interpretation of Charles Etienne's clothing—the silk to the white world and the denim to the black. *Faulkner and the Negro*, 95.

Etienne is a "lonely child in his parchment-and-denim hairshirt" (204). He is irretrievably an outsider—alien to Sutpen's Hundred and lost to the two women who, in their simplicity, fail to realize that he does not understand (indeed has no basis for understanding) his new life, the two women themselves, or their awkward protective gestures. Clytie and Judith, for all their strength and endurance, are extremely naïve woman; they are, like their father and brother, independent country people. Thus, they are unable to see the beginning of Charles Etienne's dividedness. Their naïveté and ignorance compound the boy's problem with identity and place. Both women fail Charles Etienne; he, in turn, fails them and himself. These joint failures emphasize the reciprocal nature of the tragedy resulting from defining human beings in terms of race and caste. The tragedy is social as much as private; it affects whites as well as blacks.

Charles Etienne rejects the white world, which he mistakenly perceives as being peopled by the two stern, shadow women, Judith and Clytie, who seem to need only each other. By their inability to express their feelings for him in terms he can clearly comprehend, his two Sutpen "aunts" propel Charles Etienne into a constant battle with racial barriers, which are mainly presented as social restrictions against open, public display of interracial activities. (He is reminiscent of Joe Christmas, who is similarly propelled by a restrictive Puritan disciplinarian into a rootless, embattled life.)

Charles Etienne marries a "coal black and ape-like woman" who "existed in that aghast and automaton-like state" (205). He makes his wife, a "black gargoyle" (209), an external projection of his black self. He abuses his wife's humanity, even though Faulkner presents her as physically grotesque and inhuman ("resembling something in a zoo," 209). By his treatment of the helpless woman, he dehumanizes himself and alienates himself from the rest of humanity. After a period of moving through a series of cities and towns as if driven by a fury, Charles Etienne returns to Sutpen's Hundred, rents a parcel of land on shares, and lives in an old slave cabin on the place. Nonetheless, he does not penetrate the black world. He remains as alienated from it as he is from his black wife and the Sutpen women.

Clytie and Judith succeed in making not race alone Charles Etienne's albatross, but in making his Sutpen blood heritage (figuratively Sutpen's Hundred) his private prison. The two women do not intend to alienate their ward; both love him according to their capacities as human beings. However, the problem for Judith and Clytie is that as Sutpen "twins" they do not need words, or even gestures, to communicate with each other. The two women, Clytie in particular, mistakenly rely upon Charles Etienne's sharing their kinship and their *"rapport of communal blood"* (159); he cannot. His blood is strongly rooted in the foreign environment of New Orleans, and the silken cocoon of his mother's existence there, even though his exact orientation to the city disintegrates along with the physical disintegration of his silk clothing. Their inability to understand different worlds and perceptions is akin to their father's; Sutpen, insulated from a larger experience of life, could not understand Charles Bon or his way of seeing the world.

Clytie's fierce guardianship of Charles Etienne corresponds to mythical allusions evoked by her name, "Clytemnestra." According to Mr. Compson, Sutpen "named her himself" (61), though perhaps "he intended to name Clytie, Cassandra, prompted by some pure dramatic economy not only to beget but to designate the presiding augur of his own disaster, and . . . he just got the name wrong through a mistake natural in a man who must have almost taught himself to read" (62). Mr. Compson seems inaccurate here because Clytie is not so much Cassandra, mad prophetess of doom, as she is Clytemnestra, fiercely maternal wife-mother figure of vengeance. (Rosa Coldfield appears to be the Cassandra figure.)

The allusions to the name "Clytemnestra" seem appropriate, if not precisely so. Clytemnestra is wife-mother, who out of complex motives brings disaster to her children and herself by willfully exacting revenge for her daughter Iphigenia's death. Despite the reference to Clytie's "fierceness," she does not seem to be a personality motivated by a personal fury (such as revenge). However, the mythical Clytemnestra is responsible for Cassandra's death; their two visions of reality and duty fatally conflict. Clytie is related to the mythical Clytemnestra in this sense, because she finally thwarts Rosa's efforts to control the Sutpens by taking charge of Henry. She burns the mansion rather than have Rosa remove Henry and assume responsibility for him. Shortly thereafter, Rosa dies, somehow mortally wounded by her last encounter with Clytie. Clytie's action represents a kind of dual expiation on the part of both races in the South and particularly on the part of the planter class. In burning Sutpen's Hundred with herself and Henry inside, Clytie destroys the two surviving Sutpens, who along with Judith are similar to the mythical Orestes in their attempts to expiate the old crimes, their own sins and those they inherit from their father.

While Mr. Compson speculates that Sutpen intended to name Clytie "Cassandra," he and Quentin actually describe Rosa Coldfield as "Cassandralike." Quentin sees her as having "an air Cassandralike and humorless and profoundly and sternly prophetic out of all proportion to the actual years even of a child who had never been young" (22). And before his explanation of Clytie's name, Mr. Compson speaks of the "Puritan righteousness and outraged female vindictiveness [in which] Miss Rosa's childhood was passed, that aged and ancient and timeless absence of youth which consisted of Cassandralike listening beyond closed doors" (60). Shreve, too, refers to Rosa as "Cassandra" in his description of her peculiar relationship with Sutpen: "instead of a widowed Agamemnon to her Cassandra an ancient stiff-jointed Pyramus to her eager though untried Thisbe" (177).

In linking both Clytie and Rosa to Cassandra, Faulkner reiterates that his characters flow into one another and merge with historical or mythological figures as well. The figurative association of Clytie with Rosa joins the Negro to the white southerner who is the most reactionary about race. Their union is tense because, in Rosa's words, they are "open, ay honorable, enemies" (157). Clytie and Rosa— the daughter and the sister-in-law, the slave and the "not-wife"— share a relationship with Sutpen that is as tortured as that of either Clytemnestra's or Cassandra's to Agamemnon.

When Rosa and Clytie confront each other on the stairs of Sutpen's Hundred after Charles Bon's murder, they participate in one of the most dramatic, and revealing, scenes in the work.[16] At the mo-

---

16 One measure of the importance of the encounter between Rosa and Clytie is the care Faulkner took in revising the scene. According to Gerald Langford, there were four stages of revision apparent in Faulkner's presentation of the meeting between the two women. The manuscript shows that much of Faulkner's rewriting of the

ment of their meeting, Rosa sees Clytie as an extension of Sutpen and as her own twin sister because of their joint connection to him: "the two of us joined by that hand and arm which held us like a fierce rigid umbilical cord, twin sistered to a fell darkness which had produced her" (140). Though Rosa, like Charles Etienne, rails against the order of things in her world, she recognizes the complex nature of human interconnectedness (thereby accentuating one of Faulkner's major themes). She describes herself as well as Clytie as "sentient victim" and admits the private, mysterious connection to Sutpen, who is Clytie's biological father and who gives Rosa life (that is, provides her with a *raison d'etre* which in its negative capacity links her even more closely to the negative aspect of Sutpen's indefatigable and undefeated will to duplicate himself). At the same time, Rosa acknowledges the connection between two individuals who share a deeply felt experience: "*we seemed to glare at one another not as two faces but as the two abstract contradictions which we actually were, neither of our voices raised, as though we spoke to one another free of the limitations and restrictions of speech and hearing*" (138). Rosa and Clytie are yoked so that their differences are grossly exaggerated, even though the very intensity of their union destroys ordinary impediments to communication. This yoking of "abstract contradictions" is central to the structural and thematic progress of the novel. For instance, it is one way of approaching Quentin and Shreve as creators, or Henry and Charles as friends. It is a process repeated in the narrative shared by the southerner and the Canadian as they attempt to form meaning and significance out of the legend.

Rosa's meeting with Clytie is a central scene because it reverberates all the tensions between black and white, between classes and races that have been used to define the South and to establish the major concerns of the novel. One of the most starkly honest scenes in the Faulkner canon, this meeting probes the psychological and cultural realities of race and kinship. It suggests all of the dramatic

---

scene involves emphasizing the dramatic impact of the confrontation. Specifically, Faulkner added to the section in such a way as to extend the significance of the touch, of Clytie's coffee-colored hand on Rosa's white woman flesh. *Faulkner's Revision of "Absalom, Absalom!": A Collation of the Manuscript and the Published Book* (Austin: University of Texas Press, 1971), 29–31.

meetings which take place in *Absalom* (Sutpen and the monkey nigger, Charles Bon and Henry, even Shreve and Quentin). Superseded in intensity only by Quentin's encounter with Henry, it is the single extended narration of a confrontation between black and white in a work clearly dependent upon a series of such confrontations for meaning.

Rosa, in her moments of knowing, her "epiphany," encounters Clytie as "Negro" and "woman" but also, paradoxically, as "sister": *"we stood there joined by that volitionless . . . hand, . . . I cried 'And you too? And you too, sister, sister?'"* (140). Prior to this moment, Rosa has neither recognized nor accepted Clytie as Sutpen's daughter, sister to Judith and metaphorically sister to Rosa herself. Still, Clytie is not a person to Rosa. She is "nigger" and a sphinxlike presence invented by Sutpen solely to confound Rosa; she is *"the Sutpen face . . . already there, rocklike and firm . . . waiting there . . . in his own image the cold Cerberus of his private hell"* (136).

Clytie's presence reminds Rosa that she is cut off from significant areas of life, particularly from family participation, just as the Negro, symbolically represented by the "balloon face" and the "monkey nigger," serves to remind Sutpen of his poor-white origins. It is not only that Rosa is not a wife, but that finally she is not sister, daughter, aunt, or niece. She is and remains an outsider. Begrudgingly, Rosa recognizes her own inadequacies, Clytie's essential harmony with her world, and their psychological union. But she does so by making Clytie not merely like Sutpen, a demon, but the personification of all that has prevented her full participation in life. Clytie becomes an *"immobile antagonism," "that presence, that familiar coffee-colored face"* (137), which Rosa "sees" as both an object blocking her passage up the stairs and as a force confounding her entire life.

Clytie stands for Sutpen's continuing reality and his insult to the spinster who hurls herself into: *"that inscrutable coffee-colored face, that cold implacable mindless (no, not mindless: anything but mindless, his own clairvoyant will tempered to amoral evil's undeviating absolute by the black willing blood with which he had crossed it) replica of his own which he had created and decreed to preside upon his absence, as you might watch a wild distracted nightbound bird flutter into the brazen and fatal lamp"* (138). Clytie is the proof (and for the sight-oriented Rosa, the visible therefore incontrovertible proof) of Sutpen's sexual activity, in particular his mating with someone other than "wife," with someone more animal than human, with the "black willing blood" of one of the original "wild niggers." It is an insult to the spinster that Sutpen, who represented her one opportunity for marriage (here specifically sex and children), would "grace" *even* a *nigger* but would deny her. Thus, Sutpen himself, not Clytie, has condemned Miss Rosa to ignorance and blind, futile thrusting. Sutpen is, paradoxically, "clairvoyant," and Clytie is a "brazen and fatal lamp," while Rosa is "a wild distracted nightbound bird." For all their negative capacity drawn by Miss Rosa, Sutpen and Clytie symbolize vision and light for her. On the other hand, Rosa with ironic aptness sees herself as a sightless bird enmeshed in darkness and fluttering blindly into destruction.

Clytie's command, "'*Dont you go up there, Rosa*'" (138), causes Rosa to assert the authority of her race and the superiority of her position as white woman in the South: "'*Rosa?* . . . '*To me? To my face?*'" (139). Yet even while speaking the words, Rosa knows "*it was not the name, the word the fact that she had called me Rosa*" (139); Rosa believes that "*while we stood face to face . . . she did me more grace and respect than anyone else I knew; . . . to her of all who knew me I was no child*" (139). She infers that Clytie recognizes her as "woman," intuits her female urges and sexual drives. Perhaps Clytie alone, with her "brooding awareness and acceptance of the inexplicable unseen, inherited from an older and a purer race" (138), understands Rosa's frustrated sexual energy, understands that Rosa is denied access to marriage and familial intimacy (and in this instance specifically, denied access as well to the knowledge and experience of life and death she seeks in the upper regions of the Sutpen house).

Nonetheless, Rosa perverts the meeting into a racial confrontation; she is otherwise unable to cope with its implications (that is, Clytie as a Sutpen "belongs" at Sutpen's Hundred and has a natural place in the affairs of the family, whereas Rosa, though white, is relegated to a lower, nonprivileged status). Rosa's tactic reiterates the ultimate tragedy of the Sutpen legend: the son's meeting with the father is reduced to a racial confrontation; kinship, whether physical or spiritual, may be denied when one party is "Negro."

Clytie's hand on Rosa raises the specter of "nigger" violating racial barriers. Symbolically, the gesture duplicates the larger violation attempted, according to Quentin and Shreve, by Charles Bon, the "nigger" who desires to sleep not with the abstract "white woman," but with the individual "sister" and "daughter" (which Judith personifies). Rosa experiences *"a shocking impact . . . at that black arresting and untimorous hand on* [her] *white woman's flesh"* (139). Her response is automatic: *"'Take your hand off me, nigger!'"* (140). She retreats into the sanctity of race, and to the safety of racial epithets.

In this moment Rosa exposes the process by which the individual makes "nigger" a scapegoat; it is a microcosm of the larger societal process which the community acts out in *Light in August,* and it is a tableau extending Sutpen's treatment of his son Charles Bon to the conduct of an entire society. Rosa, in attempting to convert Clytie into "nigger" and the physical embodiment of all blackness, reveals her own duality and asserts herself as the flawed component of a flawed society. Clytie is, after all, more Sutpen than black and more Sutpen than woman, primarily as a result of Rosa's own imaginative constructions, which she has made "true" in the progress of the narrative. The two visible realities that Clytie embodies ("Negro" and "woman") are denied and rendered meaningless by her "Sutpenness," which is the true abstraction confronting and confounding Rosa on the stairs. *"Yes,"* Rosa declares, *"I stopped dead—no woman's hand, no negro's hand, but bitter-curb to check and guide the furious and unbending will—I crying not to her, to it; speaking to it through the negro, the woman"* (139–40).

Since Rosa believes that Clytie is most vulnerable because of her race and the social stigma it carries, she can deny her own egalitarian emotions and subvert her own compelling logic:

> There is something in the touch of flesh with flesh which abrogates, cuts sharp and straight across the devious intricate channels of decorous ordering, which enemies as well as lovers know because it makes them both— touch and touch of that which is citadel of the central I-Am's private own: not spirit, soul; the liquorish and ungirdled mind is anyone's to take in any darkened hallway of this earthly tenement. But let flesh touch flesh, and watch the fall of all the eggshell shibboleth of caste and color too. (139)

Rosa's perception is fleeting; her spoken word, "nigger," does not coincide with her internal analysis of the meaning of touch.

Although "touch" seems emblematic of larger possibilities for interracial contact, Clytie's touch is not an ambivalent gesture. Nor is Rosa's response ambiguous; Rosa means to issue her command in terms that carry the weight of social sanction. Rosa's response to Clytie is an overt expression of Sutpen's implicit response to Charles Bon. Sutpen's drama is an internal process not witnessed by the reader, yet the essence of his complex reaction to Bon is mirrored symbolically in the extended development of Rosa's physical and emotional response to Clytie. For all of the characters, touch crystallizes the "eggshell shibboleth of caste and color" and the taboos against interracial union; touch creates, too, the necessity for southern custom and law against miscegenation (specifically here because the "secret" of the legend is solved in terms of miscegenation—actual miscegenation for the father Sutpen and intended by the son Charles Bon). Nonetheless, southern interracial restrictions, according to one theme of this novel, are not about preventing touch but rather about affirming all the negative implications of touch when they serve the ends of white society.

Clytie's reactions to this meeting are not provided; she remains as nonverbal as she has been throughout the novel; however, her presence, as a mixed-blood placed within the Sutpen family, suggests that either race or kinship must be denied if caste and color are to continue to sustain fixed meanings in a changing world. Clytie's involvement in the lives of other characters forwards the conclusion that in order to avoid self-destruction, and perhaps ultimately social disintegration, bonds of kinship on every level must be honored, even if they exist across racial lines (or most especially when they do, as Faulkner suggests both with the resolution of *Absalom, Absalom!* and with a later novel, *Go Down, Moses*). This idea of kinship, most apparent in the portraits of Clytie and Charles Bon, is, in one sense, an insightful development of the idea of family (both white and black) Faulkner first employs in *Flags in the Dust* and uses more intensively in *The Sound and the Fury*; it partakes, too, of the conception of "blood" and racial definitions from *Light in August*. Blood and family become in *Absalom, Absalom!* human kinship and interconnection[17]—larger abstractions—which Faulkner presents as confused

17 Faulkner threads the theme of human kinship and interconnection throughout the narratives. Several of the most prominent statements of this theme are: Judith's

and conflicting, but by means of them he aims toward a more comprehensive way of portraying the divided world of his South.

Clytie's meeting with Rosa is a physical reality; however, "the Negro" is a psychological reality, as encountered by Shreve and Quentin. The Negro supplies crucial, missing links of information to the two narrators most concerned with creating significance out of a seemingly hopeless conundrum of symbols. Like all the major figures in the legend, Shreve and Quentin have their epiphanies regarding the Negro; their major one has to do with Charles Bon as "Negro." These two narrators slowly unfold the tangled web of black-white interrelations in the southern family and the complex ways by which southern whites recognize and treat the black presence in their lives. With the inventions of these two narrators, the formal significance of the Negro in the novel becomes clearer.

The Negro in *Absalom, Absalom!* becomes an artistic convention used as a bridge linking fragments of information and redeeming the narrators' failures of moral insight and creative imagination. The Negro is presented as an abstraction which, in its extreme, forces the formulation of the white southerner's self and social conceptions, and ultimately impinges upon his history and art, especially on the process of creation. An observation made by General Compson during Sutpen's tracking down of the runaway French architect, and passed along by Mr. Compson, embodies an image applicable to the general presence of the Negro in the novel: "the shadows they cast taller than they were at one moment then gone the next and even the trees and brakes and thickets there one moment and gone the next though you knew all the time that they were still there because

---

idea that people are all "hitched to one another by strings" (127); Mr. Compson's belief that in assimilating the fragments of the past "we see dimly people . . . in whose living blood and seed we ourselves lay dormant and waiting" (101); Quentin's notion that no thing or person happens once "but likes ripples . . . on water after the pebble sinks, the ripples moving on, spreading, the pool attached by a narrow umbilical water-cord to the next pool" (261); and the omniscient narrator's view that Quentin and Shreve are "connected . . . in a sort of geographical transubstantiation by the Continental Trough" (258), that they are "two of them, then four" (345) because they are compounded in Henry and Charles, so that ultimately "it was not even four now but compounded still further since now both of them were Henry . . both were Bon" (351).

you could feel them with your breathing, as though, invisible, they pressed down and condensed the invisible air you breathed" (245). Even though throughout the novel the reader never knows the Negro as a major character, his felt presence has "pressed down and condensed the invisible air" breathed by the major characters and by the narrators. Thus the main attempts to give meaning to the Sutpen story by solving the mystery of individual motivation are constricted by the Negro.

Although Quentin and Shreve provide the major solution, they are preceded by Mr. Compson, who makes the first attempt to solve the mystery by resorting to the Negro to impose some rationale, meaning, or truth upon the known assortment of facts. Mr. Compson, a provincial Mississippian with an ironical view of the world (from antiquity to the present), is especially attracted to details involving Charles Bon's plaçage with a New Orleans octoroon and with the sophisticated, jaded way of life mirrored by the New Orleans episodes. He attempts to explain it all in terms of "the existence of the eighth part negro mistress and the sixteenth part negro son, granted even the morganatic ceremony—a situation which was as much a part of a wealthy young New Orleansian's social and fashionable equipment as his dancing slippers—was reason enough, which is drawing honor a little fine even for the shadowy paragons which are our ancestors born in the South and come to man- and womanhood about eighteen sixty or sixty one" (100). His pieces of the puzzle do not add up to a coherent picture ("It's just incredible. It just does not explain," 100), yet he persists in his speculation that the Negro, in the form of the octoroon "wife" and son, is at the root of the Sutpen family tragedy. Just for an instant, he has an insight that may be closer to a "truth" than his other theorizing: "Or perhaps that's it: they don't explain and we are not supposed to know" (100).

Quentin also interprets the Sutpen tragedy in terms of the Negro. He, along with Shreve, gradually finds meaning or "truth" by attributing the taint of "Negro" blood to Thomas Sutpen's unacknowledged son, Charles Bon. Quentin's conclusion suggests that Sutpen accepts an abstract view of "Negro" (and the view involves the menial, dehumanized functions set for slaves in plantation society), rather than the reality of Charles Bon as a polished, socially accomplished, cosmopolitan youth; and thus it is suggested that the problem of the Negro precipitates Sutpen's undoing.

Because often "the major burden of the southerner has been the Negro,"[18] both in the external southern world and within his own conscience, it is not surprising that *Absalom, Absalom!* turns in upon the Negro. "Almost no novel," Frederick Hoffman writes about southern fiction, "is without its Negro somewhere. But the main concern is with the problem itself. It becomes [in modern literature] a political problem and it has always been a moral one. The political and moral aspects of it conflict with each other; the tension is severe, leading to violence and death."[19] *Absalom* adds another dimension to the problem Hoffman outlines: the Negro as an aesthetic problem, as frame for the aesthetic design. What is a suggestion in *Light in August* becomes readily apparent in *Absalom*. In a sense, then, the Negro in this novel is one of the major elements of the fiction and the fiction-making process.

Southerners have traditionally in life and in literature brought physical and psychic havoc upon themselves and the South by the use they have made of the Negro. Faulkner makes double-edged use of this southern vulnerability, and at the same time shows just how impersonal and anonymous the Negro is, by having each major discovery concerning the Sutpen legend incorporate the Negro. He plays upon the formulated, accepted aspects of southern history and tradition regarding the Negro, but he provokes the recognition that the formula is, and has been, not necessarily humanitarian but of necessity pluralistic and expansive in space and time.

At one point in his narrative, Mr. Compson poses a question that seems relevant to Faulkner's own method: "Have you noticed how so often when we try to reconstruct the causes which lead up to the actions of men and women, how with a sort of astonishment we find ourselves now and then reduced to the belief, the only possible belief, that they stemmed from some of the old virtues?" (121). Though he specifically refers to "the thief who steals not for greed

18 Frederick Hoffman, *The Art of Southern Fiction: A Study of Some Modern Southern Novelists* (Carbondale: Southern Illinois University Press, 1967), 112.
19 *Ibid.*, 113.

but for love, the murderer who kills not out of lust but pity" (121), Mr. Compson touches upon a possible reason for Faulkner's explanations of the Sutpen mystery in terms of the old antagonism of southern life—the Negro, who has in fact inspired a whole code of southern "chivalric" virtues. Faulkner attempts to probe imaginatively into the causes behind the Sutpen legend, but because neither incest nor fratricide provides him with a means of transcending the inner tensions of his narrative situation, he returns to the Negro. He relies upon conventional beliefs about "Negro" to solve his narrative dilemma.

In *Absalom, Absalom!* Faulkner seems to have pulled a neat trick. Both Quentin and Shreve are convinced that they have found the "truth" of the Sutpen puzzle in the Negro, technically in their uncovering the secret of Bon's black blood. Almost inevitably their view has been accepted.[20] In a sense their resolution amounts to a discovery of the proverbial "nigger in the woodpile," a not so unexpected way for southerners to resolve the complexity of human interactions and motivations. (Shreve is, of course, Canadian; however, his notions of the South are stereotyped, literary exaggerations.) Both Shreve and Quentin, in conjecturing "Negro" as the key, reflect something basic about their conformity to the dictates of the South.

They retrace what Mr. Compson relates as the opinion of the townsmen regarding Sutpen once he became successful:

> There were some among his fellow citizens who believed even yet that there was a nigger in the woodpile somewhere, ranging from the ones who believed that the plantation was just a blind to his actual dark avocation, through the ones who believed that he had found some way to juggle the cotton market itself and so get more per bale for his cotton than honest men could to those who believed apparently that the wild niggers which he had brought there had the power to actually conjure more cotton per acre from the soil than any tame ones had ever done. (72)

The "nigger in the woodpile" to which Mr. Compson refers takes on

20 For instance, John V. Hagopian claims, "The total action of the story that Quentin and Shreve finally reconstruct shows the tragic consequences of racism." "*Absalom, Absalom!* and the Negro Question," *Modern Fiction Studies*, XIX (Summer, 1973), 207–10.

a literal meaning in the resolution as it is constructed by Shreve and Quentin. The old saw becomes one indispensable part of Faulkner's complex structure and narrative scheme.

Whether or not Faulkner accepts the implications of his method of solving the mystery, he has successfully foisted the method upon Quentin and Shreve, his two most sensitive and rational narrators. Faulkner inspires confidence in their "truth" by depicting them as the furthest removed from the legend: Quentin in terms of generations and spatial distance from his South, and Shreve in terms of his Canadian heritage and psychic environment. Yet Faulkner also partially undermines the authority of their ratiocination when he places the two in a Harvard University dormitory: "In the cold room (it was quite cold now) dedicated to the best of ratiocination which after all was a good deal like Sutpen's morality and Miss Coldfield's demonizing—this room not only dedicated to it but set aside for it suitably so since it would be here above any other place that it (logic and the morality) could do the least amount of harm" (280). The university stands for ratiocination, and from that base Quentin and Shreve respond to the Sutpen materials, but "ratiocination" is "a good deal" like the other, obviously flawed methods of interpretation.

Faulkner leads Quentin and Shreve to conclude that for the southerner and the South the Negro is inescapable: for comfort or terror, sustenance or destruction; for historiography or literature, fact or invention. Ultimately, "the nigger in the woodpile," and the process of discovering him, is simultaneously a utilitarian conception and an aesthetic creation. Just as Faulkner introduces the black religious experience specifically as a reconciliatory device at the end of *The Sound and the Fury* and as he posits Joe Christmas' transcendence into myth as a resolution of the tensions in *Light in August,* so he superimposes Bon's blackness upon the conclusion of *Absalom, Absalom!* Charles Bon's transformation into "the nigger in the woodpile" satisfies logically the inner dynamics of Faulkner's plot and themes. In all it is apparent that the only way Quentin and Shreve can unravel the meaning of the fratricide (and in the process the Sutpen legend) and Faulkner can resolve his narrative maze without destroying its intensity, and ambiguity, is to resort to the Negro, to conclude that the Negro must be at the core of it all, if the story is to carry larger humanistic significance and, thereby, justify the stylistic complexity.

In their reconstruction of the final confrontation between Henry Sutpen and Charles Bon, Quentin and Shreve assign Bon the fateful words: *"I'm the nigger that's going to sleep with your sister. Unless you stop me, Henry"* (358). The imagination of the two narrators is frozen into the clichés of southern thinking. Quentin and Shreve do not intuit the terms in which to couch Charles's decisive statement, they know. Shreve's knowledge is a result of his melodramatic vision of the South, Quentin's of his long personal and historical experience of the South.

Shreve deflates the finely tempered rhetorical reality the two have created by calling Bon in his very next reference "the black son of a bitch" (358). Somehow it all becomes very ordinary, so ordinary in fact that Shreve at last is ready to end the night: " 'Come on . . . . Let's get out of this refrigerator and go to bed' " (359). The Negro is, after all, an expected part of the tissue of southern life. Instead of penetrating something unfathomable about human conduct or life, the two narrators (and Faulkner himself for all the brilliant shape of the novel) resort to the pedestrian—though it is the pedestrian that has tyrannized conscious and subconscious levels of thought. Perhaps the problem that the Negro represents to the southern white man clouds his perceptions and constricts his imaginative faculties; however, that problem is so enduring and realistic that its power to affect mental processes does not dissipate. Even Shreve's mental capacity to make enlightened conjectures is stimulated as well as circumscribed by the Negro's actual presence in the South. Shreve comes to the legend with an image of the South's depravity, and he concludes with a confirmation of it. The South and the Negro are once again inextricably bound together, though this time it is the result of a piecemeal and tortuous logic.

Since it seems that the South has consistently validated its existence and its uniqueness by means of the Negro, it is not so surprising that in the context of the novel the narrators adhere to this pattern. Quentin and Shreve are no different from Mr. Compson, and in spite of the cluttered maze through which they imaginatively pass, they arrive at the Negro with even more certainty than Mr.

Compson. Quentin, bearer of a burdensome southern heritage, and Shreve, the outlander whose traditions and mores are even more foreign than those of the ubiquitous northerner, can invent what is for them the most meaningful tandem of thought and feeling about fratricide only when the race question enters the resolution. Miscegenation, then, becomes a more weighted issue than fratricide. Faulkner does not allow either the reader or his Harvard detectives to be content with completely acknowledging the inexplicable in human behavior; an attempt to explain must be made.

On one level, that of narrative structure, it is a long way around to a "solution." But on another level, a certain ease is apparent in the way the narrators head with an inevitable, dead reckoning to the Negro, though they themselves try to delay it and prolong the resolution in order to savor or reconstruct all the elements possible from a logical base. Their fabrications create an illusion of reality; their construct is quite believable.[21] All rational investigations lead to a basic reality: Charles Bon as "nigger."

Nonetheless, the process by which the two young narrators come to Bon as "nigger" suggests an analogy to Rosa Coldfield's poetic analysis of remembering: "That is the substance of remembering— sense, sight, smell, the muscles with which we see and hear and feel—not mind, not thought: there is no such thing as memory: the brain recalls just what the muscles grope for: no more, no less: and its resultant sum is usually incorrect and false and worthy only of the name of dream" (143). The image of the brain's recalling "just what the muscles grope for" is analogous to Shreve and Quentin's simultaneously moving toward Bon's blackness out of separate and distinct conditionings of their muscles. In re-creating the past, they are remembering what their experience of life has taught them. Different orientations to life mean little at the point where the two youths conjoin to solve the mystery. Shreve's picture of the South constructed from wild theatrics ("'Jesus, the South's fine. . . . It's

---

21 I am not forwarding the argument that there is no authority for Quentin and Shreve's conclusion regarding Bon's black blood; in this matter I agree with Richard P. Adams: "The authority for the 'fact' of Bon's Negro blood is . . . the whole tissue of hypothetical reasoning which Quentin and Shreve have woven and which Shreve in particular has pieced out with purely fanciful fabrications. . . . The result is, in a paradoxical sense, entirely realistic." Adams, *Faulkner: Myth and Motion*, 199.

better than theatre. . . . It's better than Ben Hur,'" 217) and melo-drama (probably *Uncle Tom's Cabin*) achieves completion in Bon's blackness. Quentin's picture of the South shaped by his being "a commonwealth," "a barracks filled with stubborn back-looking ghosts" (12) also completes itself in Bon's blackness.

Authority for Bon's black blood, then, is not the point. The point is rather that both for Faulkner in the construction of his novel and for his various narrators in the telling of the tale, meaning hinges upon somehow coming to the "fact" of Bon's being "Negro," when ironically he is the one character the farthest removed (by all narrative accounts) from "Negro" and "nigger" as the novel and society have presented them; even Clytie, whose Sutpen-ness primarily defines her, remains a "coffee-colored," "dark essence." Mr. Compson's images of Bon as "a young man of a worldly elegance and assurance beyond his years, handsome" (74) and as "watching, contemplating them from behind that barrier of sophistication in comparison with which Henry and Sutpen were troglodytes" (93) function effectively to separate Bon from all social images of the Negro as subordinates and servants which Faulkner incorporates into the novel.

What the narrators finally make of Bon as "nigger" is prefigured by Mr. Compson: "Bon with that sardonic and surprised distaste which seems to have been the ordinary manifestation of the impenetrable and shadowy character. Yes, shadowy: a myth, a phantom: something which they engendered and created whole themselves; some effluvium of Sutpen blood and character, as though as a man he did not exist at all" (104). It is only a short step from the conception of Bon that Mr. Compson reports to the two youths' conjecture that Bon is "nigger." (And in Rosa's confrontation with Clytie, Faulkner demonstrates how that step is taken.) Bon is "something which they engendered and created whole themselves"; he does not exist as a man, but rather, as Panthea Reid Broughton observes, as "the ultimate shape of their [the Sutpens'] fantasies, a mere embodiment of certain abstract qualities."[22] Both in the world of the legend

---

22 Panthea Reid Broughton, *William Faulkner: The Abstract and the Actual* (Baton Rouge: Louisiana State University Press, 1974), 69. Broughton's reference is specifically to Bon the suitor who is seen by the Sutpens as an object. For example, Ellen views Bon as a garment, a piece of furniture, and a mentor (*Absalom, Absalom!*, 75).

and in the world of the narrators, Bon becomes "the abstraction" and "the Negro" created to satisfy the needs of characters and narrators. His situation, like Clytie's, stresses the force and inevitability of the Negro as a presence, "impenetrable and shadowy," at the center of the South and of Faulkner's creative imagination.

Faulkner manipulates "Negro" as an aesthetic device in this novel. For example, the figure of the Negro as victim-avenger and the theme of miscegenation are two mainstays of southern fiction, and these are the two devices Faulkner ultimately employs in the major resolutions. In the apparently unreliable resolution offered by Mr. Compson, Charles Bon's miscegenation with the octoroon plays upon a traditional device for evoking sentiment—the octoroon as conventional tragic figure in southern literature. Mr. Compson describes her as "victim—a woman with a face like a tragic magnolia, the eternal female, the eternal Who-suffers" (114). The deception here is the view of a white man's "marriage" to a black woman as a barrier to his marriage to a white woman.[23] The ultimate tragedy (or trick) in the resolution offered by Quentin and Shreve turns out to be that Bon himself possesses, like his octoroon mate, a drop of black blood, or so the reader probably should believe because of Faulkner's use of the device as a "surprise" ending. The narrative deception in both resolutions is that during the course of the development the reader does not know that there is a black victim-avenger or a miscegenation theme at work, and by the end, given the speculative nature of the "truth" presented, the reader cannot be certain that there has been. Nonetheless, whether in terms of the Old South (represented by the legend) or of the New South (represented by the narrative present, the reconstruction of the legend), Faulkner depends upon myths of the Negro and the South in a wider context than that of miscegenation. He clearly ties Quentin, his father, Miss Rosa, Shreve, and all the characters in the Sutpen legend to myths of the South and to the process of mythologizing about the South.

23 Bon, as Mr. Compson speculates, reminds Henry Sutpen that both the octoroon and her child are "niggers," a fact which precludes the legitimacy of a marriage (118). The octoroon, Donald M. Kartiganer observes, "is, when necessary, the nigger who cannot possibly *matter.*" *The Fragile Thread: The Meaning of Form in Faulkner's Novels* (Amherst: University of Massachusetts Press, 1979), 85.

Absalom, Absalom! returns the reader and each of the four narrators to those myths about the southern past (the myth of racial purity is just one) out of an acknowledged helplessness and inability ever really to know or understand the South, and by extension both themselves and the past. The view of miscegenation, or a pathological fear of it, as the primary cause of destruction in *Absalom*[24] ignores the fact that miscegenation is only one piece of the larger race question and only one part of the total pattern of life presented, or invented, in the novel.

The nexus of myths about southern life and thought that play themselves out results from the internal forces at work within the Sutpens, the Bons, and those mythical figures who do not tell their own stories, and they result from the speculation of the four narrators. But these internal forces act in some immediate and far-reaching relationship to the external conditions. Maintaining the delicate balance between internal pressures and external conditions both in the fiction and in the fiction-making of *Absalom* leads to the falling back and reliance upon the myths of the South.[25] "With the crumbling of so many defenses in the present," C. Vann Woodward states, "the South has tended to substitute myths about the past"; moreover, like "every self-conscious group of any size," it "fabricates the myths about its past: about its origins, its mission, its righteousness, its benevolence, its general superiority."[26] This general process is evident in Faulkner's four narrators, who assume life stances and positions defined for them by the codes or myths of the South, which they themselves partly fabricate.

In particular, Shreve and Quentin's construction of the Sutpen legend is an embodiment and dramatization of the myths of the Negro which have imbued the South with life and death, love and hate, creativity and destruction. For them it is not slavery alone

24 Bradbury, *Renaissance in the South,* 55. Both Seiden and Charles Peavy hold views similar to Bradbury's. Seiden concludes that *Absalom* "is not concerned with the tragedy of miscegenation, but with the Miscegenation Complex." "Faulkner's Ambiguous Negro," 678. Peavy repeats this idea almost *verbatim:* "it is not miscegenation but the miscegenation complex that is the real concern to Faulkner." *Go Slow Now,* 35.
25 For a historical basis for the dependence upon myths of the South, see the study by William K. Taylor, *Cavalier and Yankee: The Old South and the American National Character* (New York: Braziller, 1961).
26 Woodward, *The Burden of Southern History,* 12.

which accounts for the South's moral deficiency. It is, as well, the white southerner's failure to respond to the black human being; he responds instead to an abstraction—"the Negro" myth. Unfortunately, Quentin's conjecture that Henry kills Bon because of the threat of the Negro points to the individual's seeking something outside of himself to hold responsible for his situation. Quentin needs the myth of the Negro in order to escape personal confrontation of complex moral problems, incest and fratricide. Sutpen, too, is guilty of a similar evasion of self when he fails to ask where he himself went wrong. Whereas Sutpen distorts his understanding of morality to fit the contours of the morally reprehensible, slave holding South, Quentin rationalizes a morally complex situation by resorting to the scapegoat sanctioned by his society. Ultimately, Quentin in the modern age repeats the mistake of Sutpen in the past. He seeks an external cause which, because of the social composition of the South, is readily available in the Negro.

Regarding the interpretation of Sutpen's story, Faulkner has observed:

> I think no one individual can look at a truth. It blinds you. You look at it and you see one phase of it. Someone else looks at it and sees a slightly awry phase of it. But taken all together, the truth is in what they saw though nobody saw the truth intact. So these are true as far as Miss Rosa and as Quentin saw it. Quentin's father saw what he believed was truth, that was all he saw. But the old man was himself a little too big for people no greater in stature than Quentin and Miss Rosa and Mr. Compson to see all at once. It would have taken perhaps a wiser or more tolerant or more sensitive or more thoughtful person to see him as he was. It was, as you say, thirteen ways of looking at a blackbird. But the truth, I would like to think, comes out, that when the reader has read all these thirteen different ways of looking at a blackbird, the reader has his own fourteenth image of that blackbird, which I would like to think is the truth.[27]

What makes *Absalom* ultimately such a fine literary experience is that it succeeds remarkably well in creating the illusion of openendedness, of expanding possibilities and realms of interpretations. Its structure and themes encourage a flexible view of the meaning of

27 Gwynn and Blotner (eds.), *Faulkner in the University*, 273–74.

the novel. An image from Mr. Compson's letter about Rosa Cold-field's death evokes the ambiguous cyclical nature of southern life and thought that Faulkner achieves in this novel: *"The weather was beautiful though cold and they had to use picks to break the earth for the grave yet in one of the deep clods I saw a red worm doubtless alive when the clod was thrown up though by afternoon it was frozen again"* (377).

Absalom engages the reader in a continuing creative process; he becomes detective and interpreter while he also experiences vicariously with both characters and narrators. This richness of possibility stands in contrast to the inadequate perspective Wilbur Cash criticizes in other southern books of the 1920s and '30s: "When we attempt to regard them as a picture of the South as everybody has done, telling the truth in detail, they fail to tell it in adequate perspective."[28] Because the nature of narrative "truth" is presented as suspect by Faulkner, the whole process of the narrative development expands the basis of the perspective from which the novel may be viewed.

In fact, in *Absalom, Absalom!* a query about the South is being answered in the working out of much of the narrative; Shreve, like others at Harvard, wants to know about the South: *"Tell about the South. What's it like there. What do they do there. Why do they live there. Why do they live at all"* (174). The novel is a response not only to Shreve's specific questions but to general questions about the South, including those that southerners themselves have. Irving Howe, for example, states:

> Faulkner in his stories and novels has been conducting a long, sometimes painful and at other times heroic examination of the Southern myth. . . . He has investigated the myth itself, wondered about the relation between the Southern tradition he admires and that memory of Southern slavery to which he is compelled to return; tested not only the present by the past, but also the past by the myth, and finally the myth by that morality which has slowly emerged from this entire process of exploration.[29]

What Faulkner does in developing a response to Shreve is to turn the question back upon itself. He makes the questioner answer himself, and Quentin, the individual supposedly supplying "answers,"

28 Cash, *The Mind of the South*, 378.
29 Howe, *William Faulkner*, 29.

is forced to admit: "'I dont know. . . . Yes, of course I understand it [the South]. . . . I dont know'" (362).

Absalom, Absalom! is in one sense a product of the major revaluation of the South undertaken after the appearance of *I'll Take My Stand: The South and the Agrarian Tradition* by Twelve Southerners. According to George Brown Tindall, "One major contribution of their [the Agrarians'] quest for tradition was a revival of concern with regional identity."[30] Both Stark Young's *So Red the Rose* (1934) and Margaret Mitchell's *Gone with the Wind* (1936) are popular historical novels and, like *Absalom*, reflections of the literary concern with regional identity. Regional identity for the southerner, regardless of his politics, is intricately bound up in the Civil War and the black presence, two distinguishing features of the South. "The War," Robert Penn Warren maintains, "claimed the Confederate states for the Union, but at the same time, paradoxically, it made them more Southern."[31] Concern with regional identity, then, leads perhaps automatically to a consideration of the southern past, so that the preoccupation with history, "the past," during the early years of the Renascence is essentially a way of mediating the difficulty of the southern transition into modern life. It is a way of responding without apology to demands like Shreve's "Tell about the South." The past does not necessarily have to be either glorified or vilified, but southern history with its constant, the Negro, offers some sense of order, stability, and pride as a point of reference during changing conditions.

One reason for the vigorous return to the past and the turning away from the contemporary South is posed in a 1933 statement by Faulkner himself:

> the South . . . is dead, killed by the Civil War. There is a thing known whimsically as the New South to be sure, but it is not the South. It is a land of Immigrants who are rebuilding the towns and cities into replicas of towns and cities in Kansas and Iowa and Il-

---

30 Tindall, *The Emergence of the New South*, 582. For a concise discussion of regional consciousness and the historical ferment of the times, see Tindall's chapter, "Southerners Rediscover the South: Regionalism and Sectionalism," 575–606.
31 Robert Penn Warren, *The Legacy of the Civil War: Meditations on the Centennial* (New York: Random House, 1961), 14.

linois, with skyscrapers and striped canvas awnings instead of wooden balconies, and teaching the young men who sell gasoline and the waitresses in the restaurants to say O yea? and to speak with hard r's, and hanging over the intersections of quiet and shaded streets where no one save Northern tourists in Cadillacs and Lincolns ever pass at a gait faster than a horse trots, changing red-and-green lights and savage and peremptory bells.[32]

Faulkner's statement is as much an affirmation of the Old South, "*the South*" he terms it, as superior to the present-day replica of the crass North (and superior to the North itself by extension) as it is a lament for what is dead. The southern past may no longer exist on the streets Faulkner describes, but by the contrast he implies that "the South" survives within his imaginative reach. The central paradox for Faulkner and other sons of the Old South is that their South, while removed temporarily from the new, is vulnerable in literature as it was in life. Slavery, the tragic flaw in the old design, complicates notions of a heroic, chivalric moral code and tarnishes edenic pictures of its glory. As a result, the sensitive, aware artist, like Faulkner, occupies an uncomfortable space between the drive toward reality and the attraction to the myth. Because of the uncertainties resulting from conflicting artistic appeals, legends, tall tales, and myths cannot so easily be isolated from "reality." The threads of southern existence derive from both myths and fabrications and from kernels of fact and truth. All of these have become intertwined and inseparable in the present, and the literature—Faulkner's *Absalom, Absalom!* in particular—reflects as much.

In spite of reliance upon myths of the South and "thirteen different ways of looking at a blackbird," the novel retains a hard and fast central core. There is no escaping the conjecture of "the nigger that's going to sleep with your sister," as Shreve has Bon identify himself (358). Faulkner may skillfully execute the illusion of myriad possible interpretations; however, he signals through his omniscient narrator's comment, "probably true enough," in order to corroborate precisely what he wishes. And one of these corroborations involves the Negro (the "nigger in the woodpile") at the center and to whom many narrative clues lead.

32 Faulkner, "An Introduction to *The Sound and the Fury*," 411.

"Negro" is a central metaphor, albeit a most difficult one to explicate.[33] Representative major black figures in the novel are all as much
white as black, and in practically every case, they are more white
than black. The visibly "white" product of miscegenation has con-
founded sight as a test of racial identity. Yet the cognitive image of
"Negro," the traditionally conceived and conventionally executed
abstraction, provides the prism through which all the black figures
are refracted.

The problem suggests Mr. Compson's consideration of Charles
Bon among the Sutpens:

> He is the curious one to me. He came into that isolated puritan
> country household almost like Sutpen himself came into Jefferson:
> apparently complete without background or past or childhood—
> a man a little older than his actual years and enclosed and sur-
> rounded by a sort of Scythian glitter . . . yet from the moment
> when he realized that Sutpen was going to prevent the marriage if
> he could, he (Bon) seems to have withdrawn into a mere spectator,
> passive, a little sardonic and completely enigmatic. He seems to
> hover, shadowy, almost substanceless, a little behind and above all
> the other straightforward and logical, even though (to him) in-
> comprehensible, ultimatums and affirmations and defiances and
> challenges and repudiations with an air of sardonic and indolent
> detachment. (93)

Bon is detached, older-than-his-years, a completely enigmatic spec-
tator. Yet Bon is far removed from Faulkner's portraits of blacks as
voices of song or laughter, an ironic chorus contrasted with the actions of whites (as in Soldiers' Pay). At the same time, what Bon represents is not clear because in the novel his very presence, "shadowy, almost substanceless," is related to the presence of the laughter
of the blacks, described as "the roaring waves of mellow laughter
meaningless and terrifying and loud" (232). Both stand for a disembodied aspect of life, some quality of existence which is at once absurd and ominous. It is a long way around to Sutpen's "monkey nigger" again, but Bon's presence, hovering "a little behind and above

33 Reed points out that metaphor is both the "central barrier" to a "comfortable reading" of Absalom and "more central to its meaning than to that of any of his other novels, because after a time metaphor is the novel's customary form of statement."
Faulkner's Narrative, 151.

all the other," duplicates the stance of the balloon face "monkey nigger":

> You knew that you could hit them [blacks] . . . and they would not hit back or even resist. But you did not want to, because they (the niggers) were not it, not what you wanted to hit; that you knew when you hit them you would just be hitting a child's toy balloon with a face painted on it, a face slick and smooth and distended and about to burst into laughing, so you did not dare strike it because it would merely burst and you would rather let it walk on out of your sight than to have stood there in the loud laughing. (230)

The Negro as a "toy balloon with a face painted on it" represents the helplessness and powerlessness of the existence of poor-whites in general and Sutpen in particular. Sutpen's awareness of the futility in taking action against a balloon, which, paradoxically, is concrete yet is insubstantial and symbolic in terms of the real world, suggests his attitude toward Charles Bon. Bon, like the balloon face, is an artificial configuration. He is the abstraction that Sutpen refuses to see or acknowledge because Bon's very presence mocks Sutpen, and any action against Bon exposes Sutpen to the possibility of that mockery being extended into the general public or community. Sutpen ignores Bon because he cannot accept Bon's reality. Like the black housekeepers in Anderson's *Dark Laughter*, Bon is and remains the anonymous "nigger" ready to burst into laughter at the slightest provocation. Acceptance of Bon would make Sutpen's design an "ironic delusion," while rejection of him foists upon Sutpen and his design an "ironic reality."

This metaphorical presence of the enigmatic "Negro" pervades the entire novel, especially the conclusion. Shreve, for example, presents the metaphor of the two niggers to get rid of one Sutpen: " 'So it took Charles Bon and his mother to get rid of old Tom, and Charles Bon and the octoroon to get rid of Judith, and Charles Bon and Clytie to get rid of Henry; and Charles Bon's mother and Charles Bon's grandmother got rid of Charles Bon'" (377–78). The metaphor suggests the omnipresence and the obstinacy of "the nigger" in the lives of white southerners. Shreve concludes his summary with the theory that, " 'You've got one nigger left. One nigger Sutpen left. Of course you can't catch him and you don't even always see him and you never will be able to use him. But you got him there still. You still hear him at night sometimes. Don't you?'" (378).[34] Despite the destructive eliminations basic to Shreve's summary and the legend, the oppressive presence of "the Negro" remains. The illusive, disturbing "nigger," Jim Bond specifically, is a metaphor perhaps for the unknowable, or the contradictions, inherent in southern life, and in life generally.

The stubborn "nigger" refuses extinction, and paradoxically, in the sense of Jim Bond's being an authentic Sutpen descendant, "the nigger" belongs; he has his place in the physical and mental space of the South. Significantly, because no one—none of the narrators, none of the participants, not even Faulkner's omniscient narrative voice which sometimes interpolates and sometimes intrudes— comes away with an understanding of the Negro as metaphor at work or with an interpretation of the meaning of the Negro, the herculean efforts (in vision, experience, and telling) remain somewhat mysterious. As long as there is one nigger left, southerners (reconstructed or not) and outlanders (sympathetic or not) alike can create myths out of the interaction of "the South" and "the Negro." Faulkner has actually left the flood gates of Yoknapatawpha open once again.

Literally, Shreve, the outlander who has vicariously experienced it all, revives the process, begins the myth anew, with his fanciful theorizing that the howling idiot and surviving Sutpen haunts the physical place (Sutpen's Hundred) and the psychological space (Quentin's dreams) that make up the South. Shreve concludes with the notion that the Jim Bonds will inherit the western world: "in time the Jim Bonds are going to conquer the western hemisphere. Of course, it won't quite be in our time and of course as they spread toward the poles they will bleach out again like the rabbits and the

---

34 According to Gerald Langford, "The most significant revision in Chapter IX is the added emphasis given to Jim Bond in the closing pages of the book." *Faulkner's Revision of "Absalom, Absalom!"*, 40. Faulkner added the image of Bond's howling to the manuscript, but the impact of the addition does not seem to be "the heritage of man's long inhumanity to man," as Langford suggests (41), but rather an enduring concern with the presence of the Negro as a symbol of the tensions in the southerner's existence. See, for instance, Langford's reproduction of the manuscript and book revisions (360–61).

birds do, so they won't show up so sharp against the snow. But it will still be Jim Bond; and so in a few thousand years, I who regard you will also have sprung from the loins of African kings" (378).

Whether Shreve is serious or not is not the question, just as whether the novel uncovers absolute fact or truth is not the ultimate consideration. With the ending as with the entire novel, it is the process that is important—the process of the mind at work creating, inventing, deciphering, conjecturing. Shreve continues the process right up to and through the ending. Shreve's image of the Jim Bonds is a fine mythologizing that is not in the least unfamiliar.[35] The myth of the Negro endures, and this is as rigid and inflexible as the old one even though it may reflect a diminishing of the traditional racial hatred and fear.

Shreve's statement is rhetorical; it is rhetoric so turned in upon itself as to be practically meaningless in its content. Only the formal context of the statement matters ultimately, because it is, like the vision of language in the novel, "that meager and fragile thread . . . by which the little lives may be joined for an instant . . . before sinking back into the darkness" (251). No amount of sorting out the ideas and metaphors helps to make the statement coherent. What is important, however, is that Shreve continues the verbal design of the novel. With his mythologizing it becomes even more apparent that *Absalom* is as much about creation and perpetuation, acceptance and rejection of certain myths of the South as it is about the needs out of which those myths materialize and are made concrete.

Shreve's prediction that "the Jim Bonds are going to conquer the western hemisphere" is not a thematic outgrowth of the content of the reconstructed Sutpen legend. His conclusion does not mesh with either the details of the legend or the attitudes of the narrators in the telling of it. Consequently, some critics have dismissed Shreve's prophecy as evidence of his flippant and condescending attitude toward the South and the legend.[36] The significant point

---

35 For example, Cash presents a synopsis of the color line that supports Shreve's prophecy as not out of joint with the times in which Faulkner created it. *The Mind of the South*, 301. That Shreve's theory bears a recognizable resemblance to ideas found in the real world simultaneously validates his theory and perpetuates the real world.
36 In an attempt to correct such views, John Middleton tries to prove Shreve's grow-

about Shreve's statement is not whether it reflects a cynical or compassionate attitude toward the materials; in either case, his conclusion simply does not grow logically out of the details of the legend or out of the details of Shreve's own personality. Nonetheless, his prediction is a direct and certain outgrowth of the method, the process, the form of the novel and of Shreve's role. (That role is to provoke and sustain Quentin's examination and formulation of his world and himself.) The prediction is a continuation of the process of creating myth, and as such it reflects quite accurately the role of the black man in southern life.

Some critics have resorted to ideological or philosophical considerations of Shreve's final statement.[37] However, Jim Bond's idiocy is less important than his transformation by Shreve, with Quentin's approval, into a bodiless presence, a voice crying in the no man's land to which Sutpen's Hundred is reduced. Jim Bond may be a portent of doom, but not in the sense that Middleton suggests when he states: "Sutpen's legacy is the triumph of miscegenation, the survival of black blood, the eventual but invisible destruction of white purity."[38] Because Jim Bond becomes merely a disembodied voice remote from any concrete reality, he represents no viable threat to white purity. Jim Bond is, too, a perversion of the black blood as well; he is a degeneration of the somehow magnificent wild niggers of Sutpen's Hundred. Resorting to Jim Bond's howling presence as the source of Quentin's unrest repeats the southern tendency to

---

ing sensitivity to the materials and the South. Middleton sees Shreve's statement as in fact the "evidence of engaged and compassionate insight"; moreover, he suggests that it is a part of Shreve's ability as an outsider "to give Sutpen's legend its largest meaning because he is able to face what insiders cannot face." "Shreve McCannon and Sutpen's Legacy," *Southern Review*, X (January, 1974), 115–24. Although his interpretation of the comment follows that of most critics, Middleton is correct in pointing out that Shreve's theory is not the result of a "detached and flippant cynicism."

37 Seiden labels Shreve's statement "overwhelmingly racist," but he gets bogged down in the meaning of Bond's idiocy and its implications: "The logic of Shreve's genetics may be abrupt, but the logic of the Sutpen tale does seem to confirm the fearful vision of mongrelization. . . . Is Faulkner playing with us here?" "Faulkner's Ambiguous Negro," 684. Hagopian, too, quite seriously states that "Jim Bond is what inevitably will come of the white man's refusal to accept the black man as both black and a man." "*Absalom, Absalom!* and the Negro Question," 210. Yet in the context of the novel, Bond is not a threat to the white man; it is not technically Bond who haunts Quentin's dreams, just as it is not Charles Bon himself who haunted Henry's life.

38 Middleton, "Shreve McCannon and Sutpen's Legacy," 122.

blame the abstraction or the myth of the Negro for the South's un- doing. Once again the myth of the Negro looms as a barrier between the individual and the direct experience of life in general and *himself* in particular. Thus, Jim Bond may indeed be a portent of doom; the very fact of his creation portends that the southerner has not yet been able to face himself without the buffer of myths, and that per- haps he may not ever be capable of so doing.

Perhaps, too, Shreve's mythologizing serves to reiterate Faulkner's inevitable "southernness." Fragmentation in a segregated world is so much a part of the southerner's life that almost invariably it becomes a part of his art. The world he lives in is not whole, and much of his artistic effort is, in fact, a quest for wholeness, for a unity in art which he knows to be impossible in life. Faulkner implies as much in *Absalom, Absalom!* with his portrayal of Rosa Coldfield's poetry writ- ing. During a three-year period, she secretly feeds her father who hides from the war in his attic; "At the same time she was writing heroic poetry about the very men from whom her father was hiding and who would have shot him or hung him without trial if they had found him" (68). Rosa's fragmented position remains the same: "for three years, feeding in secret and at night and with food which in quantity was scarcely sufficient for one, the man whom she hated. And she may not have known she hated him and she may not have known it now even, nevertheless the first of the odes to Southern soldiers in that portfolio which . . . in 1885 contained a thousand or more, was dated in the first year of her father's voluntary incarcera- tion and dated at two o'clock in the morning" (83).

Probably for anyone other than a southerner with the preparatory experience of living in a racially divided world, Rosa's position would be untenable. Even Quentin in acknowledging Rosa as "the town's and the county's poetess laureate" realizes that she wrote po- etry out of "some bitter and implacable reserve of undefeat" (11). Miss Rosa's poetry writing is unlike Miss Jenny's telling of a tale of Civil War heroics, a tale which "as she grew older . . . grew richer and richer, taking on a mellow splendor like wine" (*Flags in the Dust*, 14). Rosa's position suggests that the mythologizing of the war does not depend upon elapsed time. Her situation, feeding her father and writing heroic verse simultaneously, implies that even during the war the southerner had dispensed with the war's literal meaning and attempted to live with the experience by means of a public and heroic language of symbols and metaphors. The private experience of the war was then and remains a tension-ridden, buried experience. Rosa Coldfield is evidence of an artist's inability to reconcile the external and internal realities of southern life.

The very awareness of the impossibility of wholeness in reality causes the southerner to depict worlds or situations or people that at best only strive to merge into a whole, but never actually achieve a meaningful union. The ways in which the various narrators project the Sutpen legend suggest that there can be no wholeness in life, and they approach Sutpen from this position. Sutpen, poor white mountaineer, never completely fuses into his designated role of landed, slaveholding planter. Rosa Coldfield falls short of ever being part of a family unit or even of the community despite her poetry. Charles Bon never knows a father. Charles Etienne St. Valery Bon's shard of mirror may represent his inability ever to see himself whole.

Reality is often evaded by sacrificing clear perception and honest thinking which, in turn, are detrimental to the southerner's view of the world. His habit is "to see things as forms or large configurations,"[39] and the process of breaking these down proves fatal to his "truth" as a whole. Thus, his personality, his pattern of thought and behavior are shaped by a defense or escape mechanism involving a distortion of knowledge.

Quentin's emotional breakdown at the end of *Absalom, Absalom!* comes about as a result of the breakdown of his defense mechanism. Shreve and Quentin conclude their probing of the Sutpen legend, but Shreve turns the tables and wants to probe Quentin as a personal representative of the South. "'Now I want you to tell me just

---

39 Richard M. Weaver, "Aspects of Southern Philosophy," in Rubin and Jacobs (eds.), *Southern Renascence,* 15. In reflecting upon this problem which he encountered in the southern mind during the twenties, Oliver La Farge (ethnologist, novelist, and Faulkner's friend during his New Orleans days) has offered the opinion that "for a white man, born in the South and not specially trained, to think other than as they did would be remarkable. Every instinct of self-preservation and the deep urge to perpetuate and protect one's kind operate to develop their point of view." *Raw Material* (Boston: Houghton, Mifflin, 1945), 119.

one thing more,'" Shreve states. "'Why do you hate the South?'" (378). The reply is instantaneous: "'I dont hate it,' Quentin said, quickly, at once, immediately; 'I dont hate it,' he said. *I dont hate it* he thought, panting in the cold air, the iron New England dark; *I dont. I dont! I dont hate it! I dont hate it!*" (Faulkner's italics, 378). Shreve's analytic question shatters Quentin's forced composure. Shreve destroys the spell which their introspective process of constructing a total (that is, harmonious with all known and conjectured details) fiction has produced. The asking of the question is as much to blame as any inherent validity the question might have. The question itself is a violation of a code, and that violation is even more destructive to Quentin's uneasy equilibrium than the psychological process of putting together a compelling whole story from individually biased, fragmented perceptions.

Shreve, concerned all along with the southerner's negative identity, forges a negative affirmation of Quentin's southernness by the question and the response to it. Given the moral and psychological dualism intrinsic to southern society, Quentin, paradoxically, is telling the "truth" as he knows it. It is no illusion: he does not hate the South. The tendency, of course, is to accept that Shreve has put his finger squarely on Quentin's problem, that Quentin does indeed hate the South.[40] However, Quentin's emotional response can also be attributed, at least partially, to Shreve's violation of a code southerners tacitly agree to. Shreve, the outlander, forces Quentin to respond to a question that lies outside the boundaries of accepted social interchange. Shreve seeks a union of internal and external realities; for the southerner in this novel that is an impossibility, and both the Sutpen legend and its reconstruction are confirmations of this "fact."

Faulkner's art encompasses even while it magnifies and transcends the South as Faulkner understands and lives it. Demands for the "clarifying gesture"[41] ignore Faulkner's mirroring of a prevalent

---

40 Walter Slatoff, however, has generally read the ending of the novel perceptively: "We 'end,' then, with a psychological oxymoron of simultaneous love and hate, with internal conflict and self contradiction." *Quest for Failure: A Study of William Faulkner* (Ithaca: Cornell University Press, 1960), 201.
41 Slatoff believes that the ending of *Absalom* "demonstrates [Faulkner's] unwilling-

condition among his southerners: the virtual impossibility of personal, individual wholeness in a fragmented, racially divided world.
That condition exists as a reality for Faulkner in *Absalom,* as well as
in *Light in August* and *Go Down, Moses.* There is, he repeats in these
novels, no ready answer to the South's or the southerner's dilemma.
As long as Quentin cannot face the inner reality of his own existence, he cannot possibly resolve his own, or his society's, dilemma.

Quentin Compson, both as participant in a resolution of the
Sutpen drama and as a narrator of it, is an enigmatic figure. Faulkner has put it another way: "It's incidentally the story of Quentin
Compson's hatred of the bad qualities in the country he loves."[42]
However, Quentin is as mysterious about revealing what it is he
hates about his South as he is about what he loves. He does not
make emphatic or judgmental statements regarding Sutpen's or the
South's morality. Neither does he make specific valuations of slavery
and the South's racial dilemma. But what Quentin succeeds in doing
as a character is involving the reader in the large, complex, and
shady areas of being, almost because of his inability to provide answers, or to identify problems.

Quentin, from the outset, is a ghost because of the past; Henry
Sutpen at the end is a ghostlike apparition from the past. Together
the two remind us of Faulkner's statement that the South is "dead."
Henry, once the promise of the South's future, is a death-in-life figure who retains a deathlike grip on Quentin's imaginative and rational faculties. Henry Sutpen, Miss Rosa, Mr. Compson, and the
Sutpen legend all mark Quentin for an irreparable, nightmare stasis.
He is impotent and unable to resolve the moral dilemma posed by
the legend and the southern past; yet he has the ability to involve
Shreve actively in it. Similarly, Quentin is alienated from the southern past while at the same time completely absorbed in the South by
means of the telling of the tale. In the process of the novel, Quentin

---

ness or inability to step beyond the sanctuary of paradox, to make . . . the clarifying
'humanistic act of faith.'" *Quest for Failure,* 201. However, Faulkner does make the
clarifying gesture with Dilsey and black religion at the end of *The Sound and the Fury,*
but thereafter he seems to recognize, not the irrelevancy of such affirmations, but
their inappropriateness in the separate white world, such as the one in *Absalom,*
which dominates his art.
42 Gwynn and Blotner (eds.), *Faulkner in the University,* 71.

condemns, justifies, expiates, and absolves the South from "sin"; nonetheless, the experience of the "sin" remains.

The obscurity of the ending seems deliberate. Faulkner knows no more than he reveals; Quentin knows no more than he sees and intuits. Quentin's inability to provide tidy answers comes out in his confronting Henry Sutpen: "Waking or sleeping it was the same: the bed, the yellow sheets and pillow, the wasted yellow face with closed, almost transparent eyelids on the pillow, the wasted hands crossed on the breast as if he were already a corpse; waking or sleeping it was the same and would be the same forever as long as he lived" (373).[43]

What Quentin goes up the stairs at Sutpen's Hundred to discover is not the same thing that compels Miss Rosa; that is, he does not ascend the stairs, as Rosa does, in order to *see* for certain that Henry is in the house. The purpose for Quentin is to meet his guilt-ridden, death-in-life double, to ascertain the waste of Henry's life, to acknowledge the lost potential of the South's young manhood, and to witness the reckoning of time and futility. Quentin recognizes that Henry embodies all of the "ghosts" of the southern world which haunt Quentin himself. Even though Henry is of an earlier generation, his subjective experiences as a son of the south mirror Quentin's. Henry's suffering makes Quentin self-conscious; and Quentin suffers the more because, while meaningful synthesis is possible for him, it is not necessarily accurate or sufficient for solving his personal dilemma. When the two meet at Sutpen's Hundred, they rep-

43 If the toll on Henry seems too severe and Clytie's burning of the mansion too much of a commitment of Henry to hell or a fiery unrest in death which is out of proportion to his position in life at the end of the novel, perhaps it is due to Faulkner's own personal feelings of guilt and responsibility for his brother Dean's death on November 3, 1935. Dean's death in a plane crash occurred after Faulkner had written the first six chapters of *Absalom, Absalom!*, but before the final three. According to Joseph Blotner, Faulkner took the *Absalom* manuscript to his mother's house immediately after he learned of Dean's accident and used his work on it to keep himself from falling apart or drinking during the funeral and burial preparations. See *Faulkner*, II, 917–19. Blotner also mentions a three-page letter from Faulkner to Ben Wasson in which Faulkner claims that his heavy drinking at the end of 1935 and during early 1936 was due to guilt over Dean's accident. Faulkner was, Blotner points out, still suffering from nervous exhaustion and "unassuaged anguish over Dean's death" during January 1936. *Faulkner*, II, 928. This biographical information seems relevant because Henry's crime is fratricide; he kills his only brother, the person whom he appears to love most and the person with whom he enjoys the closest physical contact.

resent a form of self-confrontation for which the imaginative constructions of the legend throughout the novel have prepared the
reader. The horror of self-confrontation in this meeting is Quentin's
most illuminating vision. He can no longer experience his world
vicariously; the imagination is not enough, because, in this case, it
implies a retreat from reality.

Attempting to use this encounter in order to prove empirically
that Quentin did or did not learn of Bon's black blood from Henry[44]
appears inconsequential ultimately because the heart of the enigma
is not the black blood, but the unknown, the mysterious, and the
inexplicable written into Henry's wasted life and read on Quentin's
"waking and sleeping" face. Henry shows that the pariah is not necessarily the Negro and that there are fugitive southern sons, just as
there were fugitive black slaves. The black blood is a device, a red
herring in the sense that it suggests a false significance to the meeting between the two sons of the South, the old and the new, who are
linked in a death grip from which neither will emerge to tell, in specific terms, the "truth" of his existence and his experience because
neither can—given both human frailty and the inexplicable in individual motives.

Henry's guilt and Quentin's fear (of life's possibilities for him) join
in presenting a powerful image of the dark at the core of southern
life, and the southern imagination as Faulkner demonstrates. The
image has power because it is a unique turn of the tradition; the
Negro in the South (either slave or free) usually stands for the dark
that has overshadowed and blighted the South, and Faulkner himself sometimes uses this notion. However, in *Absalom, Absalom!* it is,
as the ending suggests, the southerner himself, his own mind—
conscience (Henry) and imagination (Quentin)—that encompasses
and creates the dark. The Negro, whether Clytie, Charles Bon, or
Jim Bond in type, becomes in comparison a rather benign force.

44 See the exchange between Cleanth Brooks, who argues for Henry as the source of
the information (*William Faulkner: The Yoknapatawpha Country*, 436–37), and Hershel
Parker, who claims that Quentin "realized" the information after "seeing" Jim Bond's
face. "What Quentin Saw 'Out There,'" *Mississippi Quarterly*, XXVII (Summer, 1974),
323–26. Brooks restates his position in "The Narrative Structure of *Absalom, Absalom!*," *Georgia Review*, XXIX (Summer, 1975), 366–94; rpt. in Brooks, *William Faulkner: Toward Yoknapatawpha and Beyond*, 301–28.

There is, then, in the ending a marginal pulling away from the myths of southern existence, although the retreat is not strongly verbalized. Faulkner relies upon an emotional experience (as he does in resolving *The Sound and the Fury*) to imply an abandoning of a traditional position: Look at what the black man has done to me; look at what the black man has made me do. Even though the new position is more of a felt experience than a statement, it seems to be: See what I have done to myself. This recognition, which Faulkner can present only obliquely, is one that Quentin cannot thoroughly absorb.

Whether external elements are real or imagined, the individual has to come to terms with them because they are aspects of himself. If the individual does not, he is doomed. Whether dream or waking reality, the "'Nevermore of peace. Nevermore of peace. Nevermore Nevermore Nevermore'" (373) which punctuate Quentin's thoughts after he reveals his meeting with Henry echo neither "Negro" nor "nigger," but the powerful namelessness, the metaphysical "dark" that has wasted Henry's life and promises to waste Quentin's as well. It is Faulkner's ability to portray, not the meaning of that dark in the human heart, but so surely its multifaceted existence there that contributes to the power and intensity of *Absalom*.

In this his most oblique work, Faulkner confronts the novel directly as an artistic vehicle for conveying both the form and the substance of his raw material, his imaginative South. He allows neither sentiment nor reason to obfuscate the irreparable divisions in his world; his vision is dark, and he does not attempt to alleviate the darkness by resorting to Christian verities, as he does in *The Sound and the Fury*, or to redemptive allegories, as he does in *Light in August*. What he often termed "the conflicts of the human heart" are mirrored in his characters, themes, and structure. These conflicts are irrevocably bound to both the reality and the myth of the Negro, whom he sees as inescapable in the lives and thoughts of white southerners. He exposes his characters, and himself as artist, to the full force of the stereotypes, beliefs, customs, and symbols by which the white half of his divided world projects onto the Negro the accumulated frustrations and contradictions of its existence. Faulkner's implicit admission in this novel is that his white world must have its

"Negro," because it cannot face itself without this scapegoat, this buffer which, even in its most ineffectual symbolic shape, can absorb the shock of self-confrontation. None of his subsequent novels, not even *Go Down, Moses* with its seemingly more extensive treatment of the Negro in the South, approaches with such clarity of substance and form Faulkner's "truth" of the Negro in *Absalom*.

CHAPTER VI

Set Patterns

Go Down, Moses and Beyond

The artist, whether or not he wishes it, discovers with the passage of time that he has come to pursue a single path, a single objective, from which he cannot deviate. That is, he must strive with all the means and all the talents he possesses—his imagination, his experience, his powers of observation—to put into more lasting form than his own frail, ephemeral instant of life—in painting, sculpture, music, or in a book—what he has known firsthand during his brief period of existence: the passion and the hope, the beauty, the tragedy, the comedy of man, weak and frail but unconquerable; man who struggles and suffers and triumphs amid the conflicts of the human heart, the human condition. It is not his to resolve the contention nor expect to survive it, except in the form and meaning—and the memories they represent and evoke—of marble, canvas, music, and the ordered words which some day he must leave as his testament.

Speech of Acceptance for the Andrés Bello Award, Caracas, April 6, 1961, *A Faulkner Miscellany*, p. 165.

Whereas *Absalom, Absalom!* may be viewed as the artistic culmination of Faulkner's most creative period, *Go Down, Moses* may be considered the ideological culmination of that period. His ideas about style and form, as well as subject and theme, reach a logical and emotional conclusion in *Go Down, Moses and Other Stories* (1942), which Faulkner insisted is a novel. In *The Sound and the Fury*, Faulkner discovers the aesthetic value of the divided, family-based southern world and of the religious faith of the Negro. With *Light in August*, he explores the conflicts inherent in the public and private spheres of southern life as they are related to the social and personal definitions, especially of "Negro," underpinning white southern thought. In *Absalom, Absalom!* he treats the historical and personal reasons why his divided world remains fragmented, but he develops an awareness of a concomitant fragmentation of the individual living in that world. The conflicts that he presents are both internal and external; they are exacerbated by the largeness of the Negro abstraction and the force of the Negro stereotype in their power to obscure the reality of white life and to prevent whites' confrontation of self. Therefore, although some critics, such as Myra Jehlen, view *Go Down, Moses* as Faulkner's "most searching, most artistically effective treatment of race,"[1] *Absalom* is a more appropriate choice.

In *Go Down, Moses*, however, Faulkner recognizes that history (public, cultural or private, familial) cannot be transcended, but that instead it must be encompassed. So that in this novel, not only has he grasped the artistic significance of his heritage as a white Mississippian and of the Negro in his culture, but he also has comprehended what becomes for him a way of making peace with his heritage and with the Negro. The divided world in the novel is once again the world of blacks and whites, but it is as well the world of past and present, of wilderness and civilization, of slave and free, which is at the same time realistic (in the search for objective details and attention to an historical past) and symbolic (in the reliance upon imaginative and moral lives of modern individuals). The Negro forms a bridge between the two, so that whether as an individual or as part of a family or community, the Negro offers not so much an alternative way of living, as another means of understanding the malaise affecting the whites and the land in which they live. The land, represented by the wilderness, the McCaslin plantation, and the town of Jefferson, is connected to an image of the South presented in *Absalom, Absalom!*: "a soil manured with black blood from two hundred years of oppression and exploitation until it sprang

---

1 Myra Jehlen, *Class and Character in Faulkner's South* (New York: Columbia University Press, 1976), 97.

with an incredible paradox of peaceful greenery and crimson flowers" (25). While *Absalom* achieves the full aesthetic and imaginative reach that Faulkner could make of the special circumstances of his divided world, *Go Down, Moses* assesses and distills the meanings that Faulkner could take the most comfort in believing and presenting: that is, those aspects of faith and love which can somehow save the individual from the catatonic state to which Quentin succumbs in *Absalom*.

The abstraction becomes the concrete, the individual Negro who can be verified as having lived (unlike Bon, "the abstraction . . . nailed into a box"), and with the individual Negro Faulkner returns to his premise for portraying blacks which he employs in all of the novels through *The Sound and the Fury*. Even though the separate worlds as he depicts them in *Go Down, Moses* are too closely intertwined to expect extrication, those two worlds can encompass each other in love and acceptance. They can do so in a manner similar to that suggested by the joint activity of young Bayard and Ringo in "Ambuscade": "the two of us needing first to join forces and spend ourselves against a common enemy, time, before we could engender between us and hold intact the pattern of recapitulant mimic furious victory like a cloth, a shield between ourselves and reality, between us and fact and doom."[2]

The imaginative collaboration between the white and the black youths, though part of a war game, makes it possible for both to recognize reality and fact, but also to stave off destruction by refusing to surrender their belief in something beyond reality or fact. It is a belief similar to that of Tomey's Turl and Buck and Buddy McCaslin in "Was," which opens the novel and establishes the pattern of interracial kin and blood or spiritual brotherhood. It is also a belief shared by old Molly Beauchamp and Miss Worsham, who, in getting Gavin Stevens to bring home the body of Samuel Worsham Beauchamp, compel him to acknowledge its validity in the final chapter, "Go Down, Moses." The need of individual blacks and whites to join together against the forces of time are reiterated in *Go Down, Moses* by a transition to age and maturity; for example, the youthful and

2 William Faulkner, *The Unvanquished* (New York: Random House, 1938), 4.

humorous perspective of "Was" gives way to the point of view of older men—Lucas Beauchamp, who states, "I'm a nigger. . . . But I'm a man too,'" and Ike McCaslin, who insists that God created man "to hold the earth in the communal anonymity of brotherhood."[3] The larger need of individuals to unite is also underscored by the recurrent use of marriage as a difficult, but necessary bonding for human satisfaction; Faulkner's theme of marriage, in addition, reverberates with his messages of love and faith. Importantly, then, *Go Down, Moses* illuminates the conjoining of blacks and whites that, though impossible in the earlier novels, becomes the set pattern in *Intruder in the Dust* (1948) and finally in *The Reivers* (1962).

While on a surface level *Go Down, Moses* seems to refute myths about the Negro, it actually substitutes more personal and palatable myths (similar to those in *The Sound and the Fury*) for the more disturbing cultural ones in *Light in August* or *Absalom*. Faulkner's dedication to Mammy Caroline Barr is one indication of the dominant attitude toward the Negro in *Go Down, Moses:* "To Mammy . . . Who was born in slavery and who gave to my family without stint or calculation of recompense and to my childhood an immeasurable devotion and love." The key words are *fidelity, devotion,* and *love,* which reverberate throughout the book, specifically in Roth Edmonds' recognition of Molly Beauchamp as a surrogate mother "who had given him, the motherless, without stint or expectation of reward that constant and abiding devotion and love" (117). Roth's tribute echoes Faulkner's dedication to Callie Barr, as well as the dominant characteristics of the Negro in *Soldiers' Pay, Flags in the Dust,* and *The Sound and the Fury.* While these characteristics stress the humanity of blacks, they are nonetheless reductive.

In effect, Faulkner takes the vision of the black world of faith and feeling, of love and acceptance associated with Callie in *Soldiers' Pay,* with the Strothers in *Flags in the Dust,* and with the Gibsons, especially Dilsey, in *The Sound and the Fury,* and he uses that vision as a way of seeing and understanding the black McCaslins (particularly Lucas Beauchamp, his wife Molly, and his daughter), as well as the blacks who are not McCaslins (including Rider and his wife Mannie). Faulkner also incorporates definitions of race and of the Negro

3 William Faulkner, *Go Down, Moses* (New York: Random House, 1942), 47, 257.

as a social creation which begin in *Light in August* and continue in *Intruder in the Dust;* for instance, the extended debate between Ike McCaslin and McCaslin Edmonds has a social definition of "nigger" as its thesis (295–300). *Go Down, Moses* is filled, like *The Unvanquished* and *The Reivers*, with personal memory, both the individual reminiscences of characters and the projected recollections of the author. For example, there is something of Mammy Callie Barr in Molly and something of the black male servant Ned, described in Faulkner's essay "Mississippi," in Lucas.

However, the progression in Faulkner's art and method is that he does not idealize the Negro, as he tends to do when stressing the Negro's different vision of life and living; a possible reason for this progression may be that the portrait of Clytie Sutpen and the Bon men freed Faulkner from oversimplifying the Negro and that his definition of the meaning of the Negro in the public spheres of white life in *Light in August* opened the stereotype itself to exposure (albeit in symbolic terms). In *Go Down, Moses* Faulkner seems able to acknowledge the tyranny of the cultural stereotype, especially in his portraits of Lucas and Rider, but he transforms it more fully into an underlying imaginative conception which serves his art, though he still cannot escape it. He attempts, as McCaslin Edmonds observes about the writers of the Bible, "to write down the heart's truth out of the heart's driving complexity, for all the complex and troubled hearts which would beat after" (260).

Faulkner's *Go Down, Moses* accepts and incorporates a basic vision of the world as divided and of conflict as a pervasive condition. It presents no clear resolutions to the compounded tensions of the work: hidden crimes against blood kin, legacies of slavery and injustice, rape of the virgin land, father-child conflicts, the passing of the old way of life. While these problems are not resolved, there is an uneasy truce at the end, a recognition that the individuals of the community cannot strip themselves of their collective guilt or interdependency, but they can act according to the old verities of the human heart—in love as Molly and Miss Worsham do, out of respect as does Gavin Stevens, or pity as Ike McCaslin does. Moreover, from their independent motivations, they can undertake mutually beneficial, cooperative enterprises.

All of these characters reflect human bondage, ties of emotion and tradition, which can at best be termed social responsibility.[4] Yet they come to an acceptance of themselves and one another which precludes self-destruction, emotional or moral paralysis, and dread of the future. McCaslin Edmonds implies as much when he tells Ike: "'And anyway, you will be free. —No, not now or ever, we from them nor they from us. . . . I am what I am; I will always be what I was born and have always been. And more than me'" (299, 300). Yet acceptance does not mean change. There is no resolution to the central conflicts in the lives of the white characters; Ike, for instance, does not find even the peace of expiation. However, neither do the blacks escape into a satisfactory, harmonious existence: the black woman in "Delta Autumn" recognizes the perils of her existence and loves despite them; Molly must face the burial of her grandson who has not found a promised land in the North.

Even more than a culmination,[5] then, *Go Down, Moses* is a dénouement, which brings together emotions, thoughts, and observations accumulated over Faulkner's lifetime in the South and more than a decade as a novelist. All of his subsequent treatments of blacks follow the pattern and vision established as viable in *Go Down, Moses*. Nevertheless, his tendency to rely upon the symbolic value of the Negro, both in the black world and in the white world, for developing his vision enriches the structural design and the thematic content. A major example is the intrinsic connection Faulkner establishes between the Negro and the bear, Old Ben. Obviously, on one symbolic level the bear represents the wilderness, the land itself in a relatively free and natural state. But on a second symbolic level, which moves from surface symbolism to depth symbolism, the bear represents the Negro, and becomes an analogue to the role of the Negro in this work and in the earlier Faulkner novels. The bear ex-

---

4 See Lawrance Thompson's explication of the themes of freedom and bondage in *Go Down, Moses. William Faulkner: An Introduction and Interpretation*, 81–98. An aspect of the theme of freedom which Thompson does not explore is that the attempts at freedom are primarily attempts to escape from the social structures demanded by the divided southern world.

5 Lee Jenkins views *Go Down, Moses* as a culmination in which Faulkner explicitly treats some of his fundamental themes: "man's appropriation and violation of the land and . . . his violations of the human rights of others." *Faulkner and Black-White Relations: A Psychoanalytic Approach* (New York: Columbia University Press, 1981), 221, 252.

ists in the wilderness, the natural world ("the big woods, bigger and older than any recorded document," 194), which becomes both allegorical and mythical.

In the "unaxed woods," the bear is "not even a mortal beast, but an anachronism indomitable and invincible out of an old dead time, a phantom, epitome and apotheosis of the old wild life" (146–47). Wilderness and bear combine to represent an element of human spirit. When Faulkner clarifies his conception of both the wilderness and the bear, he comes close to identifying Old Ben with the Negro:

> The wilderness to me was the past, which could be the old evils, the old forces, which were by their own standards right and correct, ruthless, but they lived and died by their own code—they asked nothing. . . . To me, the wilderness was man's past. . . . The bear was a symbol of the old forces, not evil forces, but the old forces which in man's youth were not evil, but they were in man's blood, his inheritance, his [instinctive] impulses came from that old ruthless malevolence, which was nature. His dreams, his nightmares; and this story was to me a universal story of a man who, still progressing . . . had to learn to cope with and still cope with it in the terms of justice and pity and compassion and strength.[6]

Given the appearance of Old Ben and the mythic proportions he assumes in the narrative, it seems quite plausible that Faulkner is operating in "The Old People" and in "The Bear" on literal and several symbolic levels, by drawing Old Ben as a concrete reality which is transformed by the meaning placed upon his existence (and appearance) to an abstract reality encompassing the Negro. This interpretation, in part, helps to explain the forced linking of the themes of the wilderness and of race relations for which Faulkner has been criticized.[7]

The bear, Faulkner points out, represents: "an old obsolescence that was strong, that held to the old ways, but because it had been strong and lived within its own code of mortality, it deserved to be

6 Interviews in Japan, Meriwether and Millgate (eds.), *Lion in the Garden*, 115.
7 Millgate explains the "tenuousness of the connection between the hunting episodes and the rest of the novel" as "in some measure a direct and deliberate reflection of Faulkner's conception of Ike and Ike's idealism." *The Achievement of William Faulkner*, 210.

treated with respect. And that's what the little boy did. He learned not about bears, from that bear, but he learned about the world, he learned about man. About courage, about pity, about responsibility from the bear."[8] Here Faulkner emphasizes the connection between the plantation heir, Ike McCaslin, and the embodiment of the wilderness, the bear. The lessons Ike actually learns are filtered through his contact with Sam Fathers, who "had been a negro for two generations" (164), and who hails the bear as father. As Ike's mentor, Sam Fathers encompasses both the bondage of blacks in the plantation society and the natural freedom of an older race, which in Faulkner's presentation is part of the larger configuration of the bear and the wilderness. It is not surprising, then, that in the instances when Faulkner explains his conception of the bear, he employs the words and phrases that have repeatedly characterized the Negro in Go Down, Moses.

The association of the Negro and animal imagery is not new in this Faulkner work; the association appears crudely in Soldiers' Pay, Sartoris, and sentimentally in The Sound and the Fury, in the impressionistic connection between "niggers and mules." Moreover, Absalom, Absalom! contains a refinement of this association in the extended analogy between Sutpen's slaves (the "wild niggers") and wild beasts. Importantly, too, in Absalom, Absalom! Faulkner is more concerned with the Negro as an abstraction, a primal force, rather than as a realistic character in the white world. In Go Down, Moses, Old Ben is an even more extensive use of the Negro as an abstraction, but in this case, the associative links also become abstract; nonetheless, the basic outline is clear. The Negro becomes, as a result, extraordinary and cannot be fully comprehended. Despite the vivid individual portraits of Lucas and Rider, or Molly and some minor characters, the Negro is finally disembodied from the reality of ordinary human life.

Faulkner uses the Negro in complex worlds, represented by the plantation and the wilderness, the actual world and the symbolic world, which become less stratified as civilization encroaches upon the wilderness and the past impinges upon present consciousness.

8 Interviews in Japan, Meriwether and Millgate (eds.), Lion in the Garden, 140.

Faulkner uses the Negro, too, as part of his argument for the union (tense and unsatisfactory though it is) of the divided world of the South. Thus, despite its narrative patterns and voices, *Go Down, Moses* is an extension of earlier conceptions of the Negro; its historical perspective, contrapuntal design, and thematic motifs are explicit statements both of the burden of race upon the individual, the family, the community, and the larger region and of the artistic weight Faulkner places on the Negro in his fictional world.

Selected Bibliography

Adams, Richard P. "The Apprenticeship of William Faulkner." *Tu-lane Studies in English,* XII (1962), 113–56. Rpt. in *Faulkner: Four Decades of Criticism.* Ed. Linda Wagner. East Lansing: Michigan State University Press, 1973.

————. "Faulkner: The European Roots." In *Faulkner: Fifty Years After "The Marble Faun."* Ed. George H. Wolfe. University: University of Alabama Press, 1976.

————. *Faulkner: Myth and Motion.* Princeton: Princeton University Press, 1968.

Anderson, Sherwood. *Dark Laughter.* New York: Boni and Liveright, 1925.

————. *Sherwood Anderson's Notebook.* New York: Boni and Liveright, 1926.

————. *A Story Teller's Story* (1924). Ed. Ray Lewis White. Cleveland: The Press of Case Western Reserve University, 1968.

Angoff, Charles, and H. L. Mencken. "The Worst American State." *American Mercury,* XXIV (1931), 1–16, 175–88, 355–71.

Appel, Paul P., ed. *Homage to Sherwood Anderson, 1876–1941.* Mama-roneck, N.Y.: Paul P. Appel, 1970.

Aswell, Duncan. "The Recollection and the Blood: Jason's Role in *The Sound and the Fury.*" *Mississippi Quarterly,* XXI (Summer, 1968), 211–18.

Backman, Melvin. *Faulkner: The Major Years, a Critical Study.* Bloom-ington: Indiana University Press, 1966.

Barth, J. Robert, S.J., ed. *Religious Perspectives in Faulkner's Fiction: Yoknapatawpha and Beyond.* Notre Dame: University of Notre Dame Press, 1972.

Beck, Warren. *Faulkner: Essays*. Madison: University of Wisconsin Press, 1976.

Bezzerides, A. I. *William Faulkner: A Life on Paper*. Jackson: University Press of Mississippi, 1979.

Billington, Monroe L., ed. *The South: A Central Theme*. New York: Holt, Rinehart and Winston, 1969.

Blanchard, Margaret. "The Rhetoric of Communion: Voice in *The Sound and the Fury*." *American Literature*, XLI (1970), 555–65.

Bleikasten, André. *The Most Splendid Failure: Faulkner's "The Sound and the Fury*." Bloomington: Indiana University Press, 1976.

Blotner, Joseph. *Faulkner: A Biography*. 2 vols. New York: Random House, 1974.

————, ed. *Selected Letters of William Faulkner*. New York: Random House, 1977.

————. "William Faulkner's Essay on the Composition of *Sartoris*." *Yale Library Gazette*, XLVII (January, 1973), 121–24.

Bluestein, Gene. *The Voice of the Folk: Folklore and American Literary Theory*. Amherst: University of Massachusetts Press, 1972.

Bradbury, John. *Renaissance in the South: A Critical History of the Literature, 1920–1960*. Chapel Hill: University of North Carolina Press, 1963.

Bradbury, Malcolm, and David Palmer, eds. *The American Novel and the Nineteen Twenties*. London: Edward Arnold, 1971.

Brooks, Cleanth. "Faulkner's First Novel." *Southern Review*, VI (Autumn, 1970), 1056–74.

————. "The Narrative Structure of *Absalom, Absalom!*" *Georgia Review*, XXIX (Summer, 1974), 366–94.

————. *William Faulkner: The Yoknapatawpha Country*. New Haven: Yale University Press, 1963.

————. *William Faulkner: Toward Yoknapatawpha and Beyond*. New Haven: Yale University Press, 1978.

Broughton, Panthea Reid. *William Faulkner: The Abstract and the Actual*. Baton Rouge: Louisiana State University Press, 1974.

Brown, Calvin S. "Dilsey: From Faulkner to Homer." In *William Faulkner: Prevailing Verities and World Literature*. Ed. Wolodymyr T. Zyla and Wendell M. Aycock. Lubbock: Texas Tech Press, 1973.

Brown, Sterling A. "A Century of Negro Portraiture in American Literature." *Massachusetts Review*, VII (Winter, 1966), 73–96.

————. "Negro Character as Seen by White Authors." *Journal of Negro Education*, II (1933), 179–203.

————. *The Negro in American Fiction*. 1937; rpt. New York: Atheneum, 1969.

Campbell, Harry M., and Ruel E. Foster. *William Faulkner: A Critical Appraisal*. Norman: University of Oklahoma Press, 1951.

Cash, Wilbur J. *The Mind of the South.* New York: Alfred A. Knopf, 1941.

Clark, Thomas D. *The Emerging South.* 2nd ed. New York: Oxford University Press, 1968.

Clark, William Bedford. "The Serpent of Lust in the Southern Garden." *Southern Review,* X (Autumn, 1974), 805–22.

Collins, Carvel. "A Conscious Literary Use of Freud?" *Literature and Psychology,* III (June, 1953), 2–3.

———. "The Interior Monologues of *The Sound and the Fury.*" In *English Institute Essays 1952.* Ed. Alan S. Downer. New York: Columbia University Press, 1954.

———. "The Pairing of *The Sound and the Fury* and *As I Lay Dying.*" *Princeton University Library Chronicle,* XVIII (Spring, 1957), 114–23.

———, ed. *William Faulkner: Early Prose and Poetry.* Boston: Little, Brown, 1962.

———, ed. *William Faulkner: New Orleans Sketches.* Rev. ed. New York: Random House, 1968.

———, ed. *William Faulkner's University Pieces.* Folcroft, Pa.: Folcroft Press, 1962.

Core, George, ed. *Southern Fiction Today: Renascence and Beyond.* Athens: University of Georgia Press, 1969.

Couch, W. T. "The Negro in the South." In *Culture in the South.* Ed. W. T. Couch. Chapel Hill: University of North Carolina Press, 1934.

Cowley, Malcolm, ed. *The Portable Faulkner.* New York: Viking Press, 1946.

Creighton, Joanne V. *William Faulkner's Craft of Revision: The Snopes Trilogy, "The Unvanquished," and "Go Down, Moses."* Detroit: Wayne State University Press, 1977.

Cullen, John B., and Floyd C. Watkins. *Old Times in the Faulkner Country.* Chapel Hill: University of North Carolina Press, 1961.

Dahl, James. "A Faulkner Reminiscence: Conversations with Mrs. Maude Falkner." *Journal of Modern Literature,* III (April, 1974), 1026–30.

Dewey, John. *Art as Experience.* New York: Minton, Balch, 1934.

Dollard, John. *Caste and Class in a Southern Town.* 1937; rpt. New York: Doubleday, Anchor, 1957.

Edmonds, Irene C. "Faulkner and the Black Shadow." In *Southern Renascence.* Ed. Louis D. Rubin, Jr., and Robert D. Jacobs. Baltimore: Johns Hopkins University Press, 1953.

Ellison, Ralph, *Shadow and Act.* New York: Random House, 1964.

———. "Society, Morality and the Novel." In *The Living Novel: A Symposium.* Ed. Granville Hicks. New York: Macmillan, 1957.

Fadiman, Regina K. *Faulkner's "Light in August": A Description and In-*

terpretation of the Revisions. Charlottesville: University Press of Virginia for the Bibliographical Society of the University of Virginia, 1975.

Falkner, Murry. *The Falkners of Mississippi: A Memoir.* Baton Rouge: Louisiana State University Press, 1967.

———. "The Wonderful Mornings of Our Youth." In *William Faulkner of Oxford.* Ed. James W. Webb and A. Wigfall Green. Baton Rouge: Louisiana State University Press, 1965.

Fant, Joseph L., III, and Robert Ashley, eds. *Faulkner at West Point.* New York: Random House, 1964.

Faulkner, John. *My Brother Bill: An Affectionate Reminiscence.* New York: Trident Press, 1963.

Faulkner, William. *Absalom, Absalom!* 1936; rpt. New York: Modern Library, 1964.

———. *Flags in the Dust.* Ed. Douglas Day. New York: Random House, 1973.

———. *Go Down, Moses.* 1942; rpt. New York: Random House, 1973.

———. *The Green Bough.* New York: Harrison Smith and Robert Haas, 1933.

———. "An Introduction to *The Sound and the Fury.*" *Mississippi Quarterly,* XXVI (Summer, 1973), 410–15. Rpt. in *A Faulkner Miscellany.* Ed. James B. Meriwether. Jackson: University Press of Mississippi, 1974, pp. 156–61.

———. *Intruder in the Dust.* New York: Random House, 1948.

———. *Light in August.* New York: Harrison Smith and Robert Haas, 1932; rpt. New York: Random House, 1963.

———. *The Marble Faun.* Boston: The Four Seas, 1924.

———. *Mississippi Poems.* Oxford: Yoknapatawpha Press, 1979.

———. *Sartoris.* New York: Harcourt, Brace, 1929.

———. *Soldiers' Pay.* New York: Boni and Liveright, 1926.

———. *The Sound and the Fury.* New York: Jonathan Cape and Harrison Smith, 1929.

———. *The Unvanquished.* New York: Random House, 1938.

Federal Writers' Project. *Mississippi: A Guide to the Magnolia State.* American Guide Series. Works Progress Administration. New York: Alfred A. Knopf, 1937.

Frank, Waldo. *Holiday.* New York: Boni and Liveright, 1923.

Friedman, Lawrence J. *The White Savage: Racial Fantasies in the Postbellum South.* Englewood Cliffs: Prentice-Hall, 1970.

Frohock, W. M. *The Novel of Violence in America.* 2nd. rev. ed. Boston: Beacon Press, 1957.

Geismar, Maxwell. "William Faulkner: The Negro and the Female." In his *Writers in Crisis: The American Novel, 1925–1940.* 1947; rpt. New York: Hill and Wang, 1961.

Gossett, Louise Y. *Violence in Recent Southern Fiction.* Durham: Duke University Press, 1965.

Guerard, Albert J. *The Triumph of the Novel: Dickens, Dostoevsky, Faulkner.* New York: Oxford University Press, 1976.

Guetti, James. *The Limits of Metaphor: A Study of Melville, Conrad, and Faulkner.* Ithaca: Cornell University Press, 1967.

Gwynn, Frederick L., and Joseph L. Blotner, eds. *Faulkner in the University: Class Conferences at the University of Virginia, 1957–1958.* Charlottesville: University Press of Virginia, 1959.

Hagopian, John V. "*Absalom, Absalom!* and the Negro Question." *Modern Fiction Studies,* XIX (Summer, 1973), 207–10.

Harold, Brent. "The Value and Limitations of Faulkner's Fictional Method." *American Literature,* XLVII (May, 1975), 212–29.

Harrington, Evans, and Ann J. Abadie, eds. *Faulkner, Modernism, and Film: Faulkner and Yoknapatawpha, 1978.* Jackson: University Press of Mississippi, 1979.

————, eds. *The Maker and the Myth: Faulkner and Yoknapatawpha, 1977.* Jackson: University Press of Mississippi, 1978.

————, eds. *The South and Faulkner's Yoknapatawpha: The Actual and the Apocryphal.* Jackson: University Press of Mississippi, 1977.

Harris, Joel Chandler. *Balaam and His Master.* Cambridge: Riverside Press, 1891.

————. *Free Joe and Other Georgian Sketches.* New York: Charles Scribner's Sons, 1887.

Hobson, Fred C., Jr. *Serpent of Eden: H. L. Mencken and the South.* Chapel Hill: University of North Carolina Press, 1974.

Hoffman, Frederick J. *The Art of Southern Fiction: A Study of Some Modern Southern Novelists.* Carbondale: Southern Illinois University Press, 1967.

————. *The Twenties: American Writing in the Postwar Decade.* Rev. ed. New York: The Free Press, 1962.

————, and Olga W. Vickery, eds. *William Faulkner: Three Decades of Criticism.* East Lansing: Michigan State University Press, 1960.

Holman, C. Hugh. *Three Modes of Modern Southern Fiction: Glasgow, Faulkner and Styron.* Athens: University of Georgia Press, 1966.

————. "View from the Regency-Hyatt: Southern Social Issues and the Outer World." In *Southern Fiction Today: Renascence and Beyond.* Ed. George Core. Athens: University of Georgia Press, 1969.

Holt, Grace Sims. "Rappin' and Stylin' outta the Black Pulpit." In *Rappin' and Stylin' Out: Communication in Urban Black America.* Ed. Thomas Kockman. Urbana: University of Illinois Press, 1972.

Howe, Irving. *William Faulkner: A Critical Study.* 2nd rev. ed. New York: Random House, 1952.

————. "William Faulkner and the Negroes: A Vision of Lost Fraternity" *Commentary,* XII (October, 1951), 359–68.

Hunt, John W. *William Faulkner: Art in Theological Tension.* Syracuse: Syracuse University Press, 1965.

Irwin, John T. *Doubling and Incest/Repetition and Revenge: A Speculative Reading of Faulkner.* Baltimore: Johns Hopkins University Press, 1975.

Izsak, Emily K. "The Manuscript of *The Sound and the Fury:* The Revisions in the First Section." *Studies in Bibliography,* XX, (1967), 189–202.

James, William. "On a Certain Blindness in Human Beings." In his *On Some of Life's Ideals.* New York: Henry Holt, 1900.

Jehlen, Myra. *Class and Character in Faulkner's South.* New York: Columbia University Press, 1976.

Jelliffe, Robert A., ed. *Faulkner at Nagano.* 1956; rpt. Folcroft, Pa.: Folcroft Press, 1956.

Jenkins, Lee. *Faulkner and Black–White Relations: A Psychoanalytic Approach.* New York: Columbia University Press, 1981.

Johnson, James Weldon. *The Autobiography of an Ex-Coloured Man.* 1912; rpt. New York: Alfred A. Knopf, 1927.

———. *God's Trombones: Seven Negro Sermons in Verse.* New York: Viking, 1927.

Jones, Howard Mumford, ed. *The Letters of Sherwood Anderson.* Boston: Little, Brown, 1969.

Kartiganer, Donald M. *The Fragile Thread: The Meaning of Form in Faulkner's Novels.* Amherst: University of Massachusetts Press, 1979.

———. "*The Sound and the Fury* and Faulkner's Quest for Form." *ELH,* XXXVII (December, 1970), 613–39.

Kelley, Edith. *Weeds.* 1923; rpt. Carbondale: Southern Illinois University Press, 1972.

Kenner, Hugh. *A Homemade World: The American Modernist Writers.* New York: Alfred A. Knopf, 1975.

Kent, George E. *Blackness and the Adventure of Western Culture.* Chicago: Third World Press, 1972.

———. "The Black Woman in Faulkner's Works with the Exclusion of Dilsey." *Phylon,* XXXV (December, 1974), 430–41.

Kerr, Elizabeth. *William Faulkner's Gothic Domain.* Port Washington, N.Y.: Kennikat Press, 1979.

———. *Yoknapatawpha: Faulkner's "Little Postage Stamp of Native Soil."* New York: Fordham University Press, 1969.

Kinney, Arthur F. *Faulkner's Narrative Poetics: Style as Vision.* Amherst: University of Massachusetts Press, 1978.

Kirwan, Albert D. *The Revolt of the Rednecks: Mississippi Politics: 1876–1925.* Lexington: University of Kentucky Press, 1951.

La Farge, Oliver. *The Copper Pot*. Boston: Houghton, Mifflin, 1942.
———. *Raw Material*. Boston: Houghton, Mifflin, 1945.
Langford, Gerald. *Faulkner's Revision of "Absalom, Absalom!": A Collation of the Manuscript and the Published Book*. Austin: University of Texas Press, 1971.
Lawson, Lewis A. "Portrait of a Culture in Crisis: Modern Southern Literature." *Texas Quarterly*, X (Spring, 1967), 143–55.
Levins, Lynn Gartrell. *Faulkner's Heroic Design: The Yoknapatawpha Novels*. Athens: University of Georgia Press, 1976.
Lind, Ilse Dusoir. "The Design and Meaning of *Absalom, Absalom!*" *PMLA*, LXX (December, 1955), 887–912. Rpt. in *Faulkner: Four Decades of Criticism*. Ed. Linda Wagner. East Lansing: Michigan State University Press, 1973.
Longley, John L. *The Tragic Mask: A Study of Faulkner's Heroes*. Chapel Hill: University of North Carolina Press, 1963.
Maclachlan, John. "No Faulkner in Metropolis." In *South: Modern Southern Literature in Its Cultural Setting*. Ed. Louis D. Rubin, Jr., and Robert D. Jacobs. Garden City: Doubleday, 1961.
Mays, Benjamin E. *The Negro's God as Reflected in His Literature*. Boston: Chapman and Grimes, 1938.
McGhee, N. B. "The Folk Sermon: A Facet of the Black Literary Experience." *CLA Journal*, XIII (September, 1969), 51–61.
McIllwaine, Shields. *The Southern Poor-White: From Lubberland to Tobacco Road*. 1939; rpt. New York: Cooper Square, 1970.
Mencken, H. L. "The Sahara of the Bozart." In his *Prejudices: Series Two*. New York: Alfred A. Knopf, 1920.
Meriwether, James B., ed. *Essays, Speeches and Public Letters by William Faulkner*. New York: Random House, 1965.
———, ed. *A Faulkner Miscellany*. Jackson: University Press of Mississippi, 1974.
———, and Michael Millgate, eds. *Lion in the Garden: Interviews with William Faulkner, 1926–1962*. New York: Random House, 1968.
Middleton, John. "Shreve McCannon and Sutpen's Legacy." *Southern Review*, X (January, 1974), 115–24.
Millgate, Michael. *The Achievement of William Faulkner*. New York: Random House, 1966.
———. *William Faulkner*. New York: Grove Press, 1961.
Miner, Ward. *The World of William Faulkner*. Durham: Duke University Press, 1952.
Minter, David. *William Faulkner: His Life and Work*. Baltimore: Johns Hopkins University Press, 1980.
Mitchell, Henry H. *Black Preaching*. Philadelphia: J. B. Lippincott, 1970.
Muhlenfeld, Elisabeth S. "Shadows with Substance and Ghosts Ex-

humed: The Women in *Absalom, Absalom!" Mississippi Quarterly,*
XXV (Summer, 1972), 189–304.

Myrdal, Gunnar, *et al. An American Dilemma: The Negro Problem and
Modern Democracy.* New York: Harper and Brothers, 1944.

Nilon, Charles H. *Faulkner and the Negro.* 1962; rpt. New York: The
Citadel Press, 1965.

O'Connor, Flannery. "The Fiction Writer and His Country." In *The
Living Novel: A Symposium.* Ed. Granville Hicks. New York: Macmillan, 1957.

O'Connor, William Van. *The Tangled Fire of William Faulkner.* Minneapolis: University of Minnesota Press, 1959.

Odum, Howard. *An American Epoch.* New York: Henry Holt, 1930.

———. "On Southern Literature and Southern Culture." In *Southern
Renascence: The Literature of the Modern South.* Ed. Louis D. Rubin,
Jr., and Robert D. Jacobs. Baltimore: Johns Hopkins University
Press, 1953.

Owsley, Frank L. *Plain Folk of the Old South.* 1949; rpt. Chicago:
Quadrangle, 1965.

Page, Sally R. *Faulkner's Women: Characterization and Meaning.* Deland, Fla.: Everett/Edwards, 1972.

Parker, Hershel. "What Quentin Saw 'Out There.'" *Mississippi Quarterly,* XXVII (Summer, 1974), 323–26.

Peavy, Charles D. "Faulkner's Use of Folklore in *The Sound and the
Fury." Journal of American Folklore,* LXXIX (July–September, 1966),
437–47.

———. *Go Slow Now: Faulkner and the Race Question.* Eugene: University of Oregon Press, 1971.

Peden, William. "The American Short Story During the Twenties."
Studies in Short Fiction, X (Fall, 1973), 367–71.

Pitavy, Francois. *Faulkner's "Light in August."* Trans. Gillian E. Cook.
Bloomington: University of Indiana Press, 1973.

Puckett, Newbell Niles. *Folk Beliefs of the Southern Negro.* Chapel Hill:
University of North Carolina Press, 1926.

Reed, Joseph W., Jr. *Faulkner's Narrative.* New Haven: Yale University
Press, 1973.

Richardson, H. Edward. *William Faulkner: The Journey to Self-Discovery.* Columbia: University of Missouri Press, 1969.

Roberts, Elizabeth Madox. *The Time of Man.* New York: Viking Press,
1926.

Rosenberg, Bruce A. "The Aesthetics of the Folk Sermon." *Georgia
Review,* XXV (Winter, 1971), 424–38.

———. *The Art of the American Folk Preacher.* New York: Oxford University Press, 1970.

Rourke, Constance. *American Humor: A Study of National Character.* Garden City: Doubleday, 1931.

Rubin, Louis D., Jr. *The Faraway Country: Writers of the Modern South.* Seattle: University of Washington Press, 1963.

———. "Southern Local Color and the Black Man." *Southern Review,* n.s. IV (October, 1970), 1011–30.

———, and Robert D. Jacobs, eds. *South: Modern Southern Literature in Its Cultural Setting.* Garden City: Doubleday, 1961.

———, and Robert D. Jacobs, eds. *Southern Renascence: The Literature of the Modern South.* Baltimore: Johns Hopkins University Press, 1953.

Samway, Patrick H. *Faulkner's "Intruder in the Dust": A Critical Study of the Typescripts.* New York: Whitson Publishers, 1980.

Schoenberg, Estella. *Old Tales and Talking: Quentin Compson in William Faulkner's "Absalom, Absalom!" and Related Works.* Jackson: University Press of Mississippi, 1977.

Scholes, Robert, and Robert Kellogg. *The Nature of Narrative.* New York: Oxford University Press, 1966.

Seiden, Melvin. "Faulkner's Ambiguous Negro." *Massachusetts Review,* IV (Summer, 1963), 675–90.

Skaggs, Merrill Maguire. *The Folk of Southern Fiction.* Athens: University of Georgia Press, 1972.

Slatoff, Walter. *Quest for Failure: A Study of William Faulkner.* Ithaca: Cornell University Press, 1960.

Spratling, William, and William Faulkner. *Sherwood Anderson and Other Famous Creoles.* 1926; rpt. Austin: University of Texas Press, 1966.

Starke, Catherine Juanita. *Black Portraiture in American Fiction: Stock Characters, Archetypes and Individuals.* New York: Basic Books, 1971.

Stewart, George R., and Joseph M. Backus. "'Each in Its Ordered Place': Structure and Narrative in Benjy's Section of *The Sound and the Fury.*" *American Literature,* XXIX (January, 1958), 440–56.

Stonum, Gary L. *Faulkner's Career: An Internal Literary History.* Ithaca: Cornell University Press, 1979.

Swiggart, Peter. *The Art of Faulkner's Novels.* Austin: University of Texas Press, 1962.

Swink, Helen. "William Faulkner: The Novelist as Oral Narrator." *Georgia Review,* XXVI (Summer, 1972), 183–209.

Taylor, Walter. "Faulkner: Social Commitment and Artistic Temperament." *Southern Review,* VI (Autumn, 1970), 1075–92.

Taylor, William K. *Cavalier and Yankee: The Old South and the American National Character.* New York: Braziller, 1961.

Thompson, Lawrance. *William Faulkner: An Introduction and Inter-*

pretation. 2nd ed. New York: Holt, Rinehart and Winston, 1967.

Thorp, Willard. "The Writer as Pariah in the Old South." In *Southern Writers: Appraisals in Our Time.* Ed. Rinaldo Charles Simonini, Jr. 1961; rpt. Freeport, N.Y.: Books for Libraries, 1969.

Tindall, George Brown. *The Emergence of the New South: 1913–1945.* Vol. X of *A History of the South.* Ed. Wendell Holmes Stephenson and E. Merton Coulter. Baton Rouge: Louisiana State University Press, 1967.

Tischler, Nancy M. *Black Masks: Negro Character in Modern Southern Fiction.* University Park: Pennsylvania State University Press, 1969.

Trachenberg, Alan, ed. *The Memoirs of Waldo Frank.* Amherst: University of Massachusetts Press, 1973.

Vickery, Olga W. *The Novels of William Faulkner: A Critical Interpretation.* Rev. ed. Baton Rouge: Louisiana State University Press, 1964.

Volpe, Edward. *A Reader's Guide to William Faulkner.* New York: Noonday Press, 1964.

Waggoner, Hyatt. *William Faulkner: From Jefferson to the World.* Lexington: University of Kentucky Press, 1959.

Wagner, Linda W., ed. *Faulkner: Four Decades of Criticism.* East Lansing: Michigan State University Press, 1973.

———. "Jason Compson: The Demands of Honor." *Sewanee Review,* LXXIX (Fall, 1971), 554–75.

Warren, Robert Penn, ed. *Faulkner: A Collection of Critical Essays.* Englewood Cliffs: Prentice-Hall, 1966.

———. *The Legacy of the Civil War: Meditations on the Centennial.* New York: Random House, 1961.

Weaver, Richard M. "Aspects of Southern Philosophy." In *Southern Renascence: The Literature of the Modern South.* Ed. Louis D. Rubin, Jr., and Robert D. Jacobs. Baltimore: Johns Hopkins University Press, 1953.

White, Ray Lewis, ed. *The Achievement of Sherwood Anderson: Essays in Criticism.* Chapel Hill: University of North Carolina Press, 1966.

———. *Sherwood Anderson's Memoirs: A Critical Edition.* Chapel Hill: University of North Carolina Press, 1969.

Williams, David. *Faulkner's Women: The Myth and the Muse.* Montreal and London: McGill-Queens University Press, 1977.

Wittenburg, Judith Bryant. *Faulkner: The Transfiguration of a Biography.* Lincoln: University of Nebraska Press, 1979.

Wolfe, George H., ed. *Faulkner: Fifty Years After "The Marble Faun."* University: University of Alabama Press, 1976.

Woodward, C. Vann. *American Counterpoint: Slavery and Racism in the North–South Dialogue.* Boston: Little, Brown, 1971.

―――. *The Burden of Southern History.* Rev. ed. Baton Rouge: Louisiana State University Press, 1968.

―――. *Origins of the New South, 1877–1913.* Baton Rouge: Louisiana State University Press, 1941.

―――. *The Strange Career of Jim Crow.* New York: Oxford University Press, 1966.

Wright, Richard. *White Man, Listen!* Garden City: Doubleday, 1957.

Young, Stark. *So Red the Rose.* New York: Charles Scribner's Sons, 1934.

Index